D0142009

LF

Beyond *Spoon River*

THE DAN DANCIGER PUBLICATION SERIES

Beyond *Spoon River*

THE LEGACY OF EDGAR LEE MASTERS

by Ronald Primeau

UNIVERSITY OF TEXAS PRESS
AUSTIN

ALBRIGHT COLLEGE LIBRARY

Copyright © 1981 by the University of Texas Press
All rights reserved
Printed in the United States of America
First Edition, 1981

Requests for permission to reproduce material from this work
should be sent to Permissions, University of Texas Press,
Box 7819, Austin, Texas 78712.

Poetry from *The New World*, by Edgar Lee Masters, © 1937 by Edgar
Lee Masters, is reprinted by permission of Elsevier/Nelson Books; also
reprinted by permission of Elsevier/Nelson Books is poetry from
Masters' *More People*, © 1939 by Edgar Lee Masters, and *The Fate of the
Jury*, © 1929 by Edgar Lee Masters. We are very grateful to Ellen C.
Masters for permission to quote from the other works of Edgar Lee
Masters.

Portions of chapter 4 which appeared in *Mid America V*,
ed. David D. Anderson (East Lansing, Mich.: Midwest Press, 1978),
are reprinted by permission. Portions of chapter 6 which appeared in
The Old Northwest 1, no. 2 (June 1975): 141–156, are reprinted
by permission.

LIBRARY OF CONGRESS CATALOGING IN PUBLICATION DATA

Primeau, Ronald.
  Beyond Spoon River.
  (The Dan Danciger publication series)
  Includes bibliographical references and index.
  1. Masters, Edgar Lee, 1869–1950—Criticism and interpretation.
2. Masters, Edgar Lee, 1869–1950—Books and reading.
3. Influence (literary, artistic, etc.).   I. Title.
PS3525.A83Z83   811'52   80-25825
ISBN 0-292-70731-2

811.52
P953b

180209

22.50

FOR SARAH

180209

Contents

Preface

How a poem gets itself started is a problem which has long baffled and intrigued students of literature. In question-and-answer sessions following public readings, poets are asked where they get their ideas, why and when they write, what they do when they can't write, and what they would recommend to people who are trying to write. Writers are interviewed about their education and family background, their geographical environment and daily routine, and the books which have most influenced them. Such questions reflect our abiding interest in the creative process.

At various times in literary history, critics have intensified the search for origins. We seem right now to be entering such a period. After a long insistence on the "objectivity" of "the work itself," critics have returned to lengthy investigation of the personal and subjective dimensions of literary genesis. Commentators look for the germ of a poem's idea, the background of its narrative and characters, and the progressive stages of its conception and composition. Even the motivations and intentions of an author—so long taboo in the face of affective, intentionalist, pathetic, and other fallacies—are once again regaining prominence.

As we approach with caution the study of literary genesis, we find ourselves turning to the ancients. In leapfrog style, our concerns have jumped over the New Critics' alleged "objectivity" as well as the romantics' investment in various theories of genius. Classical rhetoricians examined closely the elaborate stages of search and discovery that were required before a speaker even began the actual process of composing a speech. Classical invention was a study in the psychology of creativity. Building on the work of the ancients, modern rhetoricians have adapted classical invention to modern communication theory and recent discoveries in linguistics, aesthetics, and cybernetics.

The study of literary influence has in our time moved away from the simple tracing of sources. Classical theory in any culture has always required that authors seek out enlarging influences, that they absorb the riches of the best models and imitate in order—paradoxically—to become truly free. But the emphasis is no longer merely on what books writers read but on how, in the process of their reading, they reinterpret past works and traditions. What had for so long been treated as static cause–effect "borrowing" is now seen as a dynamic interaction between an organic text and an active reader. The notion of borrowing is giving way to a modification or transformation of what has gone before. Literary influence is becoming synonymous with revisionist reading.

Recent developments also in reader-response theories have further shifted attention away from static influence to the dynamics of the reading process. The influence of *A* on *B* clearly depends as much on the response of *B* as on the source *A*. Reader-centered theories acknowledge that readers at least in part create what they read and that the present in large measure creates the past.

These and other recent developments in rhetoric and critical theory suggest new grounds for a long overdue reassessment of the legacy of Edgar Lee Masters. Masters' place in American literature has so far been limited by his reputation as a "one-book author." With its innovative style and startling themes, *Spoon River Anthology* was a smash hit when selections ran in Reedy's *Mirror* in 1914. A year later the full-length book, published by Macmillan, was a financial and critical success. Dozens of reprintings, a Broadway play, and numerous paperback editions demonstrate the fame and popularity of the one instantly recognizable work of a man who was called "an aboriginal American poet."

Spoon River Anthology has been read, performed, praised, attacked, debated, even censored for over sixty-five years. Generations of readers with widely differing values are attracted to the work. But between 1916 and 1942 Masters wrote over fifty other books—most of which are unknown even to his admirers. Exactly how a writer can be an instant "phenomenon" with one book and then collapse into near obscurity is a complicated question of how literary traditions and values take shape, change, disappear, and then return.

Masters maintained a lifelong commitment to the classical tradition and its emphasis on rhetorical invention. The evidence from his early schooling in Lewistown as well as his later training and experience in the legal profession demonstrates that he knew classical rhetoric and its application in practical forensics. From his observations in his autobiography, in the pages of *The American Mercury*, and in several published interviews, we know that he was accustomed to studying and carefully analyzing the influences on his own development as a poet. His wide reading of nearly the whole of Western literature occupies a central place in the shaping of his own themes and style. His record of that wide reading and its effects on his literary output is the basis for the reinterpretation of Masters' role in the development of modern American literature.

This book will begin that reassessment. Chapters 1 and 2 review Masters' statements on literary influence and evaluate his place in the critical climate of his own time. Chapters 3 through 7 are devoted to his reading of Greek literature, Goethe, Emerson, Whitman, Shelley, and Browning. In the Greeks and Goethe he found magnitude, heroism, and strength of conviction. Emerson taught him to distrust the influence of all but his own self-reliant mind. Whitman held out the possibilities of a truly American mythos. Whitman and Emerson were, for Masters, correctives to the poetry of his time which he little admired. In Shelley he sought a vision which matched his own aspirations as a poet. Shelley steered his political and philosophical concerns into visionary hymns to human potential in other realms. Browning helped to objectify his expanding visionary insights in a controlled dramatic frame. Masters' own popularity suffered in part because these were not the most popular sources of the thinking of his own time. But in unspectacular yet special ways, these authors helped him to understand much about poetic composition that was either misunderstood or out of fashion in America at the turn of the century and for some time after. Finally, Chapter 8 explores Masters' midwestern heritage in light of recent reinterpretations of regionalism.

Masters was a tireless reader, a strong critic, and a revisionist. In his wide reading of Western literature, he dissected the origins of American letters and, in the process, made room for himself in that tradition. Far from being a one-book author, Masters contributed much to the American literary tradition that is just now coming into view.

I am especially grateful to Ellen C. Masters for her special insights and for her patience in responding so promptly and thoroughly to all of my inquiries. John C. Hepler (Central Michigan University) got me started on this project when he gave me a copy of an unpublished poem in Masters' own typescript. Jack Stillinger (University of Illinois) has been an abiding influence on much that led up to this study. His wisdom, example, and enthusiastic support have been abundant. For much close reading and helpful conversation, I am indebted to several colleagues. David D. Anderson (Michigan State University), Maurice Beebe (Temple University), Harold Bloom (Yale University), David L. Frazier (Miami University), and Herbert W. Martin (University of Dayton) offered welcome advice and encouragement. Peter A. Obuchowski (Central Michigan University) brought great expertise and invaluable friendship to his tireless reading of this manuscript. His wide-ranging knowledge helped me in ways too numerous to note individually. Carol Swan and her staff of student typists stood by me through several revisions. I have been fortunate often to enjoy their patience, good cheer, and unswerving dedication. Above all, I thank my wife, Katherine, who puts up with more than I care to describe here and each day brings everything back to what is most important.

Selected References

Abbreviations used in the text are designated in parentheses.

1915   *Spoon River Anthology*, Macmillan (*SRA*)
1916   *Songs and Satires*, Macmillan (*SS*)
1916   *The Great Valley*, Macmillan (*GV*)
1918   *Toward the Gulf*, Macmillan (*Gulf*)
1919   *Starved Rock*, Macmillan (*SR*)
1920   *Domesday Book*, Macmillan (*DB*)
1921   *The Open Sea*, Macmillan (*Sea*)
1924   *The New Spoon River*, Boni and Liveright (*NSR*)
1929   *The Fate of the Jury: An Epilogue to Domesday Book*, D. Appleton and Company (*FJ*)
1930   *Lichee Nuts*, Horace Liveright (*LN*)
1933   *The Serpent in the Wilderness*, Sheldon Dick (*Serpent*)
1935   *Invisible Landscapes*, Macmillan (*IL*)
1935   *Vachel Lindsay: A Poet in America*, Charles Scribner's Sons (*L*)
1936   *Poems of People*, D. Appleton-Century Co. (*People*)
1936   *Across Spoon River: An Autobiography*, Farrar and Rinehart (*ASR*)
1937   *Whitman*, Charles Scribner's Sons (*W*)
1937   *The New World*, D. Appleton-Century Co. (*NW*)
1938   *Mark Twain: A Portrait*, Charles Scribner's Sons (*T*)
1939   *More People*, D. Appleton-Century Co. (*MP*)
1940   *The Living Thoughts of Emerson*, Longmans, Green, and Company (*E*)
1941   *Illinois Poems*, The Press of James A. Decker (*IP*)
1942   *Along the Illinois*, The Press of James A. Decker (*AI*)
1942   *The Sangamon*, Farrar and Rinehart (*S*)

Beyond *Spoon River*

1

An Omnivorous Reader

MASTERS AND INFLUENCE

Masters' classical education and training in forensics keyed his sensitivity to analytical rigor and taught him to enjoy looking for and dissecting the influences on his own thinking. His background in philosophy as well as his practical experience in the courtroom made him introspective, even self-conscious, about his own theories as he worked them out. Although only a few of his books show the direct effects of trial experiences, nearly everything he wrote displays a lawyer's appetite for theoretical exchange.[1] His comments about authors from the past and his own career often took on the cast of a legal debate. At times, he presented discussions of his wide reading like a series of courtroom exhibits offered as evidence to help his readers reach a verdict.

For Masters, reading was an energizer which provided new ideas and literary models against which he measured his own goals, accomplishments, and failures. He learned through imitation, identification, and transformation. He often revised sources even as he acknowledged a debt to them. He was never reluctant to rewrite history, to reclaim overlooked accomplishment, or to disclaim ill-conceived repute. His Emersonian passion for originality engaged him frequently in struggles with his literary ancestors that led to denials of all influence in the name of self-reliance.

Throughout his entire writing career, Masters saw reading as a way to learn from and revise the past. His reading was, as well, an indispensable means of self-expression. Each of these dynamics of his creativity must be studied more closely in his own statements.

Across Spoon River is the most detailed record of Masters' development as a reader and poet. He describes himself in his early days as "an omnivorous reader" who spent much time in the library "feeding a hungry mind." He later considered his teenage years as a time of "largely wasted and misused energy" except for the friends he made and "the books I found mostly for myself." His acquaintance at that time with the daughter of a Presbyterian clergyman introduced him to books which he would read again and again throughout his career. The minister's two libraries quickly became further sources of nourishment. "Whatever he had was thrown open to me," Masters recalls, "and I tried to read everything in both libraries, with the result that I soon became badly stuffed, and had to rest to digest the material" (*ASR*, 85, 86, 89–90).

In one of his earliest recorded commentaries, Masters outlined his views of classical imitation: "It has been my wont, indeed, to read a passage that particularly tickled my fancy, until I had a clear conception of the contained idea, and then, closing the book, to essay to reproduce it in the same terms." Of course, this procedure is straight out of the classical and neoclassical doctrines of imitation for the purpose of liberating one's own creativity. "The result was often discouraging enough; for while I got the thought down with tolerable accuracy, I failed in that effect of arrangement which, perforce, constituted the strength of the passage as a whole. At other times I have copied pages from my favorite books, and when I have come to write at some future time, many of the words which were strikingly used, I found to my glowing satisfaction, were unconsciously added to my own vocabulary, and flocked willingly to assist me in the etching out of my thoughts."[2] Over four decades later he continued to assess the influences on his earliest writing:

> There was a time in those years when I aspired to be a short-story writer, and many that I wrote bore the influence of Poe. The poems I published bore the influence of no one. What with setting type and sending dispatches I always had a little money in my pocket, with which I was buying what books I wanted: a Shakespeare for thirty-nine cents; an Epictetus for nineteen cents, and Emerson's essays for a few cents, and a Seneca, a Marcus Aurelius, and Poe's stories, which I read again and yet again.[3]

Masters also had definite opinions about how poets are influenced. Like most poets, he didn't think much of narrowly conceived source study. As early as 1915, he wrote to Theodore Dreiser: "I think it is a low order of criticism to be forever tracing out a man's artistic derivations. . . . I never read a line of Crabbe in my life until a month ago, and I never heard of Robinson until the *Anthology* was finished, and never read his book until this fall." Almost twenty-five years later, again in a letter to Dreiser, he compared "how adult critics want to get at your origins—and then maybe mock them" to the way children want to take a watch apart "to look at the works." Obviously, the implication is that neither the children nor the critics are able to put back together what they took apart. His opinion of such critics is less than happy: "By God I do hate these reviewers."[4]

But in spite of his distaste for conventional studies of "artistic derivations," Masters constantly analyzed the origins of his own thinking and made in the unfolding of that genesis a substantial contribution to American aesthetics. Throughout his career "influence" became an increasingly expansive image for the influx into the poet of power, energy, magnitude, and an almost mystical vision. He referred often to influence in its etymological origins as an opening up to an influx of power. He spoke of "roots" and "nourishment," of "intellectual stimulus," of an imagination that could be "fed by abundant oil" (*ASR* 77, 89, 287).

Masters believed that writers should search for their inspiration in the classics. He described frequently the feeling of an energy flow as a burst of power that would flood in on him each time he experienced anew one of the giants of the past. Most often, that "inspiration" came as a breakthrough following a long struggle. What looked automatic was really a result of hard work and thought over a long period. *Spoon River Anthology* was a product of that kind of incubation:

> As my career as a poet seemed stayed or stopped altogether, I began to dream of writing one book, a book about a country town, but which should have so many characters, and so many threads and patterns in its texture that it would be the story of the whole world. This came into my mind within a short time after I got to Chicago, as something to do later, when I had more leisure, as a book to write which should be my first and only contribution to the literature of America. In 1906 I went to Europe, and at that time I had the plan for this book thoroughly matured. It was never written; instead the *Spoon River Anthology* was written, as the result of that long incubation, and upon that matter of architecture as it happened.[5]

That "incubation" is a difficult process which goes to the heart of his understanding of literary influence.

Masters identified two distinct steps in the creative process. First, at the conscious level, writers had to read widely, study rigorously, and strive to perfect the tools of the trade. Secondly, the results of all that hard work had to be given the necessary time and space in which to develop. Experience, time, thinking, and rethinking would then shape "the architecture of the writer's work according to the foundation which had been fixed":

> As the Fall of 1914 came along, and as my memories of the Sangamon country and the Spoon river country became more translucent and imaginative under the influence of pale sunlight and falling leaves, I departed more and more from the wastrels and failures of life and turned more and more to gentle combinations of my imagination drawn from the lives of the faithful and tender-hearted souls whom I had known in my youth about Concord, and wherever on Spoon river they existed. As December came I was nearing exhaustion of body, what with my professional work and the great drains that the Anthology was making on my emotions. The flame had now become so intense that it could not be seen, by which I mean that the writing of the pieces did not seem to involve any effort whatever; and yet I should have known that I was being sapped rapidly. I had no auditory or visual experiences which were not the effect of actuality; but I did feel that somehow, by these months of exploring the souls of the dead, by this unlicensed revelation of their secrets, I had convoked about my head swarms of powers and beings who were watching me and protesting and yet inspiring me to go on.[6]

Masters repeatedly insisted that the poetic "flame" could be ignited only after arduous "months of exploring." Recent research on the psychology of creativity sheds light on his theory of that obligatory interaction between inspiration and the ritualized stages of preparation.

Most writers, painters, or scientists who have commented on how they create insist that inspiration requires regular habits of hard work combined with the best environment. Ritualized patterns of conscious-level activity seem to activate the indefinable powers of creativity below consciousness. What is often thought of as mere busywork courts the muse, and such routine discipline prepares the inventor to seize the moment of breakthrough when it appears. The recorded observations of creative people support that necessary interplay between the conscious and subconscious processes.

In *The Creative Process* Brewster Ghiselin has summarized the conscious and subconscious activity which turns up in the recorded observations of so many creative people. Scientists as well as poets, Ghiselin has found, invent new material first through the force of hard work at the conscious level followed by a period of "incubation" in which their subconscious processes continue to work on what had begun at the conscious level:

The secret developments that we call unconscious because they complete themselves without our knowledge . . . are induced and focused by intense conscious effort spent upon the material to be developed or in the area to be illuminated. Though the tension of conscious striving tends to overdetermine psychic activity, to narrow it and fix it, such tension gives stimulation and direction to the unconscious activity which goes on after the tension is released. The desired developments are usually delayed for some time, during which presumably something like incubation is going on and attention may be profitably turned to something else. Then without warning the solution or the germinal insight may appear.[7]

These successive stages of overstriving, conscious release, and incubation can be found in Masters' view of reading as a classical absorption of the riches of the past. But after the strenuous efforts, the release produced for Masters an almost mystical state:

Often, after writing, during which I became unconscious of the passing of time, and would suddenly realize that it was twilight, I would experience a sensation of lightness of body, as if I were about to float to the ceiling, or could drift out of the window without falling. Then I would go out of the room and catch up one of the children to get hold of reality again; or I would descend for a beer and a sandwich. These nights I was playing on the Victrola the Fifth Symphony of Beethoven, out of which came the poem "Isaiah Beethoven," and such epitaphs as "Aaron Hatfield," "Russell Kincaid," and "Elijah Browning."[8]

The work habits which Masters ritualized spanned his two very different careers as lawyer and poet. What he considered to be a hectic work schedule in the law office detracted from the time he wanted to study, read, and write. At the same time, however, the daily routine of busywork intensified and fixed his work habits in ways that were bound to help his reading. Appointments with clients, research in the law books, and actual court trials provided the competition which only increased his appetite for poetry and made him all the more eager to read and write. When he did find time to read his favorite poets, he would read intently for what he considered too short a time. The return to a demanding schedule then forced his thinking about literature into subconscious-level thinking where in some senses it was freer to experiment and grow. His actual reading was intense and rigorous, but the release necessitated by the demands of a wholly different career pushed his reading responses out of the more restricted conscious-level ranges. The struggles which inevitably ensued from trying to be a practicing attorney and a poet on the side may ultimately have been among the most productive influences on his literary career. His poems show the effects of liberating, at times exhilarating, struggle.

Masters' classical education made him remarkably "upbeat" about the positive effects of reading on his own ability to write poetry. But reading great literature had more than the usual enticement for the small-town boy who wanted to enlarge himself, for the overworked lawyer who wanted a vision outside the courtroom, and for the believer in American ideals who saw the principles of democracy caving in around him. The search for literary sources was, in such circumstances, a strategy for survival against forces that threatened to stifle his goals and ideals.

On the meaning of literary influence, Masters was alternately comic and meditative. He could make light of the many times when, working in the law office, he would hide poetry or philosophy behind the legal volumes so that if his father came in suddenly "he would not catch me with Locke or Shelley" (*ASR*, 78). When he had to sneak his reading on the side, he felt oppressed by an environment that allowed little or no time for reading. A good portion of his autobiography becomes an answer to his ever-recurring central question as an artist: "Why was I not obliterated?" (402). *Across Spoon River* is an odyssey of Masters' developing imagination for which influences and the overcoming of influences proved the most illuminating map.

Masters framed many of his meditations on influence in the always gnawing and sometimes nearly destructive oppositions he felt between his career as a lawyer and his longings to be a poet. When he was still in high school, he recalls later, he was told by a teacher that "the law and literature were oil and water" (*ASR*, 288). He expressed often his opinion that a writer needs an encouraging environment. He lamented: "My sister was not a Dorothy Wordsworth. She was proud enough of me, but her influence was not inspiring" (286). He sometimes felt also that he was trapped "in a business which destroyed every imaginative impulse, and took all my strength and all my time" (209). This kind of brooding became almost bitter at times: "Here was I with my head full of Greek, with my memory swarming with Chaucer and Keats and Petrarch, and I meant nothing to these egotistical experts in their line" (151–152).

Masters' concern with the effects of an unfavorable environment on a writer was not limited to the confinement of his profession. In a moment of what is in many ways an unparalleled rejection of his own origins, he insisted that any kind of growth depended on the overcoming of oppressive and perverse obstacles: "But no less I feel that no poet in English or American history ever had a harder life than mine was in the beginning at Lewistown, or among a people whose flesh and whose vibrations were better calculated to poison, to pervert, and even to kill a sensitive nature" (*ASR*, 410).

Unfortunately, the poison metaphor has been picked up and given an undeserved prominence in the inflexible portrait of Masters' career given to us by many of his critics. The picture shows a sour and crabby man, trapped in the village, beaten down by oppressive forces, poisoned to death by his own bitterness. The truth is almost exactly opposite. The theme of confinement and oppression occupies a major place in Masters' autobiography in order to call attention to his emphasis on reading as a way to spring loose from traps of all sorts. The failure to see that he stresses the overcoming of obstacles much more than the obstacles themselves has had serious consequences in determining Masters' place in American literary history.

One lesson Masters thought writers must learn from a reading of the classics is how to survive in a society not particularly conducive to the development of artists. He actively sought strong, positive influences as a survival strategy for growth as a writer. In fact he often discovered the greatest strength in the process of overcoming obstacles. The ability to thrive in the midst of adversity was central not only to his self-concept but also for his theory of literary creativity:

> All this shows, no doubt, that part of me which has never been at rest, but was always moving, and indeed moving toward a visioned end. That part of me has not been obliterated by any distraction, or disaster, or by discouraging days. Many men would have been broken completely by those years of mine between 1919 and 1929; but I went on writing books. Many men would have been sunk to their eyes by that spiritual mud through which I walked from 1900 to 1915; but I kept my nose up where I could breathe, and trudged onward. Why was I not obliterated? [*ASR*, 402]

His answer to this crucial question forms the basis of over fifty books which came from his pen. Slowly he understood that what he always thought to be oppressive was actually a source of liberation for his creative powers.

Recalling later a time when he was intensely despondent, he saw the positive side of what he earlier had loathed:

> I pitied myself too that with all my aspirations and efforts I had been so caught and tangled down, and shoed with lead, and held

9

back as in a nightmare. I did not know that day by day I was living a life that gave me vast understanding of human nature and of the world. It is clear that I should not have had more numerous or significant facts of life brought before me in newspaper work; whereas if I had lived a cloistered life I should not have learned much besides books. [*ASR*, 209]

While he was confronted by the most debilitating experiences, Masters' growth as a poet continued to feed on the nourishment of his literary ancestors. He actually felt himself withdrawing from distractions: "I have felt that after all distractions, all detours, I would return to the full possession of myself. But in ways of daily living and associating with human beings I have been two persons: first that person who has been annoyed, fatigued, even degraded by inferior human contacts, by experiences, amorous and other, alive with contaminations—I have been this person, at the same time that I was that other person existing aloof and untouched by demoralizations" (*ASR*, 399–400). He survived by repeated close reading of his literary ancestors and by keeping intact above all else the life of imagination: "I have lived in the imagination. Perhaps this is the deepest secret of my nature, namely, that imagination has been the controlling influence of my life; and that I have not lived among facts of economics, among buildings of brick and mortar, among the concrete matters of worldly success" (398).

Masters' central image for this survival mechanism was what he referred to as a third eye, his flashlight of imagination: "The law had been an X ray to me, and many kinds of chemicals; the law, and my contacts with so many varieties of people. And now imagine a human being with one great eye in the center of his forehead with which he saw everything with realistic clearness; but suppose him in retention of his two normal eyes, which in their normality saw beauty where it was not, and truth where it had never been" (*ASR*, 317–318). Masters is describing in his own sensibility an actively transforming agency akin to what he calls "the flashlight of imagination" (398). That visionary light is always nonetheless problematic: "That was I who saw people with penetration . . . but who with dreaming eyes looked down paths without seeing the tangles all in all, Pyrrhonist as I was about life and success." There follows an oversimple and offhanded comment that contains astonishing insight into the strengths and weaknesses of Masters' contrary literary impulses: "All through my poems there run the two strains of realism and mysticism. I wrote with my cyclopean eye many of the portraits of Spoon River, and with my dreaming eyes I wrote 'The Star' and 'The Loom'" (318).

Even after his reading countered the pressures of his daily living and presented the possibility of enlarging his literary sensitivity, Masters faced the problem of how to respond to those influences. When the daily routine and the world of reading tried to crowd each other out, he would pause and call for the question: "All the while material for creative work was accumulating so fast within me that I was on the point of bursting. I had seen and lived so much, and read and thought so much. What was to be done with it?" (*ASR*, 285).

In answering this crucial question Masters became a revisionist. When he read Shelley or Whitman or Dickinson, he was eager to correct the current opinions of critics and to reassess past reputations in light of his own discoveries. We are better able to understand Masters' revisionist approach to his sources with the help of developments in the aesthetics of influence since his time.[9]

In modern criticism, literary influence has gone from being a pattern of static cause and effect to a gestalt of dynamic configurations. We have learned from Eliot's "historical sense" that included "not only the pastness of the past but its presence,"[10] Lionel Trilling's "sense of the past" that is altered in its "transmission,"[11] and Claudio Guillén's discussion of influence as "displacement."[12]

In a series of works about literary influence, Harold Bloom has described the creative anxiety felt by later writers when they confront precursors. For Bloom, influx is a flood from the past. Poets write in order to keep from drowning. To him, literary history is "indistinguishable from poetic influence, since strong poets make that history by misreading one another, so as to clear imaginative space for themselves."[13] Walter Jackson Bate is similarly concerned with the poet's "accumulating anxiety" over the weight of past accomplishment. Bate's notion of "the late-comer" is very like Bloom's heroic "ephebe" who must always "rally everything that remains." But whereas Bloom sees the anxiety as a falling away, a creative "sorrow" unable to match the greatness of the precursor, Bate holds out hope for the artist's "readiness" to turn to a past that might become "truly active and liberating without also becoming intimidating." All this leads to what Bate sees as "the greatest single cultural problem" we face: "how to use a heritage, when we know and admire so much about it, how to grow by means of it, how to acquire our own 'identities,' how to be ourselves."[14]

Masters' fascination with the sources of his own development lines him up securely with Bate's arguments about how post–eighteenth-century poets dealt with the overwhelming burdens of past accomplishment. Masters felt the pressures of originality when he tried to Americanize his Hellenist values or when he found himself behind Whitman trying to make a new culture or when he wanted to transplant Shelleyan mystical hymns into the coarser, tougher soil of the Illinois prairies. The "massive achievement" of Goethe energized his own conception of beauty, and yet he felt burdened because he could never outdo the vision of Helen in *Faust*. How could he not feel at least slightly intimidated when he says that in Goethe can be found "all that I have felt of love, both as a giver of life and as a forecast of a higher sphere, as a delusion, a satiety, and a deathless force" (*ASR*, 408)? He often felt the anxieties of his role as "late-comer"; yet he never wavered from the neoclassical view that following behind the great is a first step in the freeing and enlarging of one's self. Though burdensome in Bate's sense of the gnawing presence of a modern insistence on originality, Masters' constant reading and his habits of measuring himself against Homer, Whitman, and Shelley ultimately released powers within him through which he could more fully be himself.

Masters could never understand why American readers had shamelessly misunderstood Whitman; his own reading of "America's Hesiod" attempted to restore his accomplishments. Emerson's beliefs had been exploited for nearly a century when Masters set out to re-write his legacy. With the help of Emerson's essays and journal entries, Masters found more in Goethe than the Anglo-American tradition has so far allowed. The neglect of Shelley was almost total when Masters included hundreds of allusions to the "eternal hymns" in his prose. Even Browning was popular for entirely the wrong reasons, Masters thought, when he began tuning his own dramatic pitch on the power of the monologues. In an enterprise doomed to misinterpretation from the start, Masters set out to rewrite the legacy of the Greeks by showing the Judeo-Christian tradition to be a mere interruption in the higher, richer culture of Hellenism. These and other attempts to alter the existing order of the literary tradition of the whole Western world resulted from Masters' constant and vigorous reading, his revisionist stance on the meaning of tradition and the canons, his expression of new interpretations in his critical statements, and his absorption of those new interpretations into his own poems.

The problems which arise in this revisionist view of interpretation and influence are, of course, many. Bate has raised several issues that are disturbing and challenging. He questions, for example, the biases caused by (1) "our vocational interest in presupposing that there is a relatively clean cut influence of ideas on artist," (2) the introduction of new standards in any age that reduces immediate competition with the past, (3) the tendency of writers to choose their influences by reducing immediate predecessors to size and turning to older ancestors instead, and (4) problems in the general retrenchment of creative possibilities—all related to what he refers to as "the burden of the past" with its "accumulating anxiety" and the question posed for the poet *What is there left to do?*" The questions Bate raises for the study of influence arise from the reductionism and "epiphenomenalism" of our naive assumptions. Are we often "noting several things that occurred at the same time, connecting them, and saying that one produces, or at least helps to produce, the other?" And is the past "richer and more vivid because we select only the highest possible moments and then coalesce them into a more condensed unity than any actual experience could ever provide?" Do we, in short, persistently manicure or inflate the past in order to shape or reshape it into a pattern we can more readily understand and accept?[15]

Masters thought so. He saw that kind of manicuring and inflation of reputations everywhere he looked. Throughout his entire career he had a healthy disrespect for the critical machinery which shaped traditions and decided what was and wasn't worth reading. Without using the philosophical terms, he attacked the reductionism inherent in almost any "school" of thinking which necessarily reduced the expanse of poetry to a manageable package that would fit preconceptions. (In 1942 he told a *New York Times* interviewer that he didn't want "to be tied up with anyone, with any group.")[16] His own incessant reinterpretation of long-standing figures is evidence alone for his skepticism about how reputations were achieved. (He had little or no use for American heroes such as Lincoln and Twain, for example.) His final verdict on what Bate calls "epiphenomenalism" was strikingly similar to Bate's much later and much more elaborate insights. In his biography of Whitman, Masters noted, in passing: "Whitman in his unfettered originality shook off stock verdicts of his day. He knew that Shakespeare, the Bible and any book whatever, can be so constantly studied that it takes on elements of beauty and greatness which it does not really possess. For myself, I am sure that Shakespeare and the Bible have reached their pre-eminence as the result of long years of study, propagandum, and commentation" (*W*, 237). Masters regularly blended this kind of embattled rewriting of the past into his more serene conversions of classical riches to his own use.

Masters was always combative. Whether in the courtroom or discussing the literature he loved or hated, he never hesitated to take a firm stand. Perhaps the foremost battle at the center of Masters' views on literary influences is his typically Emersonian struggle against influence itself. After spending nearly three hundred pages in his autobiography on the sources contributing to the development of his poetic career, he feels an inclination to sweep them all away with one burst of self-reliance: "I was the chief influence in my own career" (*ASR*, 287). True enough; and his immediate return to the discussion of sources shows that he meant the statement not literally but rather as an assertion of the independence of mind he thought Americans badly needed. In that same spirit he responded to the *New York Times* interviewer's question about the influences on his career with the preposterous statement that he had "no relationship" with earlier poets. A reading of his poems or his own statements about influences shows that he didn't mean that disclaimer. But as a poet who practiced "imitation" in the classical sense and at the same time felt both the modern pressures to be original and the Emersonian ideal of self-reliance, he simply had to say it.

Emerson influenced almost every American writer since his day—even while he was telling everyone to avoid being influenced. Masters believed in the imitation of classical models, and yet his idol Emerson said "never imitate." In a fascinating essay "Emerson and Influence," Harold Bloom calls the legacy of self-reliance in American culture "the only poetic influence that counsels against itself, and against the idea of influence." [17] Masters' wide reading in Emerson and the effects of that reading on his poetry will be discussed extensively in chapter 4. But it is significant to note how what Bloom calls "the war of American poets against influence" created another chapter in Masters' struggle against the accomplishments of the past. No matter how strongly his classical view of imitation took hold, he was always most comfortable with the Emersonian heritage of self-reliance. But for Masters that nudge toward the self as final arbiter of taste and value never meant originality at all costs. Instead he was content to go on absorbing and transforming past riches; he was patient enough to wait for the larger, freer "self" to emerge rather than accept the first "self" that came along.

Despite his loud cries on behalf of the Emersonian push away from Europe and toward the unique culture of the new world, Masters' refusal to overthrow past traditions completely became a cause of much misreading of his work. He wanted to be original—an unavoidable quest for almost any post-romantic poet. But he also knew Greek culture well enough to understand the notion of the communal singer or the poet-prophet whose individual identity was of little consequence. He felt the pressures to produce new material at any cost far less than most of his contemporaries. He was relatively free of the typically modern anxieties when he absorbed what proven models from the past had to offer or when he willingly reinterpreted sacred assumptions about those models.

In addition to wide reading in the history of literature, other influences in Masters' education contributed to his views on how a writer grows in response to people and events. He understood clearly that not all influences are cosmic broodings or powerful floods of energy, and he often noted the benefits derived from seeing the universal in concrete, local truths. In "Masters and Some Mentors," Charles E. Burgess has studied "the role of the communities of Masters' youth in the artistic and psychological stimulating of his expression." The concrete particulars in Masters' poems created a "verisimilitude" through which he achieved "universality."[18]

Burgess also reviews the mesh of styles which Masters achieved through his apprenticeship to a "vast body of literary, historical, journalistic, and even scientific writing." To the long lists of Masters' reading in the classics Burgess adds "the robust, didactic prose of the journalists, ministers, and lawyers who traced the history of the region, or explored questions within their own professions; the curiosity of those who sought to explain the natural world; the frail and grasping search for poetic expression by the companions of Masters' youth." And there were the other local influences such as professional people "who found in the practice of letters an outlet for talents larger than they needed in their profession." The influence of that complex struggle to write "on the side" in Masters' own career is obvious. Burgess concludes that local influences also provided competition for "one of America's most argumentative and combative of modern poets."[19] As in all accounts of his reading, the competitive dimension of his poetic invention was fierce and liberating.

Another form of struggle with his sources can be found in Masters' attitudes toward what might be called influence by indirection. His accounts of how he wrote *Spoon River Anthology*, for example, describe influences avoided as much as influences sought. His famous correspondence with Reedy was frequently a dialogue containing advice which he sometimes accepted and other times turned back. For example, it was Reedy who urged Masters to read the *Greek Anthology* and use it as a model for a new American mythos: "All the while there was implicit in Reedy's criticisms the idea that I should do something distinctively American, that my experience and background should not go unexpressed, and should not be smothered under verses of mere skill, which did not free what was really within me."[20] These exchanges were in 1907. It was some of the best advice Masters ever received, and he knew how to respond to it.

The influences Masters avoided also nourished his developing aesthetics. When he rejected Reedy's advice, he knew why. In "The Genesis of Spoon River" he recalled one of his few refusals to go along with the promptings of his editor:

> There was nothing new about free verse except in the minds of illiterate academicians and quiet formalists like William Dean Howells, who called Spoon River "shredded prose." Reedy understood all these things as well as I. He knew that Imagism was not a new thing, though he kept urging me to make the Anthology more imagistic, and I refused, except where imagism as vivid description in the Shakespearean practice was called for. I had had too much study in verse, too much practice too, to be interested in such worthless experiments as polyphonic prose, an innovation as absurd as Dadaism or Cubism or Futurism or Unanimism, all grotesqueries of the hour, and all worthless, since they were without thought, sincerity, substance.[21]

Masters knew the classics well enough to be certain of his dislike for what he saw happening in American literature.

Ultimately, Masters felt that the deepest influences from reading could be experienced only when the reader brought books into contact with the passions and sufferings of real people and events. In the final analysis, he saw literary influences as "rich schoolings for the mind and heart." He likened the interaction between the reader and the source of influence to a kind of "erotomania" which becomes for two lovers "a severe schooling" and a deepening of emotional powers. The struggles required to convert the riches of the past to one's own uses are often strenuous and painful; but the conversion unlocks "the secrets and the agonies of all the world's lovers" (*ASR*, 312–313).

Nowhere is Masters' revisionist sense of reading and literary influence more apparent than in his theory of biography. Alongside "the hysterical unrealities and demoralizations which accompanied and followed the World War," he observed, there arose "a marked activity in biographical writing in America, and in the recreation of dramatic periods in its career." A "sick and feverish people" rushed to get "the truth told before it was too late."[22] Whether a propagandist for a cause such as war or a corrective to past distortions, the biographer must interpret constantly shifting data in the flow of historical developments.

This dynamic interaction of past and present is at the center of

Masters' views on biography as well as his theory of influence. First there is the imbalance which unduly sways interpretation: "The populace everywhere is afflicted by manias, and not less so in America than elsewhere. Here we are inclined to be wildly for a man or wildly against him, changing in a day from one extreme to the other. This cannot be without vast mendacity, and that mendacity gets into our books." At the same time there is a solution to the problem: "But meanwhile some one is keeping a journal, as Emerson did, in which there is a sane record of men and affairs. That becomes a correction in later days. Or documents put aside in mad days turn up to prove that war originated in causes far different from those to which it was ascribed at the time, and to which it has long been ascribed."[23]

It is, then, the job of the biographer, the historian, the literary critic, and the student of influence to reexamine the flow of events and set the record straight: "The world would not be where it is today if all along there had not been those obstinate and pugnacious spirits who could not bear to see history falsified, and leading men of the past kept in the dust-bins of time to be more and more sifted over with refuse." The dynamic interplay of evolving human events demands a revisionist reading from the later age trying to make sense out of developments:

> To take these figures out and to clean them is to make them rallying points of cultural progress, forces of correction and readjustment, and inspirations to a wisdom which reshapes. They may stand again as types for emulation, and as figures between past times and present times, for useful comparison. Or some of the gilt may be taken off figures too much gilded. In either case the country is set going straight. That is the idea behind the best biography.[24]

That is also the kind of correction and adjustment Masters had in mind as he struggled to understand the influences on his own development.

The critical views which grew out of his wide reading and a desire to revise what he thought was a distorted Anglo-American tradition will receive much more extensive treatment in later chapters. His sustained and complex consideration of the dynamics of literary influence forms the basis of his hitherto neglected contributions as a critic.

17

2

"While Homer and Whitman Roared in the Pines"

MASTERS AS CRITIC

Petit the Poet's wisecrack about versifiers who prefer trivial formalities to visionary singers is Masters' most famous critical statement. Petit regrets his own concern with "little iambics" while he missed the tragedy and heroism all around him (*SRA*, 89). That sentiment recurs frequently in Masters' interviews and essays, as well as his autobiography. It is also the kind of remark which gave him the reputation of a quarrelsome man with explosive opinions. But on closer inspection, Masters' seemingly spontaneous outbursts reveal a definite pattern. What appears to be merely the anger of a cynic turns out to be penetrating insight on the state of poetry in our culture in the first few decades of this century.

Masters often noted what he thought was wrong with the literature of his time. He offered several choice remarks, for example, about the "haughty exclusiveness" of many literati who gathered themselves into "unctuous" and "pretentious" clubs and produced verse that was "largely derivative and warmed over." He was very good at this kind of put-down, but his observations offered much more than saucy commentaries about what was wrong with America's poetry. His criticism traced what he found to be best in the American tradition as he knew it. He sketched a theory of poetry based on the primacy of the visionary as well as the necessity of realism. And he presented coherent and detailed recommendations about what he thought poets ought to be doing.

Not surprisingly, with over seventy years of hindsight we find it easier to understand Masters' critical theories. When he started writing around 1910, poetry was not enjoying much popularity. But soon Carl Sandburg, Amy Lowell, Vachel Lindsay, Robert Frost, T. S. Eliot, Ezra Pound, and Harriet Monroe's *Poetry: A Magazine of Verse* changed all that. By the time *Spoon River Anthology* appeared in 1915 Masters found himself embroiled in controversies and in the midst of a poetry boom. As an observer of the developments of the time as well as a participant in their making, Masters the critic deserves our attention.

The primary texts for a study of Masters' criticism are his biographies of Whitman, Twain, and Lindsay, his own autobiography, and several articles.[1] There were also the usual poems on poetry—a form of criticism that often reveals the most about a poet's goals and values. In all, a voice can be heard with much to say about realism and inspiration, experimentation and the classics, imitation and originality, regionalism and the universal.

Masters' first critical theories appeared in "Learning to Write," an article published in *The Writer* in 1889. The essay is the first documentation of his classical education and the role of that training in the formation of his theories about poetic composition and critical standards. The article appeared when the twenty-year-old Masters was helping his father in the law office, writing for the Lewistown *News*, and reading all the books he could get his hands on. What he refers to as "the higher principles of rhetoric" were a large part of his study at the time. In sum, "Learning to Write" is about the necessary interaction of thought and style and the role of reading and imitation in the compositional process. He stresses simplicity as "the primordial essential of good style" and notes that many who were considered geniuses often revised their works as many as sixty times. His classical emphasis on "simplicity, energy, elegance, and rhythm" and his insistence on imitation, revision, and the supremacy of thought are early indications of themes that were to develop throughout his career.

"The Poetry Revival of 1914" is an on-the-spot appraisal of a movement by one who was almost, but not quite, a participant. Masters goes on the attack in this essay against publishers and poets who produce "correct verse written without inspiration." At the same time he celebrates the "freshness and realism" of poetry of the "commonplace" and explains why the Revival must "acknowledge the paternity of Whitman." Beginning with his analysis of Stedman's *American Anthology* (1900), he traced the accomplishments and failures of the "new poetry" of his own time.

Masters heartily approved of Stedman's Emersonian directive that America's poets must "seek inspiration from within" and not from the "masters to whom all resort for edification." Stedman singled out Whitman, Emerson, and Poe as the American poets from whom "the Old World had most to learn." He called for a modern American poetry "native to the American scene."[2] Stedman was the kind of critic and editor Masters greatly admired.

In the face of "largely derivative" and "correct" verse "written without inspiration," Masters saw in the 1914 revival a return to the genuine American tradition that began with Whitman and Emerson. He felt that turn-of-the-century verse had been taken over by "the dilettante interests of Stone and Kimbal of Chicago" and others. The revival, for Masters, brought poetry back to "a freshness and realism which did not seem poetical to the reigning Stoddard-Gilder-Aldrich school." The Imagists' attempt "to find a new word and the exact word and to discard the words blurred by use or the word which failed to express sharply the intended meaning" was "not a novelty" but a return to the natural speech of Shakespeare or Burns. The "fresh, audacious novelty of words and imagery" that he found in Sandburg was—in Masters' view—a revival of the essential American native spirit which had for too long dropped out of sight.

Most of "The Genesis of Spoon River" is about the personal and poetic influences on the writing of the *Anthology*. But in reflecting on the difficulties he had breaking in, Masters once again comments on what he thought was wrong with the literary establishments of the time:

> Because American poetry had been taken over by jewelers like Aldrich, and fourth raters like Gilder, and by clerical sonneteers and lyricists whose merit was a constrained attitude unrelated to any revelation, but kept down for the sake of form, art, yet with intent to be poetical, correct and in the tradition of English verse; because the publishing houses were all in the East, and didn't want books of verse, and would scarcely take one from a Westerner; because, in brief, the art was strangled and despised, or was made the concern of precious coteries—because of all this, and my own laborious law business, I stood embattled."[3]

When Reedy came along, he introduced Masters to the *Greek Anthology*. The rest is well known. Perhaps even more significantly, Masters recalls his counsel to "do something distinctively American." Reedy hoped that the American "experience and background should not go unexpressed, and should not be smothered under verses of mere skill." The theme was the same. In order for American poetry to survive and thrive, the poet must avoid the pitfalls of technically correct verse and return to the native stock that broke from the courtly Muses of Europe.

In *Across Spoon River*, most of Masters' beliefs and attitudes about poetry are stated and elaborated at some length. There the earlier attacks are full-fledged. And there his theories of what imaginative writers ought to be doing are more detailed.

20

Masters was never fond of critics. While helping Sandburg find a publisher for *Chicago Poems*, he noted that "the state of poetical criticism was at a low level at this time, for America was coming out of the slumber into which it had been sunk by the various Knickerbocker schools." Not that he ever felt the criticism to be at a very high level. "As poetry is a living expression of life," he continued, "it cannot be judged by erudite schoolmen who are prone to measure whatever is done by the masters of the past." In defense of Sandburg, Masters judged that he "was beaten with cudgels at first" and then was "given a part of the rotten eggs that were intended for me, and which could not always be cast at me because of the popularity of *Spoon River*" (*ASR*, 369–370).

Erudition in critics seldom impressed Masters. About "a scholarly professor of influence" who had personally attacked him, he observed that such critics "have read nearly everything and know the history of literature; yet having eyes they see not." He assures readers that he "could fill a page with the names" that he was called, and counters mud-slinging by quoting Goethe's autobiography for an axiom upon which he built throughout his career: "I honor both the rhythm and rhyme by which poetry becomes poetry"; "but what is really deeply and fundamentally effective, what is truly educative and inspiring is what remains of the poet when he is translated into prose. What is left is the pure essence, which beauties of form may strive to simulate when absent, and when present only serve to conceal." Masters fell back on this quotation often to dismiss the distortions of the formalists and to account for the best of "what is done in free verse when it is excellent" (*ASR*, 370).

Masters' reactions to the critics can be summarized in his remarks about the reception of volumes after *Spoon River*. When *Songs and Satires* appeared he thought that the critics "wanted more *Spoon River*." He felt they "had sharpened their pencils" for the sequel and that they were ready to dispute whatever direction he followed: "If I had gone on in the *Spoon River* manner they would likely have said that I had but one set of strings; in fact, when I published *The New Spoon River* in 1924 these same spirits lamented that it was a fall off from the *Anthology*, and that one book of its kind was enough."[4] As his correspondence with H. L. Mencken shows, Masters valued and actively sought honest and even severe criticism. But for "stupid," "personal" attacks of "obvious malice" he felt "unforgiving contempt."

Always more than personal, his contempt grew into theories which went against the currents of the times. He had a healthy sense of reticence about publishing his earliest poems; even then he concluded that the journals were "stuffing their covers with wheatless straw, such as sonnets on themes a thousand times treated." With cautious modesty he adds "what I wrote was fresh and original, if nothing else" (*ASR*, 192). While he tried unsuccessfully to publish *A Book of Verses* a few years later, he proclaimed that poetry was "all in control of formalists in the East, and was at a very low ebb" (253). It was a time of the "haughty exclusiveness" of the "dilettanti" in "the Little Room" in Chicago (336). Later Masters recalled with embarrassment his own membership in the Twentieth Century Club, "an unctuous and pretentious group to which I belonged when I was groping for my way and made many detours by mistake" (344). From such groups poets "sprang up . . . like woodland violets in April." But there were also the "mushrooms" and "the School of the Half-Wits" where "the half-educated and the half-formed" took pens to paper. Such stuff, he recalls, "convulsed me to the core of my being" (348–349).

One series of convulsions followed Amy Lowell's "descent upon Chicago" after "a poem, so called, which she had then just written on the theme of herself taking a bath gave the press just what it wanted in the way of colorful sensation." He likened her to "an Italian diva" and when he went to visit her he described her as "enthroned in state" at the Congress Hotel. After smoking cigars together, they had a difference of opinion about "literary judgment" and parted hastily (*ASR*, 347).

In later years Masters voiced the same kind of indignation about critics who "can't help themselves." In 1938 he told August Derleth that critics were "little men all mixed up with ideologies—with abstracts." They always want to "criticize your work on the basis of your social consciousness." He called this "damned nonsense" and "a wild obsession" and added that he hadn't any use for "isms" unless it was "good old fashioned Americanism." He conjectured also that many critics didn't read the parts of *Spoon River* that "wouldn't fit in with their line." And when Derleth asked him about the poets writing in the late thirties he answered that he couldn't read most of them at all: "Those fellows have nothing to say, and they say nothing as obscurely as possible."[5]

The deliberate obscurity of the poetry of the time continued to infuriate Masters in his later years. In 1942 he told Robert Van Gelder in a *New York Times* interview that modern poets have "no principles, no individuality, no moral code, and no roots." He dismissed the poetry of the time as "worthless" and likened it to "air plants." When asked in the interview about whether he was part of a school, he answered that he didn't want "to be tied up with any one, any group." And again he called for a literature that was "not imitative, that stands alone, that is strong, that leans on nothing outside itself and permits nothing to lean on it."[6] As often was the case, these attacks can be reduced to his view that for almost a century America's poets failed to heed the advice of Emerson and Whitman.

In *Whitman*, he elaborated on precisely what went wrong. For Masters, Whitman was the neglected prophet who was driven in his later years to sing "songs of sublimation and escape." When "America departed from its path," the "spirituality" Whitman inspired gave way to the "imperialized" republic and "the breeding place . . . of special privilege." As mercantilism and centralization overtook the "songs of liberty," Whitman's mystical optimism gave way in later writers to "satire and anathema" (*W*, 307–309).

This scenario is at the center of Masters' populist politics, but it is also his explanation for why Whitman was so shamelessly degraded in the twentieth century and why the possibilities of a truly native American culture had to collapse. In arts and letters the counterpart of these "executions against the last hope of liberty in this world" becomes the colonization of poetry. The parallels must be stated in Masters' own words:

> The bearing that all this has on poetry is clear enough. What happens is that plotters get all the money by legalized privileges and partial laws. They then go on and make the culture of the country, both by surrounding every one with materialism, and by further laws and court decisions to make their possessions secure and on the increase. Soon the thinker finds himself cramped and in want. The creator, the poet, the minds who can save the country, are struck down or rendered dumb or bitter. Budding Virgils and Homers are nipped, but Juvenals grow up. For resistance, not to say revolution, is outlawed in America. Free speech is banned, and protesters must steal through the interplexus of things forbidden. To do that they must pick words which deceive the swine or which are regarded by them as mere poetry and of no dangerous moment. All this has happened in America, and much of it since Whitman died. [*W*, 309–310]

Masters' constant return to Whitman brings out what is central in his attacks against the reigning literary establishments—whether in 1900, 1914, or 1942. "Governmental independence" matters little if poetry and criticism continue to be produced in "an intellectual province." His conclusion is unmistakable: "The emancipation from this foreign rulership, for which Whitman wrote so many brave words in

ALBRIGHT COLLEGE LIBRARY 180209

verse and prose, has not yet by any means come to pass." And behind his harshest attacks on what was going on in his own times, Masters held on to the unswerving optimism of Whitman about "the life forces that are never destroyed or reduced" (W, 312, 313).

That optimism kept him from producing any Juvenalian satire about what was wrong with modern poetry. Instead, Masters the critic had a good deal to say about what should be happening if the poets of his time were to be able to hear the roar of Whitman and Homer.

Most of the chapters in this book will be concerned with influences on Masters' poetry. Not surprisingly, these same sources often turn out to be the elements of tradition Masters felt were most ignored in modern movements. His critical views tended to be unpopular in art because he admired many of the old poets who were out of favor and had no use for most current trends.

The most important lines of tradition for Masters were always the classics. Homer, Aeschylus, Sophocles, Goethe, Shelley, Browning, Whitman, and Emerson were the writers he returned to after he tired of everything else. Like his grandfather, he caught the cadences of the King James Bible and the language of Burns. When he was nineteen he read Spencer, Huxley, and Hume. At the age of twenty he read through the canons of English literature as well as Montaigne and translated Goethe and Homer. In those early days too he read a paper on Whitman before the Fulton County Scientific Association. The gist of the paper he described later as Whitman's "conception of America as the field of a new art and music in which the people would be celebrated instead of kings" (ASR, 336). The catalog of ideals admired by Masters the critic is very long. Mary Fisher taught him rhetoric. He admired Tolstoy and Dreiser, Milton and More, Mill and Bacon; he read Swedenborg again and again. Always there was the "Homeric dignity" of Whitman.

Pieced together in this list of wide reading and clear-cut opinions are some very definite ideas about the nature of poetry and the role of the poet. What dominates in these rather diverse statements is the primacy of vision, an unmistakable commitment to realism, and a theory of "erotomania" as the physical manifestation of spiritual correspondence.

Speaking of Harriet Monroe, editor of Poetry, Masters noted that she always stood for "fresh creation." He admired her also because she was beyond slavish adherence to the formalism Masters despised: "She knew that poetry is thought and feeling, imagery and music rather than rhyme and meter" (ASR, 347). This was an important distinction for Masters, and he elaborated further on the differences between "the poetry of fancy" which "lulls and lifts" and "the greatest poetry" which "founds itself upon the truth which is the beautiful" and which "proves the laws of the spirit of man." For Masters the "truth" of poetry was the unifier of all other disciplines, the passion of his life "to which philosophy and science and history have been but handmaidens." The access to that truth came through the energy which breaks through to vision. From his college days to the mystical hymns of the thirties and forties, he "thrilled to harmonious words and tried to write them" himself (413).

For the meaning of poetic vision, Masters again looked to Whitman. Since Whitman was "trying to put all of America into poetry," he was "driven into catalogues, which are a way of presenting to the eye of imagination the content of the vision." His follow-up on this point is even more fascinating. This vision—a hymn for a new day of democracy—made Whitman great: "It was not his poetical skill, not artistry, not even his own successful achievement. Over and over again later he said that he merely gave directions. He was never the Homer of America; at best he was our Hesiod, writing *Works and Days* in terms of what America was and meant, and what its rightful destiny was" (*W*, 60, 61).

Masters' visionary poet was Emerson's prophet. "A poet of great vision," he conjectured, "never realized in words or poems, may be a poet no less of greater achievement than one who fully expresses the content of his imagination" (*W*, 76). And he later goes on to describe Whitman's "aggregate" imagination which transforms "swarms" into a "vast vision." Masters warns readers they may miss Whitman's strength if they become distracted by his lack of precision. The mark of the visionary becomes "poetic feeling" and "emotion, which is the basis of poetry and its rhythms" (304, 305).

In *Across Spoon River* Masters observed that he saw running through his own poems "the two strains of realism and mysticism" (*ASR*, 318). He saw no conflict between these two strains in Whitman, and he therefore tried to combine them in his own poetry. The mystical was always the way to vision—whether it was in his early monologues in the graveyard or the invisible landscapes of later years. Tired of imitative verse, he enthusiastically greeted poetic realism wherever he found it. As a critic also, Masters found that poetry which realistically explores the local can be an effective access to the mystical awareness which is vision.

As early as 1889, Masters was advocating simplicity of style as necessary "to write of the truths of every-day life correctly and pleasingly." Speaking later of the "revival" of 1914 he pointed to a "freshness and realism" suitable to the "wonder" of "the commonplace, the everyday things."[7] Of course he tried to capture the rhythms of ordinary speech in *Spoon River*, and he hoped to use the microcosm to explore the human condition. While on vacation from his job in Chicago, Masters read *Sister Carrie* and found in it "a refreshing realism, and honesty that meant something" (*ASR*, 284).

As he often did, Masters used a metaphor from science to describe more fully that sense of realism he thought appropriate to the poet. He had observed how scientists could alter the genetic pool of fruit flies by using X rays or how cyclopean eyes could be similarly created in frogs. He was fascinated by the way nature itself could be altered by chemicals. His own cyclopean eye or X ray was, he felt, the law and his contacts with people. He felt that his experience in the studies of the law and in counseling people gave him a special access to the problems of day-to-day living. He likened his legal training to having "one great eye in the center of his forehead with which he saw everything with realistic clearness." But at the same time he had his normal eyes of the dreamer-poet who "saw beauty where it was not and truth where it had never been" (*ASR*, 317–318).

This doubleness of the realistic mystic was the tension he saw at the center of the best poetry. In his own work he sought to exercise and somehow to blend "the cyclopean eye" and "the dreaming eye." He was happy that he "saw through people with penetration" and was able to "weigh arguments and facts judicially" but troubled because with "dreaming eyes" he "looked down paths without seeing the tangles all in all." These were "the two strains of realism and mysticism" that Masters felt must always feed upon each other (*ASR*, 318).

Most of the poetry Masters liked contained large doses of what he meant by realism. He didn't think the style was in any way new. Realism for him didn't begin with Howells or Crane or even Rabelais. He didn't like it when he was described by critics as a Crabbe-like realist. He didn't think that the Imagists had begun a new "movement." To Masters, the Imagists were merely insisting on what the best poets had always demanded: the right word at the right time. What made realism in any way new at the time was the way in which poets had for so long strayed from what poets should be doing. Sandburg's "refreshing realism" illustrates this return to common sense: "He was not following the poetical idiom, the stock imagery and the often-repeated subject matter of the prominent poets then writing. He was off on an entirely new trail" (*ASR*, 335–336).

Masters' insistence on the poetry of the commonplace was also reinforced by his reading "the prose poems of Turgenev and the

French schools." He especially liked their "simplicity" and the way "they turned from the stock themes of poetry: . . . They concerned themselves with everyday things and people, with familiar tragedies and joys in the present world. They were far away from everything American except Whitman and Stephen Crane and Horace Traubel, and even from Emily Dickinson who was not greatly known in 1914, though I was then familiar with some of her poems, and admired them without reservation" (*ASR*, 342–343).

Again Whitman was the focus of what was real and vibrant in the American tradition Masters knew best. Masters offers some advice to students of American poetry. "The way to get Whitman's beauty," he counsels, "is to consider his comprehension, the multiverse that he sees, the love for nature that stirs him with such mystical simplicity of heart." Here is the blend of realism and mysticism at its best. Masters wanted readers to see Whitman's "plainness, without figures, without ornamentation." A lawyer, trained in forensics and classical figures, consciously chose an "American poetry, plain as the prairies, level as the quiet sea" (*W*, 320, 321).

It is not surprising that these kinds of critical judgments were unpopular at the time *Spoon River* was published or in the thirties when Masters wrote for *The American Mercury* and recorded his views in his autobiography. Masters himself noted that World War I ended the era of Spoon River. The popularity of *The Waste Land*, published in 1922, started a vogue for a different kind of mysticism—a vision coming from esoteric sources more than everyday things. Curiously enough, Ezra Pound, who championed the poet's responsibility for "the cleanliness of the tools," admired Masters greatly; and the Imagism of T. E. Hulme and others was very similar to what Masters referred to as realism. But as Karl Shapiro has shown, Whitman wasn't able to thrive at a time when D. H. Lawrence was considered "ignorant" and when the likes of Milton and John Donne were about to be reinterpreted in critical canons where the best poetry was the most difficult brainfood.[8] In a provocative look back to Eliot and Masters, Ernest Earnest has contrasted the "learned" verse of the Eliot School with its "abstruse symbols" to the "more accessible" poetry that "does not overinflate an experience." Citing the Village Atheist's famous dictum that immortality is an achievement for which man must "strive mightily," Earnest quips: "Unfortunately for his later reputation Masters did not render this in Sanskrit."[9]

Perhaps Earnest and Shapiro overstate the case, and surely William Carlos Williams' observation that *The Waste Land* "set me back twenty years" must be weighed carefully. But such skepticism about the stranglehold attained by the academics shows why Masters' critical stance on realism didn't get a large hearing.

For many years in American poetry, realism was to go one way, mysticism another. Myth came to mean foreign tongues, distant sources, difficult themes with deep philosophical and theological overtones. At the same time, much realism went the way of local color and regionalism. Most of the difficult "mythopoeic" documents ceased to be read outside the academies, and the critics and scholars in control of distinguishing "masterpieces" from the run-of-the-mill dismissed the regionalists as mere popularizers.

In the midst of such disparity, Masters stuck with his commitments to both realism and mysticism. The way he thought he could blend the two can be seen most clearly, first, in his unwavering exploration of the universal in the local, the macrocosm in the microcosm and, secondly, in his theory of "erotomania" and Emersonian correspondences. The former accounts for his successful but often misunderstood reputation as a regionalist; the latter coaxed him into what critics have forever insisted was his "preoccupation" with sex.

Devotion to a region was always, for Masters, a species of realism. He celebrated the land of his origins not to champion one area in competition with another but to record in detail his observations about what he knew best. In his essay on Emerson he admitted that Concord for Emerson was not going to be much different from the small town of his own youth (*E*, 1–41). He was not arguing for the uniqueness of his experiences as much as attempting to fulfill the poet's responsibility to observe the experiences of every day. In this, Chaucer was remote enough to be admired in Masters' day (though maybe for the wrong reasons); Wordsworth was an embarrassment for almost everyone; Whitman was out of fashion; but regionalism at least had a chance.

Masters didn't talk much directly about the Midwest in which he was born and raised. But he wrote hundreds of poems that both celebrated and chastised the people and ideas of the place of his origins. Strangely, critical response to what was referred to as his "cynical" and "poisonous" attitudes overlooked the deepest kind of indebtedness and love motivating his attacks.

The man accused of bitterness was actually very protective of the Midwest he grew up in. Coming face to face with the difficulties of making a living solely by writing, he complained that poetry was "all in control of formalists in the East." The same kind of pride in origins forced him to become annoyed with Sandburg. He even called "Chicago" a "mere place of interesting extravagance" because, to Masters, the poet "did not know Chicago, except as a city of packing plants, and criminals, and dirty alleys" (*ASR*, 253, 337).

Masters felt that the spirit of place—the prairie, Chicago, or the Midwest on the whole—was broader and deeper than most regionalist tributes would allow. The breadth of locale in his own experience is predominant in his breakdown of the pattern of his life, recorded in his autobiography. First there were the pastoral scenes of the prairie, the sunsets, the sounds of the meadow, and the accompanying "longings" for the infinite. Then there was his education, personified by the classically trained yet Emersonian free-thinking Mary Fisher. Curiously, Masters mentions her three times with reference to regionalism. He singles her out as the one who "had started many of us to reading, had inoculated us with freethinking, by directing us to the study of Emerson, and to the reading of Ingersoll's lectures which were enormously popular in those days in that part of Illinois" (*ASR*, 79–80). Again in his own essay on Emerson he praises her for enlarging the thinking of so many raised in Lewistown. And yet when her unenthusiastic note about *Spoon River* reached him he shows displeasure at what came across in her as insecurity or snobbery: "She was a type of the Midwest who tried to rise out of it; and depictions concerning it did not interest her" (67).

Displaced midwesterners or inhabitants of any region who would rather be elsewhere were not new then or now. And Masters was attuned enough to critical thinking to know that the kind of regionalism he was talking about would be misunderstood. While writing *The Great Valley* he "wanted to interpret and memorialize Illinois and the country which had given so many distinguished men to America." Only now can we see just how accurate his pessimism was: "It will be many years, if ever, before those poems and those of *Toward the Gulf*, written the next year, receive the attention which a people of self-conscious culture give to such portraits and epics of a land" (*ASR*, 375). The key word here is "self-conscious." Masters understood clearly the dangers of such epics, and this may be another instance where hindsight and today's growing interest in regionalism will again make him look very good indeed as a critic.

In his listing of the "figures" that made up his life pattern, Masters listed Chicago as an influence that counterbalanced the prairie: "That city carried me out of overintrospection, it brought me face to face with people, it got me into a life of action, and thereby helped to aid my intellectual digestion; it cured me of the pathos of the country, and by doing that it started me toward that ruggedness of physical health which was naturally mine as the son of my father, and which I have kept more or less, despite nerves, from that day to this" (*ASR*, 404). Also while he was living in Chicago, the decidedly midwestern agrarian movement helped Masters coalesce his earlier studies and led him to write "many poems of people." His sense of the region was ultimately a mixture of the meditative prairie and the rugged action of the city. Again he experienced a combination of mysticism and realism.

In addition to countless poems celebrating the land of his origins, Masters also wrote *The Sangamon* for Rinehart's series "Rivers of America" (1942). The book is a history of the region and its people, complete with several fascinating maps and artists' sketches. There is also a good deal of autobiography in the book, and often the prose breaks out into an exuberant chant in honor of "prairie peace" (*S*, 6), the thrill of sunsets on the plains, "olfactory ecstasy" from aromas of the farm (81), and the "supernatural character" of the landscape (136).

In many ways *The Sangamon* is a philosophical treatise on landscape poetry. The river itself is a symbol of "good and useful lives lived along its shores" and a tribute to the "beauty of its prairies that sleep and bloom and wave their grasses to the passing winds." It flowed "where little villages slept, mesmerized by time, where man came and went unnoted and unsung" (*S*, 235). This seemingly nonliterary book about a river turns out to be an important document in the body of Masters' critical thinking. This river song is his "Nature" and the record of experimentation at his Walden Pond. Consider his invitation to the reader very early in the book: "I am sure that if you should drive through Menard County strange dreams would come to you, and moreover those dreams would tally with mine. If so, does not something float out of that soil, and are not the past people of this region double-lived, having this place on earth and some place beyond, like the poets dead and gone of Keats?" (6–8). Masters always considered that soil his "nurturing spot of earth," his "spiritual home" still "brooded over" by the influence of folks long gone (30–31). The spirit of place "catches the imagination like a strange touch on the very heart, the very spiritual being of prenatal memories" (87). What he calls "earth places" stir feelings beyond explanation. He recalls that "the silence and the pastoral beauty of the country there bring one into a trance." He is cautious, yet certain about the deeper symbols: "It may be that I idealize it, but at any rate it has a magical appeal to me quite beyond my power to describe" (116).

But the silence and magical memories are not always happy, and Masters' critical sense reveals much that is bittersweet in his devotion to the spirit of place. In the Sangamon Valley, the prairie "defies change and the works of man." And that defiance will often "speak a silent language of past generations." For all his "love of the prairies," Masters is also wary about how "some of the pioneer women grew melancholy under the influence of their unchanging mood." The same prairies produce a bewilderment in the quest of ultimates. This yearning also shows in a different kind of landscape: in "the faded eyes, the drooped eyelids of some of the old women of Sandridge" after "years of gazing over the level stretches of grass to the rims of a forest that seemed to bound a happier land" (*S*, 16).

This same bittersweet yearning is embodied in the symbol of New Salem Hill: "One feature of the landscape is the broad prairie to the west, which stretches to the sunsets under a memorial light in which the Illinois meadow larks fly and hide and sing, breaking the silence of eternity which broods over the land with music that speaks of 'old unhappy far off things and battles long ago,' and of happy things as well, of hopes and love, of goodness and simple devotion to nature and truth" (*S*, 160). Those far off things tell the story of Jay Bishop whose life and death were later to haunt Masters. Bishop's untimely suffocation in the pit of his outhouse became for Masters "a symbol of what many little towns do to weary citizens who walk the square and pine for larger life, or different life" (57). This sounds more like the poet whom critics called "poisonous"—but here it tells both sides in a book mostly celebratory.

For Masters, exploration of the region of one's origins was a species of realism. He believed, with Coleridge, that a poet might "steal from himself all the natural man." The poetry of everyday things necessarily led to the landscape, and the land invariably led to relationships with the people raised in that soil. Just as Emerson's and Thoreau's regionalism helped them discover a theory of correspondences, Masters found that the infinite was to be found in the intimations of the prairies and the mystical awareness made possible by physical love. No discussion of Masters the critic would be in any way adequate without a closer look at his highly misunderstood ideas on love and sex.

Reviewers generally objected to Masters' discussion of his sexual affairs as well as to what they felt was an inordinate amount of his poetry devoted to biological love. He was fully aware of the labels attached to him—"poet of passion" and "a poet who was immersed in sex"—but he preferred to think of himself as "a poet who expressed the ideal phases of the erotic impulses" and "a priest of the Uranian as well as of the Dionaean Venus." It's just that he saw the way to

Urania through the Dionaean: "I had never been able to see anything wrong in erotic indulgence." Rather, "beauty in women was one manifestation of the divine influences that controlled the world." The erotic impulse was "luminous," "mystical," and ultimately "transcendent" (*ASR*, 251, 250).

Now if this sounds merely like a typical though elaborate "love" of one "on the make," consider repeated allusions to his love affairs as "a severe schooling in what was practically erotomania." Through "emotional concentration" as well as "the secrets and the agonies," he felt that his "emotional powers were enormously deepened" (*ASR*, 313). The deepest resources of physical love provide, for Masters, the most available source of man's vision of the transcendent. On the question of this access to indefinable truth, he turns to Goethe who "celebrates the eternal womanly, and love as the all-uplifting and all-redeeming power on earth and in heaven." This intimation of the eternal is therefore for man "revealed in its purest and most perfect form through woman" (*ASR*, 408).

Though this all sounds very Platonic, Masters didn't read Goethe in any dualistic sense. Lest anyone forget that he is celebrating sexual union, Masters uses repeated images from biology—including the detailed accounts of the path of sperm, the cycles of a zygote and the mystical side of the physical process he described. Yet his emphasis is on "the mysteries of creative beauty." And Swedenborg, Emerson, and Goethe taught him to express that indefinable cosmic mind in the language of correspondences:

> Goethe declares here that in the transitory life of earth love is only a symbol of its diviner being, and that the possibilities of love, which earth can never fulfill, become realities in a higher life which follows, and that the spirit which woman interprets to us here still draws us upward. So here is expressed all that I have felt of love, both as a giver of life and a forecast of a higher sphere, as a delusion, a satiety and a deathless force. [*ASR*, 408]

This theory of the life forces released in the physical union of love goes a long way toward explaining some of the controversies of Masters' own life as well as his more provocative poems and critical pronouncements. His poems about sex are almost always an expression of correspondences. Whitman was misread in the same way, and Masters' transcendentalism is again quite naturally at its best when he is talking about his hero.

Masters makes his point very clearly in defense of his literary ancestor: "Never has a man so fully expressed his cosmic longing as

Whitman did, flinging to the winds all reticences, and daring to use words and images which shadow it forth. He incurred the risk of being mocked, of being grossly interpreted by the vulgarity of the world" (*W*, 148–149). As it turned out, "risk" was an understatement. Somehow when writing about Whitman, the critic in Masters was always most clear on that cosmic longing: "Whitman here is hinting at those profound intimations of nature, of man and love, which visit all deeply imaginative souls. He is catching the flashing lights of realms afar and around us, and doing it, as only it can be done by the experience of love which is union, merging with the infinite through the finite" (148). In Whitman's poems he found "the awe, reverence and beauty of life, as they are expressed in the human body, with the physical attraction and delight of physical contact" (296). Transcendent and mystical truth must be expressed through what is real; no dualism here. The blend of the mystical and the physical was foremost in Masters' account of how "Whitman fought for the modern point of view which has discarded chastity as the perverted ideal of Asiatic mysticism." Whitman celebrated physical union: "He spoke for sensuality, not the life of wayward and hedonistic indulgence, but for man's and woman's spirit playing through the body and thereby ministering to the spirit and finding itself" (323). The discovery and expression of self were at the center of everything Whitman wrote and became foremost in Masters' repeated allusions to the mystical nature of physical love.

Masters thought the best poetry dealt in the transcendental by exploring everyday things; it was mystical yet realistic; it opened out into expansive vision by coming to know the truths contained in the land and the spirit of place. Further critical judgments on these points can be found in the differences he points to between the revered Mark Twain and his friend Vachel Lindsay.

Masters chided Twain and praised Lindsay on many of the same counts. Twain "lost his home" when he abandoned Missouri for Connecticut; Lindsay was a poet of "rich localism." Twain was "not a real satirist" because he lacked vision; Lindsay used his "Swedenborgian faculty" to "bind together the whole visible scene of life by some unifying tie or principle" (*L*, 273). Twain was, in Masters' eyes, the opposite of much that his heroes Emerson and Whitman stood for; Lindsay was often very close to their reincarnation on the modern scene. A close look at how and why Masters reached these conclusions will fill in much more detail on his own stance as a critic.

Reviewers called *Mark Twain: A Portrait* (1938) "inaccurate," "incomprehensible," and even "stupid." The reviews cited its lack of originality, coming after the famous arguments of Van Wyck Brooks. Surely the book will not take its place at the head of Twain scholarship, but its energetic analysis is a strong expression of what Masters valued in the native American literature he hoped to see flourish.

Masters' attacks on Christianity had long upset reviewers. But his quarrel with Twain was not so much an indictment of Christianity as an exposé of sublimated religious indoctrination that Twain couldn't escape: "He never became what he wanted to be as a free spirit, a free thinker, and that was true because his impressionable years had been indelibly fixed by village theology and maternal piety." The result was serious, as "he never became a clear character with respect to religion and philosophy." When he did protest, it was always to "curse and rail, like the typical infidel." This deep repression forced him to drag "the ball and chain of Christian theology to the last" (T, 16). The consequences on his later thinking were severe: "He never had what Whitman called religion, namely a confidence in Nature and Cosmic scheme. In consequence peace never entered his heart. He was a Christian by the fact that he saw life as evil. He was an infidel by the fact that he first denied God and then cursed him for being able to be denied by a mind that looks over the suffering, the folly of men, and the tragedy of death" (167). Masters was disturbed by the skewed vision created by the effects of severe repression. More than an attack on Christianity, his anger at Twain is a plea for the "magnanimous man" of Goethe, Emerson, Whitman, and Nietzsche:

> His observations on the Bible never got beyond his pointing out its patent absurdities. The Christian mythology was so deep in his mind from the Hannibal days that in fifty years of thinking and writing he never did more than bring up arguments against it, as a man will do who is struggling to draw away from something that he wants to reject from his life, yet is unable to do so. This is the whole of his intellectual emancipation from superstition. All his epigrams and dialectics are directed against fables that are not worth noticing. He had neither the courage nor the insight to see, as Nietzsche did, that Christianity is a poison. [T, 214]

Masters' critique obviously goes beyond his displeasure with religion and is consistent with his rejection of triviality, orthodoxy, and formalism in poetry and literary criticism.

The popularity Twain enjoyed disturbed Masters on several counts. He was, Masters felt, incapable of poetic vision because he had "no philosophy of life, no compelling ideals, no political principles, no theory of the literary art and faith, no belief in man, in liberty, in institutions, in possible progress for the race, in the potential influence of civilizing processes." Lest his readers feel that something is left out, Masters adds that "the cause of Twain's spiritual collapse was that he had no genuine convictions about any important thing" (*T*, 169). He frequently accused Twain of attacking the wrong people. To Masters, Twain went after "manikins," "small frauds," and "petty cheats," while "great mountebanks and influences who were devouring his country had his friendly and unsuspecting association" (85). And although he "loved the river" he gave up his home out of "subliminal fear that he had lost the lofty position to which fortune had lifted him in the East" (85). His thinking was "indicative of the unformed spirit, the mind in the making, the immaturity that is American"; thus "Twain never touched the deeper waters of the sweep of things" (240).

Above all, to Masters, Twain was a victim of "American Philistinism"—the total opposite of Jefferson, Emerson, and Whitman. While Whitman, the seer, "told his country what was the matter with it," Twain was "making money by burlesquing the follies of the human race." Whitman exposed "rank hypocrisy" and "the depravity of the business classes"; Twain "walked amid the idiocy and the stench of the times making faces" (*T*, 98, 100). Here's the difference:

> The quackeries that flowered in Emerson-transcendentalism, in Whitman's optimistic chants, comparable to the dynamo that evolved from electricity observed in a piece of rubbed amber, in the twitching of a frog's leg, came to riotous buffoonery in Twain. There was money in it, treasure. To choose preposterous characters, to depict absurd situations was as funny as to use phonetic nonsense. America has always given more to her clowns than to her legitimate performers. Twain knew this. [*T*, 100–101]

The differences were crucial to Masters: "All the while we wish that he had done for America as a satirist what Whitman did for it as a poet" (178). And again: "Whitman, believing in a Hegelian progress, in Darwin's deductions about life, could well stand up for the stupid, the disinherited, the criminals. Twain, gathering evidence for a kind of infidel Calvinism, could let the world shift for itself, yet curse the destiny that fixed man in irrevocable tragedy" (247–248). These differences spoke to the essence of what Masters thought the poet should be doing.

Perhaps Masters was so upset with Twain because he also saw greatness in him. In fact, Twain had a lot of what Masters held in high esteem. In *Innocents Abroad* Twain's ridicule of Europe and his "abandoned humor" produced what Masters called "real eloquence fresh and original" (*T*, 64). Similarly, in *Life on the Mississippi* Masters saw "the eloquence of silence," "the haunting sense of loneliness, isolation, remoteness," a "tranquility" which is "profound and infinitely satisfying" (148). In Masters' view, the book "comes as near being the great American epic as anything we have." He elaborates: "Whitman rolled the word *Mississippi* under his tongue and spoke of it as a theme for great poetry. Twain captured some of its poetry and wrote a book that can scarcely be forgotten, though it is not sustained to the end" (152). Finally, Masters thought of *The Mysterious Stranger* as "Twain's supreme tale, a work of marvellous imagination, and wrought out in language full of energy and eloquence" (221).

Such praise for Twain was mixed. Less restrained was Masters' approval of Lindsay, whom he called "America's greatest lyric poet." One major artist's assessment of another cannot be overlooked, and the critics proclaimed *Vachel Lindsay: A Poet in America* (1935) as "important," "profound," and "definitive." Masters set the tone for the kind of document he produced by frequently calling it a Wordsworthian record of "the growth of a poet's mind" (*L*, 161).

To Masters, Lindsay was in the line of Whitman. He showed a "passion for restless wandering." He was a visionary "in search of the soul of the U.S.A." (*L*, 9). His mind "ran always to symbols, figures, pictures, and resemblances, and with a Swedenborgian faculty he strove to bind together the whole visible scene of life by some unifying tie or principle" (273). Masters traced Lindsay's unifier to the "essentially American religious spirit" which brought "union in disunion such as binds a family by blood ties which cannot be shaken off and is even more powerful in domestic strife." Because he was "totally immersed" in this religious culture, Lindsay was, in Masters' eyes, "the most rational poet that America thus far had had" (251).

Masters' study is rich in the detail of Lindsay's life and includes hundreds of lengthy quotations from his letters and notebooks. He considered his friend "a pure instance of the poet by profession, who had devoted all his life to the preparation and the practice of poetry" (*L*, vi). His estimate is at once a panegyric for his friend and a public statement of support for the poetry he believed in:

> If I could write one sentence that would magnify the vision of readers to a clearer reading of Vachel Lindsay's art and its problems it would be this: Not in England, and in a measure with leisure, as was the case with Tennyson; but in America and

against poverty, and the fatigues of a life of lecturing, did Vachel Lindsay pour forth his wholly original songs, songs more numerous than those of Poe, and nearly equal to the bulk of Whitman's. [*L*, viii]

In numerous commentaries strung between quotations from the journals, Masters stressed Lindsay's insight, the "self-made mythology" of his Gospel of Beauty and his Map of Vision, his "power of lyricism" which enabled him to produce a "species of poetry in which a kind of madness was the engine of miraculous achievement" (217).

Masters greatly admired the courage that spoke through Lindsay's poems. "He was never like a poetaster looking for something to write about, and working with virtuosity on his technique," he noted. Rather, "it was in his nature to make war upon the whole tone, temper and morale of post–Civil War America." A sense of urgency emerges in his poems as "a sensuality concerned with beauty, truth and reality floods the soul with peace and satisfaction" (*L*, 287).

Above all it was the realism Lindsay combined with his visionary stance that dazzled Masters. It was his devotion to the spirit of place that set him on the way to "catching the American voice" (*L*, 287). Lindsay was "the voice of that mythical America of Colonial heroisms and splendors"; he was "the celebrant in free and sinuous measures" of native American heroes, the "bard of the Indian," the "comic muse of the Negro." Though he had no classical education, he was most American in his close study of the land, the people, and the region of his origins. Many of his poems were accurate and moving records of what Masters called a "rich localism" (373–374). At a time when poetry steeped in place was hardly in vogue, Lindsay the regionalist was afforded an impassioned defense by the lawyer-poet who was also a neighbor in the soil.

Masters recognized that Lindsay's ancestry, education, religion, morals, and taste were identifiably "Middlewest." He maintained that "if ever an American poet was nurtured to sing of his land for it in words and images deriving from nowhere except from the soil which bore him, it was Vachel Lindsay." Here Lindsay was a "collateral relative of Whitman" who "independently and in his own original way carried out some of the instructions in which Whitman was insistent all his life" (*L*, 34). And here, at a time when literature was controlled by editors and publishers in the East, Masters' defense of Lindsay the midwesterner reaches a high point: "The country then needed to see itself part of the time in the mirrors of nonmetropolitan environment, and to know that Fifth Avenue is not America all in all" (135).

Being a poet in the Midwest was in no way easy. Lindsay had to stand up to the cultural heritage of what Will Durant called the "European America" of the East "where the older stocks look up respectfully to foreign aristocracies" (*L*, 371). Even after his early success, the trap waited for Lindsay:

Not being Eastern American he made in fact only a slight impact upon it; and after the first excitement about his poetry he was treated with supercilious indifference, and the field which he had broken and harrowed and sowed was taken and reaped by pro-English artists. He found that there was no union of spirit and mind in America; and that his own West cared more for the East than it did for the West, and cared more for Eastern poets than for him who had striven to give Springfield and Illinois a soul. [*L*, 371]

Life itself in the Midwest scarcely made things easier for its poets: "Many have been the gifted youth in Illinois who dreamed these Lindsay dreams, but never sang them. They were crushed by materialism, they were broken by Philistine persecution, they were suffocated by the Fat Prairie, and hunted down by the factory spirit." But somehow Lindsay survived what he called "the usual Middle West crucifixion of the artist." He rose above satire to sing of "Mystic and Magical Springfield, the city to be" (271). What Masters thought Lindsay was up against is a further gloss on his own theories of the state of poetry at the time:

What New York says about a book is imposed upon Chicago, and over the country goes the judgment of the financial capital of America 3000 miles from one of its most populous states and a thousand from its center of population. The voice of America west of the Hudson is only the ululation of an echo. It is possible for someone who has only traveled in the Mississippi valley to write a story of the Mississippi River, and to have the writing so coached and advertised and hailed in New York that Missouri and Illinois will take up the cry, and drain their own firsthand knowledge of their own country. As there are no sovereign States, there is no independent judgment. [*L*, 366]

By now it should be obvious that Masters and Lindsay were in many ways kindred spirits. Masters' commentary on his friend's critical judgments is, therefore, a good reflection on his own thinking. A final look at their mutually shared views might begin with this interesting analysis prompted by the skeptic in Masters' philosophical side:

Philosophers and poets are likely to carve out of the shifting air and mist of life's manifest a sphere of interpretation, and say here lies the main interest, here is the place from which the whole landscape of life can be viewed and appraised. Not only that but every poet can make his empire thus created the very substance and meaning of the whole. It is like taking into a phial some of the sea's water, and calling it all that can be said of the sea as to quality and essential substance. [*L*, 315–316]

In the mood of this warning, Lindsay calls for "a poem, a poem that is grand and wonderful as the whole race." And again Masters quotes him: "The great poem has yet to be written. . . . The man who is too much in harmony with his time is a compromiser. . . . True criticism of art can never consist in the mere application of rules. It can be just only when it is founded on quick sympathy with the changeful efforts of human nature" (104).

In many ways, Masters found in Lindsay exactly what he was looking for in poetry and criticism on the whole. His tribute is also an appropriate summary of his own thinking:

He was not interested in theories of sensuous flow, in presenting images for their own sake, in inducing hypnotic conditions by repetitive rhythms, in refinements, in exoticisms, in neo-romanticism, druidism, dadaism, paroxysm, or vitalism. His interest, his passion, was America, the American heroes, American democracy, beauty, and religion; and in finding the soul of the U.S.A. and giving it voice. So on the one hand he was oblivious of the dead corpse of poetry lying about him mesmerically squeaking for culture, technique, and form; and on the other hand he did not hear the raging schools quickly arising about him. . . . From the beginning poetry with Lindsay was not technique, not fine writing, not culture, but it was courage, faith, vision, great belief in American democracy. [*L*, 288]

In his inimitable way, Masters' portrait of Lindsay touched on most of what he thought was wrong with the literary scene in his time; and he makes bold suggestions on what the American poet must do to survive and be worthy of the name.

No brief review of Masters the critic can examine all his strong and at times controversial opinions. But a definite pattern can be found in his autobiography, in selected critical articles he wrote about poetry in his time, in his biographies of Whitman, Twain, and Lindsay, and in his river song, *The Sangamon*. Like most poets, Masters wrote a good many poems about poetry. The views he expressed in his prose are consistent with his criticism in verse—from the pronouncements at graveside in the *Spoon River Anthology* to the fullness of prairie songs in *Illinois Poems*. Whether it is Petit the Poet in *Spoon River*, Lord Byron talking to Doctor Polidori in *Starved Rock*, or the mystical, mute dreams of Black Hawk in *More People*, the subject is poetry in its myriad forms. Masters' theories on poetry are consistent with the views of many of his critics. Cesare Pavese sees the mystic in his "Dantesque yearning" and his "exasperated and surrealistic normality." Earnest stresses the realism of his "accessible poetry." Charles Burgess links many of Masters' opinions on literature to his training in forensics. Henry Hahn finds a curious mixture of optimism and somber brooding filtered through the influence of the "graveyard school." [10]

Masters never strayed far from his writer's sense in his role as critic. In his appraisals of achievement and failure, he never abandoned his understanding of the difficulties of composition. In his review of *Vachel Lindsay*, Sherwood Anderson called the book "a story of a writer, by a writer, for writers." [11]

Boldly and often with refreshing humor, Masters took a cutting edge to what he felt was wrong with the poets and critics of his time. In reviewing the sources of his own inspiration, he often rewrote literary tradition to tell it the way he felt it should be told. He spoke out especially against formalism, Eastern snobbery, and imitation of Europe. His goal was always the poet's mystical vision, and he saw the access to that visionary awareness through a realistic portrayal of everyday things, close study of the people and places of one's origins, and the union of physical love which opens the consciousness to a direct perception of the transcendental.

"I Am a Hellenist"

MASTERS, GOETHE, AND THE GREEKS

By the time he enrolled as a student at Knox College, Masters had read "a good deal of the Greek classics in translations." In order to enter the college he was required to begin the study of Greek in the prep school; at the same time, he decided to resume his study of German, which he had begun years earlier. Thus began his fascination with the cultures of Greece and Germany—an interest which grew into a lifelong devotion to Homer, Aeschylus, Sophocles, Euripides, and Goethe. Years of translating and repeated reading of the classics helped Masters sharpen his tools, opened up to him the classical spirit of what he called "magnitude," and provided access to his ever-deepening mystical vision.

It is a matter of record that the *Greek Anthology* was the immediate source of the *Spoon River Anthology*. Reviewers of the time were quick to note Masters' indebtedness.[1] In dedicating *Toward the Gulf* (1918) to William Marion Reedy, Masters explained exactly what he saw in that ancient text. He found in the epigram "sad revealment" and a "touch of irony," and he hoped to absorb from the Greek language and symbols what he called "the humanism and dignity of the original." His attempt was to transfer these elements into his own *Anthology*, in the process creating something "if less than verse, yet more than prose." What Masters hoped to accomplish was to take the Greek epigrams "ironical and tender, satirical and sympathetic" and combine them with "the form and spirit" of Homer. Using the classical machinery of an ancient culture, he wanted to examine closely "the life around us as we view it through eyes whose vision lies in heredity, mode of life, understanding of ourselves and of our place and time." Ultimately he hoped that the force of the Greek spirit would help him create "an epic rendition of modern life."

In the introduction to the Collier paperback edition of *The New Spoon River*, Willis Barnstone has reviewed the influences of the *Greek*

Anthology on the achievements in *Spoon River Anthology*. Barnstone describes the advantages of using the ancient form of the epigram to release the power of Masters' Kafkaesque portrait of the modern world. The "objectivity" and "frankness," the tragic reflections of "sun and darkness" combined to contribute to the "fresh, rough diction," the "uncompromisingly irreverent and dark mood" and the "poetic exploitation of the common and the banal" in Masters at his best.

As Barnstone points out, the advantages of using the *Greek Anthology* as a model were many. The anthology format was a good solution to the "esthetic problem of how to extend the lyric voice successfully beyond Poe's forbidding one-hundred line barrier: how to write a long lyric poem without lapsing into narrative or descending into boredom." Moreover, the epigrammatic structure suggests the intimacy of confessional verse in a dramatic frame. Such dramatic monologues make possible "a voice of social conscience with the passion and aesthetic shape of individual confession." Barnstone reminds us also that Masters found in his reading of the older anthology an interrelatedness of voices blending to a unity, a pervading mood of "bitterness and misanthropy," and the common theme of the descriptive influences of urban and industrial values. Solidly based in the classical form, Masters' lyrics were freed to explore more accurately and fully the modern and the mundane.[2] All this must have been at least a part of what Reedy had in mind when he urged Masters to prepare himself to write a distinctively American poetry by reading more of the Greeks.[3]

Throughout his entire career, however, Greek culture meant much more to Masters than anything the *Anthology* had to offer. Aeschylus and Homer were always his inspiration and energizing force. In 1942 he told a *New York Times Book Review* interviewer that he reread all the Greek plays every two or three years. Describing himself as "a Hellenist," he contrasted the expanse of the Greeks and the narrowness of Americans: "The great marvel of the world is Greek civilization. They thought in universals, as did the Elizabethans. We are provincial in our thoughts."[4] These contrasts are easy enough to understand, and they add up to a rather typical appraisal of Hellenism.

But with the help of several startling metaphors, Masters took his reading of the Greeks a bit further. In the same interview he suggested that esteemed writers like Howells, Garland, and Twain suffered from the opposite of Hellenism: "Some one should write an article on America's Cinderella complex and the many men it has destroyed. The man in the country dreaming of being the guest of honor at a city banquet. The Cinderella complex—the destroyer of virility, of sound workmanship and honest thought."

In *Vachel Lindsay* (1935) Masters expanded the comparison into a full-scale analysis of Greek and American ideals. He acknowledged that one of Lindsay's purposes was to "amalgamate a vast and loosely articulated nation into a spiritual whole, to which appeals could be made which would touch all nerves simultaneously and evoke the one exact cultural response." Masters shared his friend's desire to "shape men and a new state by an irresistible influence of art." But he pointed out that in Greece the people were "unified by games and song and language." Pythagoras and Plato urged the "building of the soul to the strains of music" in order "to tune the ear to the music of the spheres, the harmony of the universe." The contrasts are obvious: "Lindsay knew well enough that the America and the Springfield which he would reshape were not places of a common blood, common religious center, nor, outside of baseball, a gathering for a game or games in which all the people participated." In short, Masters observed, "America has lacked a god fitted to harmonize the whole country" (*L*, 267–268). Masters felt that a rebirth of the Greek spirit might supply that god for the new world.

In explaining "what Lindsay was trying to say," Masters filled in the outline of his own reading of Greek philosophy. In short, he combined Plato's ladder and the theory of love as "the cornerstone of the ideal state" and linked Lindsay with the similar chant for unity in Whitman. Plato felt that anyone who had a foreshadowing of ultimate beauty was charged with "the enthusiasm of ideas" and experienced the poet's madness. In order to come into possession of that vision, the poet had to become attuned to higher rhythms and then make it possible for others to participate in the "highest activities" and the "life of deepest satisfactions." Masters contended that Americans must go sing and dance and build monuments to the higher ideals: "The Greeks danced, so should they dance in Lindsay's Magical Springfield; and themes should be danced, as they were long ago in theatres scooped out of the hills. . . . The western glory thus should rise; and if it does not, the cities were doomed" (*L*, 270–271). Ultimately Masters wanted to use the Greek models and then push off from them into "Whitman's fine dreams" of "inventing for America classical allusions of her own, and of making for America her own mythology which passed the understanding of sensible people" (*L*, 270–271).

In *The New World* (1937) Masters pleaded for America's "rise to nationhood" through "verse which celebrates Democracy and the magnanimous man." Again the model he used was classical Greece:

> Greece may instruct the New World in this wise;
> Greece by her verse transformed the city-states
> Into one nation, one Hellenic mind.
> Rome by an imitation of the inimitable,
> And the mouth honor to Hellenic gods,
> But with no native legends never rose
> To verse or art that spoke the Roman mind,
> And made the Roman State.
> The New World, too, with neither myths nor gods,
> With no traditions save those of the People,
> With never a theme distinctive, save the People,
> Must sing the People or go down to time
> As a nation songless,
> Or a nation which never found its soul.
>
> [NW, 267]

Masters clarifies exactly how the New World should follow that classical spirit in his repeated distinctions between Hellenism and Hebraism. In explaining the basic differences, he accused Lindsay of misrepresenting Greek culture by overlaying on it "the spirit of Jerusalem" and thereby confusing "a genuine passion for their intellectual heredity" with "his own kind of evangelism and religiosity" (L, 265). Masters rejected "the Hebrew culture with its moralizing and its millenniums, its prophets and its asceticisms, its oriental and extravagant imagery." He found it strange that, "in the name of apocalyptic wrath," Lindsay would support "a mendicant, a wizard, a wandering preacher, a hater of the rich, a foe of Rome, and a trampler of the cities" (L, 209).

What Masters found to be "beyond Lindsay's understanding" was at the core of his own reading of the Greeks. Always at the center was "Apollo, the god of fate with avenging arrows, the god of poetical creation, the leader of all the Masses, the founder of towns and civil institutions, the Sun god whence all life comes." Masters liked Lindsay's Swedenborgian sense of symbol and ultimate unity; however, as Masters saw it, Lindsay chose the wrong unifier. For Masters, Christianity was "far from that Dorian Apollo, the god of order, of music and beauty, who presided over the philosophy of Pythagoras and was selected to rule Plato's city of the Perfect." Even Lindsay's "restlessness" was not prompted so much by a vision of the absolute as by a "characteristically American" wandering that lacked "a calm god like the Dorian Apollo." In all, Masters recommended lifting ourselves "above the heredity and educational saturation" of the Bible and celebrating instead with Homer and the Greek tragedians, "a civilization and culture greater than any since its day" (*L*, 209, 268, 216).

Never one to be accused of hedging, Masters clarified on many occasions exactly what he thought was wrong with the Judeo-Christian world view. The following lengthy passage from *Across Spoon River* deserves full citation as a significant statement of his Hellenism:

> With years and study I came to the definite conclusion that the Bible should be thrown away, and utterly eliminated from human interest, except as literature, so far as it is literature, and that Hellas should take control of America. In spite of New England theology America started under the influence of Hellas. Thomas Jefferson's was the great mind and vision that tried to commit America to the beauty and the rationalism of Hellas. Two summers ago after reading H. L. Mencken's excellent *Treatise on Right and Wrong*, I read Aristotle's *Ethics* for the first time; and it revived my conviction that what America needs is the magnanimous man, not the man of charity of St. Paul. In a word I think that Christianity has falsified and enervated the world, America included. It has bred the hypocrite, who was a far less prevalent character in pagan days. I think I can say this with as much justification in reason as I could say that a great pestilence and a vast slaughter in war were disasters to the world. To my mind there is hardly an utterance of Jesus that is sound and true, while his mind and his character are inferior to those of Socrates, Confucius, Aristotle and Plato. [*ASR*, 401]

Masters attacked this falsification and hypocrisy by the subject of another biography—Mark Twain.

Even though the Missouri satirist made a reputation on ridiculing Christianity, Masters felt that, in spite of himself, "Twain judges man's life and destiny upon earth by really accepting the Bible tales, by viewing them not through the eyes of Confucius, Lao-tze, or Socrates, not through the philosophy of Athens and Plato, but through the eyes of Israel and Jesus and Paul." For Masters, Twain was another example of a flimsy American "Cinderella" hero badly in need of a classical vision. A sense of Greek mythology could have helped him see what Masters called a Bible that preached "absurd things about the Cosmic Mind and enforced their acceptance . . . with incantations and witchcraft." Masters felt that American culture needed the struggles of the Greek gods rather than "the idiocies of the Bible" (*T*, 233).

Greek literature set Masters in pursuit of magnanimity, energy, beauty, and the tragic vision which releases a typically classical fullness of experience. His prose writings throughout his entire career describe what he found in Greek symbols. In Aeschylus' vision he saw "a titanic dedication to the hope of uplifting the human race." He compared Heraclitus to the mysticism of the Buddha (*L*, 183–184, 269). His collection of Emerson for the Living Thoughts Library includes three pages of Emerson on the fables of Prometheus, Orpheus, Proteus, Hercules, and Apollo (*E*, 45–47). He repeatedly compared the songs of Whitman to Homeric hymns, and he once called Homer's songs the greatest poetry of all time. In a tribute to Whitman, Masters explained the triumphant sensuality which he found in Hellenism: "He spoke for sensuality, not the life of wayward and hedonistic indulgence, but for man's and woman's spirit playing through the body and thereby ministering to the spirit and finding itself" (*W*, 323).

Alongside his reading of the Greek philosophers and dramatists, Masters kept open the pages of Goethe. In an epilogue to his autobiography he attributes to Goethe a summation of "all that I have felt of love, both as a giver of life and as a forecast of a higher sphere, as a delusion, a satiety and a deathless force." Masters read the last chorus of *Faust* as a celebration of "the external womanly, and love as the all-uplifting and all-redeeming power on earth and in heaven." In years of reading *Faust* he constantly experienced a further energizing force for his classical vision: "Goethe declares here that in the transitory life of earth love is only a symbol of its diviner being, and that the possibilities of love, which earth can never fulfill, become realities in a higher life which follows, and that the spirit which woman interprets to us here still draws us upward." This higher life is, of course, at the center of Masters' "Hellenism," but it is a vision which the energy of Goethe always renewed. He pauses to underscore the significance of that renewal: "I dwell upon this subject because I feel that a good deal of my secret is contained in it, and I would be glad if I could fully express it" (*ASR*, 408).

Goethe showed the lawyer-poet how to express that secret. Writer, lawyer, and scientist, Germany's most universally acclaimed genius offered Masters a personal model of accomplishment. When he read books hidden behind legal briefs in his father's office, the young Masters must have admired the accomplishments of the multi-careered Goethe. He praised Goethe's training in forensics which created in him an unwavering logic that disciplined his most energetic quests after the infinite. (Masters once even chided his hero Whitman for not possessing the logical restraint of Goethe.) Goethe's interest in plant life and anatomy also has a parallel in Masters' repeated use of extended metaphors from science to explain metaphysical processes. Even the burdens of administrative duties when Goethe worked at the court in Weimar would have bolstered Masters' confidence and determination when his own daily grind in the law offices threatened to destroy his career as a writer.

Though Masters' most frequent allusions are to *Faust*, several of Goethe's lesser known works point to further affinities between the two authors. *Götz von Berlechingen* (1773), a play about a failed peasant revolt, parallels Masters' interest in populism. *Hermann und Dorothea* (1789) is set in the village of Goethe's own times. Goethe's influence on the *Sturm und Drang* movement and the lessons he learned from his teacher Herder also provided clues to how he helped Masters express "the secret." Herder's almost mystical identification with the truths available only in the landscape and in the soul of the folk led Goethe to the kind of nature hymns which Masters heard on the Illinois prairies. This combination of "storm and stress" and mystical calm appealed to Masters' own commitment to the pain-bought process of energetic quest and serene contemplation.

In *Across Spoon River*, Masters recalls that he had read Goethe's *Dichtung und Wahrheit* and *Conversations with Eckermann* as early as his Lewistown days. He recalls regular visits to the home of a man of German descent who knew German literature well. There he spent evenings discussing Goethe, Schiller, and Heine. Before moving to Chicago he also wrote a sonnet "On Reading Eckermann's Conversations with Goethe." The sonnet was published in *A Book of Verses*[5] and initiated a series of allusions to Goethe that was to span three decades of Masters' writings.

Masters never wrote a biography of Goethe, but his series of books on Lindsay, Whitman, and Emerson contain elaborate discussions of Goethe's accomplishments as a writer and critic as well as an assessment of his importance for major figures in the American tradition.

Masters found in Goethe a "mystical faculty, which saw into the heart of things more clearly than the intellectual eye." With this mystical power Goethe had what Masters called an "intuition" which "goes straight to the core of an object or a person and lays hold of its essential." This mystical breakthrough was slightly different from the Greek sense of the journey of the soul where the vision is less clear and certain. The contrast is elaborated in Masters' appraisal of Lindsay's shadowy vision alongside Goethe's intuitive penetration.

Where Goethe's vision shoots straight through to the essence of people and objects, Lindsay looked primarily to "the outer appearance of things, the garb of nature, the language and the inarticulateness of human beings, and the unexplicable shadows and filaments which clothe the life of man." Thus Masters identifies Lindsay's very Platonic sense of shadows, the forms which "have something back of them of which these are in a way the hieroglyphics, to use a word that he often employed to shadow forth his speculations and his dreams" (L, 59).

Lindsay was much more Greek than German, in Masters' reading. His vision lingered in the Platonic shadows where Goethe's immediate penetration would always be too awesome. Masters' distinctions between these two different kinds of vision reveal as much about his own views as they do about his friend Lindsay. His sense of the magnitude of the absolute always formed an inseparable part of his "Hellenism." But the access he found to that vision of the absolute was decidedly more Goethe's than Plato's. His own sense of the mystical owes a great deal to a romantic energy in Goethe which became a part of his attitudes toward people and places in his later works. Masters identified in Lindsay a mystical quest, a "journey of the soul by the inner ascent" to "the presence of God." He was, therefore, a "soul seeking beauty," and that mystical vision above all made him a poet.

What Masters called Lindsay's "religious quest" also glosses his own debts to Goethe and the links between that debt and his Hellenism. The mystical religious vision of Lindsay or Whitman, Goethe or the Greeks was, for Masters, beyond the capabilities of any philosophy: "for what a man sees he sees; and what he desires with his whole heart to possess cannot be made untrue by satire or analysis." The "religious" mysticism that Masters found in Goethe was not an orthodoxy or creed but "a moral conviction and passion by which man is linked to cosmic forces, to something beyond the daily life of materialistic effort, and by which life is dignified and uplifted." This is the pain-bought vision which Masters expressed so often in his later poems; it is the "soul seeking beauty," the "innate urge, besides which talents, smartness, erudition, culture are nothing." For Masters, this urge burst forth in Greece in "the courageous eye of Sophocles" and later in "Shelleyan Prometheanism." He found it also in "the eighty years' toil of Goethe" (L, 60–61).

The overall picture of Goethe which emerges from Masters' comments provides considerable insight into his own values and attitudes. He admired Goethe, Homer, Shakespeare, and Whitman as nation-builders, prophets and voices of the people (L, 315). Masters had considerable empathy with the "abandon" of Goethe's desire in his later years to "purposely offend" what he felt had become "technical caprices," to violate foolish conventions and run his language outside "the technical grooves" then in fashion.

Two years later in *Whitman* his adulation for Goethe grew. Calling the second part of *Faust* "one of the world's great poems," Masters was drawn especially to "the soul weariness of Faust and his extrication from that by a rejuvenation." He journeyed with Faust in each reading, drawn in by the romantic energy and power to "heights where it was . . . difficult to conceive what was fairest and best." Goethe brought Masters' Hellenic vision to these kinds of heights, and yet an important qualifier shows how that mystical vision held on to the classical sense of limits: "Something in the quality and limitation of the human mind compels it to stick to men and the earth" (*W*, 103–104). That awareness of limitation guided Masters to look for the mystical in the concrete realities of the people and the landscape.

Masters got much of his Goethe through Whitman. In reflecting on Whitman's task in cataloging "the image of a whole land," he cites the passage

> Only themselves understand themselves and the like of
> themselves
> As souls understand souls
>
> [*W*, 306]

as a "paraphrase" of Goethe's "You are like the spirit which you comprehend." He also read *Faust* over Whitman's shoulder and found what Whitman called Goethe's "centering life in self—in perfect persons—perfect you, me: to force the real into the abstract ideal: to make himself, Goethe, the supremest example of personal identity: everything making for it: in us, in Goethe: every man repeating the same experience." Whitman found the Greek and Roman teachers emphasizing the self—but always (Masters felt) in a moralistic sense. Goethe, on the other hand, "seemed to look upon personal development as an end in itself." Masters concurred with this celebration of self in the interest of "beauty, erudition, knowledge—first of all, . . . culture." And he seconded Whitman's enthusiastic heralding of Goethe as "the most profound reviewer of life known . . . the first great critic and the fountain of modern criticism," the bringer of "the soundest philosophy of the modern world" (*W*, 241–243).

Masters also read Goethe through the eyes of Emerson. *Representative Men* was one of Masters' favorite books, and when he edited a selection of Emerson's writing for the Living Thoughts Library, he set aside a good deal of space for Goethe. Included are Emerson's commentaries on Goethe's "versatility," his humanizing of the devil in *Faust,* and his presentation in "the Helena" of "a philosophy of literature set in poetry." In his introductory remarks, Masters noted again his own liking for Goethe's "delicious sweetness and wisdom which dealt not with costume and condition, but with the spirit of life." Masters' praise is for Emerson as much as Goethe, and he provides an outline of how the vision of Goethe was to enter—through Emerson and Whitman—into the best of the American tradition as he saw it: "In a day when Goethe was suspect, when the portrait of Mephistopheles was considered devil worship, Emerson sounded the praises of Goethe in some of the truest and profoundest utterances that have come forth concerning the great genius of the nineteenth century" (*E*, 28). Emerson called Goethe's Mephistopheles "the first organic figure" that had been added to literary mythology "for some ages." Making the devil "real," "modern," and "European" located the symbol in time and space and forced man to look for the evil forces "in his own mind, in every shade of coldness, selfishness, and unbelief that, in crowds, or in solitude, darkens over the human thought" (28). Masters quoting Emerson on Goethe is a good gloss on the darker vision of the Spoon River poet.

Emerson had reservations about Goethe, and his qualified praise elicits from Masters some revealing insights into his own views. Emerson felt that Goethe could not attain "the highest unity" because he was not devoted to "pure truth." He was too much a realist, overly devoted to human culture for its own sake. In Emerson's words, Goethe—like Whitman—placed too much value on existence for its own sake. Emerson's view provoked an interesting response from Masters: "It may be that Goethe's earthiness, his erotic interests, his love of the good earth, of physical well-being, affected the ascetic side of Emerson in the forming of his estimate" (*E*, 28).

In these remarks Masters was defending his own values as well as Goethe's. But he was also touching on one of the paradoxes of his own age. Critics debated throughout the twenties and thirties the relative merits of what they came to see as the excesses of the nineteenth century. Modern poetics of the early twentieth century took a decidedly anti-romantic bent that became impatient with talk about "pure truth" and "higher unities." Some critics called for a return to the classics to combat the abuses and failures of romanticism. Masters, too, preferred the hard classical line to artless obscurity and pointless formalism. At the same time, however, many of the moderns—Masters included—never abandoned the romantics' belief in poetry's access to mystical vision. The poetry and criticism of the time bear many of the scars of that struggle between the romantics and the anti-romantics.

In many ways, Goethe was for Masters an important link between the classical vision of Greece and a modernism which had been strongly influenced by European romantics. Masters objected strongly to a great deal of what had transpired in the name of romanticism, and he agreed with much that was said in the wave of anti-romanticism usually identified with the writings of Irving Babbitt, T. S. Eliot, and T. E. Hulme.[6] But as other "isms" came along to replace fledgling romanticism ("Imagism," "Surrealism," "Vorticism"), Masters was just as impatient with them and chose to stick it out with Goethe and the Greeks.

There are many basic differences between Masters' reading of the classics and the "classical revival" predicted by Babbitt, Eliot, and Hulme. Masters agreed with the Imagists' call for a return in poetry to what was "plain, hard, and forceful." He also shared their rejection of what Hulme called "sloppiness which doesn't consider that a poem is a poem unless it is moaning or whining about something or other." [7] But Masters' favorite English and American poets (Shelley, Browning, Whitman, and Emerson) were "romantic" by anybody's definitions, and he worshipped Goethe; yet he read the Greeks all his life and described himself as "a Hellenist." What looked like a contradiction to many in Masters' own time is simply further support for what we *now* recognize as the paradox of the "anti-romantic romanticism" of the modern classical vision. A brief look at the writings of T. E. Hulme, a chief exponent of the classical revival in modern poetry, will help explain exactly how Masters absorbed Goethe and the Greeks into a new synthesis.[8]

It is necessary to summarize only briefly the history of romantic thought to identify the tradition that Masters helped shape and then passed on to his successors. In a line from Kant through the German idealists—especially Hegel, Fiche, Schelling, Schiller, and Schlegel—culminating in England in developments in eighteenth-century aesthetics and early nineteenth-century poetry, the romantic stance developed clearly identifiable views on the function of the mind and self in creating the realities of human perception. The role of the mind in structuring that reality became a dominant motif in philosophy in general as well as in aesthetics, Hegelian dialectics, Schelling's transcendental idealism, Coleridge's organicism, British empiricism (especially through Locke and Hartley), and Wordsworth's "creative sensibility." In this framework, what is often taken to be the "classicism" of Eliot and Pound is but a short-lived deviation from a still developing tradition, and modernism becomes a further development in the romantic preoccupation with the mind's creation of reality. Masters' anti-romantic romanticism is a significant contribution to that tradition in America (with its foundations in Whitman and Emerson); the corrective he learned from the Greeks and Goethe helped him avoid succumbing to what he saw as the excesses of "romance."

The many attacks on romanticism early in this century were warnings against abuses and at the same time strong defenses of the best and most durable elements of that romantic sensibility. Anti-romantic railings of fifty years ago appear to us now as a necessary defense of what was most viable in romantic poetry.

T. E. Hulme's famous essay "Romanticism and Classicism" (1924) is a good example. His basic distinction is between classicism as an adherence to what is fixed and romanticism as an aimless grasping after infinity in the world of the impossible. Hulme's metaphor of flight is almost archetypal: "What I mean by classical in verse, then, is this. That even in the most imaginative flights, there is always a holding back, a reservation. The classical poet never forgets this finiteness, this limit of man. He remembers always that he is mixed up with earth. He may jump, but he always returns back; he never flies away into the circumambient gas."[9] Masters liked this kind of image of excursions into the unknown. He used it often—most notably in the kites soaring high above the Illinois plains. The kite flies over Spoon River, and in his later years in the Chelsea hotel the kite becomes Masters' image of soul transport; he closes his eyes in New York and sees himself flying his kite over the prairies. The excursion releases intimations of the mystical that make the person standing on earth choke with longing. But Masters' kite—like Hulme's balloon—stays attached to the earth. It never flies off unattached, and the journey back is aided in this kind of anti-romanticism by the classical vision of Greece.

Hulme's call for a classical revival reflects critical thinking around the time of *Spoon River Anthology*. Hulme is typical of the reactions against the excess then current. His call for a return to the classics and his support for precision in poetic imagery were part of the mounting reactions against the abuses of late-nineteenth-century verse. The young Masters went to the classics for the same kind of corrective. He liked the solid, unwavering mythology of the Greeks, but he refused to react against the energy of a Goethe. Throughout his career, Masters used his sense of the classics to rediscover Whitman and Emerson.

But Masters' Hellenism did not go the way of Hulme. The reaction against romanticism represented by Hulme simply went too far for Masters. The kind of classical revival Hulme called for discarded too much of what Masters cherished. Where Hulme asked for concrete imagery dealing with the truths of the commonplace, Masters saw no need to discard the corresponding truth of the visionary. Where Hulme wanted to get rid of sloppiness, Masters saw no need to take mysticism with it. Hulme wrote: "A reviewer writing in *The Saturday Review* last week spoke of poetry as the means by which the soul soared into higher regions, and as a means of expression by which it became merged into a higher kind of reality. Well that is the kind of statement that I utterly detest." Masters, on the other hand, cherished that kind of statement. Hulme wanted "to speak of verse in a plain way as I would of pigs: that is the only honest way."[10] Masters spent a career trying to make poetry plainer than most of the critics and literati of his time would allow. And he even wrote a few poems about pigs. But he saw no need to give up using the terms "soul" or "higher realities" in order to prove that he was plain.

While this brief sketch oversimplifies Hulme and his contributions to modern aesthetics, the contrasts between his views and Masters' reveal just how important the classics were to the small town midwestern lawyer who wanted to break into the literary establishment. Hulme describes what he thought the Greek poets were doing:

> The ancients were perfectly aware of the fluidity of the world and its impermanence; there was the Greek theory that the whole world was a flux. But while they recognized it, they feared it and endeavored to evade it, to construct things of permanence which would stand fast in this universal flux which frightened them. They had the disease, the passion for immortality. They wished to construct things which should be proud boasts that they, men, were immortal. We see it in a thousand different forms. Materially in the pyramids, spiritually in the dogmas of religion and in the hypostatized ideas of Plato. Living in a dynamic world they wished to create a static fixity where their souls might rest.

This classical drive for "fixity" to combat the terrors of "flux" is countered by a very different modern view according to Hulme: "Now the whole trend of the modern spirit is away from that; philosophers no longer believe in absolute truth. We no longer believe in perfection, either in verse or in thought, we frankly acknowledge the relative."[11] Masters would not have considered himself *that* "modern." He would have admitted enthusiastically to having a bad case of the immortality disease. He thought passion was the energizer of everything. He didn't need Hulme to tell him that absolutes were suspect (he knew Nietzsche and many others); the philosophers he learned most from didn't hold much stock in "fixity." Masters simply didn't read the classics the same way Hulme and many others of influence in his time did, and his reading of Goethe alongside the Greeks kept alive his faith in the possibilities of romantic vision.

Hulme's disgust over how thoroughly readers had been conditioned to moaning and whining might offer some insights into why Masters had trouble breaking into the poetic establishment of the time. To show just how bad things had gotten by 1924, Hulme warned that when the classical revival "does come we may not even recognise it as classical." The state of criticism "has got so bad now," he continued, "that a poem which is all dry and hard, a properly classical poem, would not be considered poetry at all." Masters had to contend with that state of poetic taste when he read the Greeks. Romanticism had collapsed from exhaustion, Hulme contended, "yet the critical attitude of mind, which demands romantic qualities from verse, still survives." The result of this survival could explain some of the reactions to what the modern Hellenist was trying to do in his own writing: "If good classical verse were to be written tomorrow, very few people would be able to stand it."[12]

Masters wrote the kind of hard, precise classical verse which Hulme described; yet he also espoused the romanticism which Hulme despised. In working toward his own kind of romantic classicism, Masters reflected the debates of his age. Unable to lose sight of the romantics' vision of higher realities and unwilling to let go of his firm grasp of classical limits, Masters combined mysticism and realism into the hybrid form of his dramatic lyric. Continued reading of the Greeks and Goethe enabled him to maintain the balance between these "classical" and "romantic" tendencies over the years.

That Masters was influenced by the *Greek Anthology* has been noted by critics since the earliest reviews of *Spoon River Anthology*. The larger Greek influence throughout his career extends beyond what can be summarized here. But a brief look at how Masters relied on the classics at pivotal stages of his career will clarify some of his intentions and begin a much needed reassessment of some of his little-known works.

From *A Book of Verses* (1898) to his posthumously published poems (written in the thirties and early forties), Masters frequently alluded to, and captured the spirit of, Greek mythology. When he worked on the newspaper in Lewistown and then as a student at Knox College, he often wrote apprentice poems inspired by his reading of Greek philosophers and dramatists. In his earliest volumes there are tributes to Psyche and Vulcan, Sappho and Helen of Troy. The tributes to Helen suggest hints of the monody tone and the notes of the eternal quest of ideal beauty. For the most part, the earliest poems are evidence of Masters' interests at that time, though the classical themes and allusions are neither extensive nor fully developed. *The Blood of the Prophets*, published under the pseudonym Dexter Wallace (1905), is a series of exercises in classical imitation.[13]

Songs and Satires (1916) was the earliest collection other than *Spoon River Anthology* in which the larger dimensions of Masters' "Hellenism" came into his poems. "Helen of Troy" was a tribute to the timeless symbol of the energy Masters saw in ancient Greece. In the same volume, "The City"—a portrait of Chicago—is steeped in Masters' understanding of Greek culture. The narrator follows the sun god Helios around on his daily journey through the windy city. Everywhere in the modern urban landscape he finds only remnants of the old culture long since overtaken by the abuses of the Judeo-Christian tradition. The norm for values in the poem is Helios' vision of truth, given substance through symbols from Greek mythology. But when Helios awakens from a dream and traverses the city streets, he finds that in "every heart flamed cruelty like a little emerald snake." The modern city, steeped in contemporary culture, is a displacement of Hellenic values, a fall from higher realities. In many similar poems, Masters' absorption of Greek mythology energized his symbols of the landscape and provided the norm he used to measure the modern collapse into fragmentation.

In softer tones, the Greek impulse permeates *Toward the Gulf* (1918). Masters dedicated the volume to William Marion Reedy, the man who first got him interested in the *Greek Anthology*. The title poem opens the book with an epic song cataloging "the age and the country in which we live" (*Gulf*, xiii). The song rolls through rivers and fields and "symphonic" whisperings of "the voices of freedom." Ultimately the symbol of change and growth and the quest itself is the Mississippi, "Father of Waters" who "flows forever, / Making land forever, reclaiming the wastes of the sea." This "Wholly American" symbol of freedom recaptures the Greek spirit of a "new Ulysses" who will not turn back "till the thing is done" (1–8). The possible rejuvenation of the American spirit from age to age depends, in Masters' view, on renewing this Hellenic spirit.

The symbols of *Toward the Gulf* are based on the Greek access to higher realities. "Heaven Is but the Hour" (76–81) is a love poem about Plato's ladder to Beauty and the higher realities reflected in physical union. Again the human condition is explained alongside the classical norm and the dulling of a dream is Masters' critique of the dislocated values of his own time. The same haunting symbols speak through the museum pieces in "Victor Rafolski on Art" (82–90). Again Zeus and Venus outlast pulpits and editorials and court rulings and laws which "strangle life." And again the fire of classical passion burns straight through modern values. Rafolski's sardonic self-indictment is worthy of the *Greek Anthology*:

> I have stolen beauty
> To keep from freezing in this arid country
> Of winter winds on which the dust of custom
> Rides like a fog.

From the dedication to Reedy to "the epic stuff" of "Bertrand and Gourgaud" (157–167), *Toward the Gulf* looks for the birth of a new nation created out of the spirit of classical Greece.

Three years later in *The Open Sea* (1921) Masters' attempts to transplant the motifs of classical Greece in the midwestern soil become more overt. In several poems the speakers elaborate on a desire to remake themselves in the likeness of the Greek gods. In "Ulysses" (*Sea*, 225–231), the aging quester returns from his journeys and tries to answer Telemachus' queries about why he was gone so long and why he returned when everything was so exciting with Calypso. Telemachus is stunned by the tales of the Cyclops, Aeolus, the Sirens, and Hades; he is overwhelmed by stories of Apollo's oxen, Hades' horrors, Circe, tales of "the wayward ways of the streams / That flow round earth, the winds and waters / Of passion, wisdom, thought and dreams." But Masters' Ulysses values most the enduring joys of union between man and woman. The long journey was necessary, Ulysses tells his son, because he "needed the planets, / And suns of the spring to live, mature." Along the way of the quest, however, there were "secrets of cunning, / Cruelty, strength, and much that you use / In the battle," but the essential core of man's relationship with woman was missing. At last he found that the restless urge drew him back home, because all the travels "are not food, they are not wine; / They are not heat that stir the secret / Core of the seed of a man, be sure."

Telemachus' inability to understand makes the poem work, as the returning quester Ulysses tries to explain to him what he calls "the core of the deepest truth." He doesn't really expect his son to understand because he is "a boy yet." The half-understanding auditor only gives more energy to the father's dream, memories of the island of Ogygia, and Calypso's promise of eternal youth. But the catalog of joys and beauties Ulysses recites for his son is interrupted in every stanza by his caution "But even I found this growing old." Telemachus doesn't understand the sense of place, home, and the long-standing pain-bought relationship developed over the years by his parents. Ulysses doesn't want immortality at the price of what is most valuable to him, and he doesn't expect Telemachus to understand until he too has made the journey as well as the return. Ulysses' classical energy turns inward, and the mystical vision deepens: "I find this doorway good, Telemachus, / As a place to dream and a place to rest."

In tune with this domestic setting and the sense of place and family, the quest of *The Open Sea* turns increasingly inward toward the mystic's contemplation. "Invocation to the Gods" (*Sea*, 248–252) calls upon the energies embodied in the Greek deities to deepen that vision of fullness and expanse. First the speaker asks Aphrodite to right the waywardness of the modern world which has abandoned classical values:

> We are sunk in a slough of our shame;
> We are torn with denials and fears,
> Who have turned from thy altar,
> And rejected thy worship
> And mangled the gift of love
> For the ritual of Mary the Virgin.

That displacement of the classical ideals with a guilt culture stressing shame and fear is a central theme in Masters' attempts to revive the spirit of Greece.

The next invocation is to Pallas Athena "whose temple yet stands enthroned rock-bound above / The grotto of Mary of Galilee, / Eternal symbol!" She is also asked to bring "the healing of harmonious thought" to a dislocated contemporary scene. Apollo is called upon as "lord of music, lord of words and sounds," and Zeus, "broad souled as nature" and subject to fate, is summoned to bring redemption "through truth which frees through being known, / Not faith in truth which is not known." In a lengthy prayer, Zeus is invoked for all that is atypical in what Masters sees as Judeo-Christian distortions:

> No stirring envy like a man of war
> To make all peoples worship thee, O Zeus!

> Nor preaching words of gladness to the meek;
> Nor opening prison doors
> To sound the day of vengeance,
> To make all peoples worship thee, O Zeus!
> Nor saying, eat the riches of thy foes,
> And suck their milk;
> And make them plowmen;
> And take dominion over them and power.

"Invocation" celebrates the passing of that world and yet hopes to recall its essential spirit in the new land. Despite the great loss, so long as "the hunted ghost of Delphos steals / From land to land" there is hope. But the poem makes the consequences clear:

> Thy lyre has been weighed in the balances
> Of the money changers, and rejected.
> The Prince of Peace has brought the sword
> Even as he prophesied.
> All peoples are at strife
> Between his ritual and the will to life.

The dislocation brings its traumas as the human spirit holds on, nonetheless, to a glimpse of what is lost:

> Vengeance, hypocrisy and darkness
> Are over us, we are vipers
> Coiled in a cistern.
> We wait for blood in the moon,
> For darkness in the Sun,
> For a voice from clouds of glory:
> Depart from me, accursed; into fire.
> I shut the gates of heaven
> And burn the world with wrath!

The final plea is an urgent statement of Masters' Hellenism:

> Thou in Olympus tombed
> With all thy sons and daughters,
> Palace no more, a footstool
> For Jehovah of Judea,
> Come back that we may re-make ourselves
> In the likeness of thy face.
> O, father Zeus,
> Wake when Jesus shuts

The gates of heaven,
And take us to Olympus!

That impassioned cry for renewal epitomizes Masters' classical values further energized by Goethe's vision of Helen. It suggests what Hulme would call a classical revival that has passed through romanticism. Masters held out great hope for the revival of that spirit in the New World. He foresaw that men and women might remake themselves by catching the spirit of Greece in the silence of the midwestern prairies.

"Pentheus in These States" (*Sea*, 253–261) is a reworking of classical myth, a recreation of the Dionysian spirit on the plains. The poem is a "meditative hymn," a song of "the daimon" in quest of the mysteries of Orpheus. Pentheus is a pioneer who comes "In coon-skin caps and jeans / Into this wilderness, spanned / By mountains, to this home / Of the Corn-mother, clothed in variable greens / Of barley, oats and wheat." From all of Europe came the immigrants in a wave "like flame that follows flame" with "new dreams" that "stir the Spring awakening and the quest." "Swarming sallies" moved westward "attending Dionyse, / And seeking realms of Nature to be free." The burst of energy released by the wave of new freedom swells with the classical vision:

Rocks sealed with frost and ice which prisoned
The secret wine of Life new sensed and newly visioned
Flowed when the Spring of a great Age, and its Herakles,
Fire of the Sun of Liberty, melted the locks
Of ancient and forbidding rocks
Binding the torrent: human and divine
Strength and adventure: Maenads and Thyiades,
Bacchae, Bassarides:
Spirits and evangels of new wine.
Mad Ones: armed for war.
And Rushing Ones: defying Strife.
Inspired Ones: trailing the Star
Of larger life.

The remaking in the image of Greek deities seems within reach in "Pentheus." The new quest will be energized by the spirit of democracy. Shame and guilt can be set aside as once again it is "the Mystery, the delights / Of living and of thought, which moulds and wields, / These hunters, fur-capped, like the devotees / Out of the

Thrace of old, worshipping and defending / The wine-grower, and temple-builder, Dionyse." The "larger life" can once again be reshaped in the New World in a feast of life. Even the new theologies are reinterpreted when "Dionysiac Christ" passes the cup.

In a stirring bacchanalia, "false salvationists," "foul-breathed ranters of Duty," and "preachers of Denial and of Death" are replaced by a "feast of Life" that brings "rapturous elation" and an "intenser life in soft intoxication." The classical myths bring the energy of healing to the sickness of modern metaphysics. The "Orphic lips" and "sun-lit wings" of the Greek spirit bring rebirth through Dionysus. They go on "living, rejoicing in Life's thrilling spring, / Not grieving in its autumn and decline, / Bridal, not funeral wine / In the hour of memory and of parting." The classical myths replace fears with the "illumination" of "Nature's secrets," and the "intoxication / In which our souls are paradised" may yet triumph over "the oafs and boors and lunk-heads of the land, / And the bigot, Puritan, / And the martyrs to the martyrdom of Pain."

Masters reaffirms his hope in this rebirth of the classical spirit in the tribute, "Monody on the Death of William Marion Reedy" (*Sea,* 285–289). The mood of the poem carries that Sapphic quality which Masters admired and perfected in the mysticism of his later poems. The symbols of Reedy's accomplishments pick up where the enthusiasm of "Invocation" and "Pentheus" leave off. Here the life forces are made concrete in the accomplishments of one man.

Masters had celebrated Reedy's Greek spirit previously in his dedication to *Toward the Gulf,* and in "William Marion Reedy"—an early poem published in *Songs and Satires*—he reviewed the *Mirror* editor's wide reading based in the classics. In the Monody, Reedy becomes a symbol of the Greek gods re-created; Pentheus come to life in American letters. Reedy's death brings memories of "the feast of Life" and the lesson that "immortality / Is not a promise, but a threat." Reedy "lived with books" and "saw with clairvoyant eye" piercing through to the core of "unquenchable fire, / Walled with impenetrable ice." Masters confesses a "mystic brotherhood, which can rise / From kindred spirits."

What they had most in common—and the force behind Masters' exuberance—is a devotion to what Masters called "The Spirit of Greece." Reedy showed him that it was possible to hold to the vision by "viewing the misty age / Atop a pillar of Zeus, and holding fast, / Through change and weariness, to work, in spite / Of clear conviction, nothing can assuage / The soul's desire." In Masters' view it took the classical vision to satisfy the modern world's "soul hunger."

It took the spirit of Greece to answer the tough question: "If soul father us could soul not do / For souls of us what water for our thirst / Accomplishes?" The classical view says *yes*, in spite of the agony:

> Promethean, this you knew:
> The restless search with which man's soul is cursed;
> Yet brooding on it, still you dreamed
> Of a city for all nations, consecrate
> To the creative spirit of God in man;
> Guardian angels were to you revealed
> In labor with man's fate,
> Uplifting the human spirit, like a flame,
> Consoled, redeemed,
> Strengthened and purified and healed,
> To the silent, eternal life from whence it came.

That is the vision of wholeness which Masters saw in Reedy: the humanistic spirit of Greece, transplanted into the new ideals of pioneers on the midwestern prairies. Reedy achieved the immortality described by the village atheist. He became absorbed into the "quietness" where the dead find peace and "loose the bands / Of some intenser rhythm." Even spinning inward, the Promethean energy "turned within to a realm more deep, / Where death's great secret seemingly was known / As some clear, mild Simplicity!" That simplicity is the final, irreducible core of the classical spirit. The fullness and mildness at the end of the quest was, finally, Reedy's legacy for the moderns:

> I stood alone
> Empty of hand, save for the heritage
> Of what you were:
> A voice, a light, a music of deep tone,
> Which life made richer, and the age,
> And something of heaven employed
> To be for us our best interpreter.

As Masters' vision matured, those deeper tones from Greece would become increasingly prominent.[14]

The deeper tones began to surface in 1924 when Masters returned to the people of Spoon River. In scope and tone *The New Spoon River* captures more of the Greek spirit than its celebrated predecessor. The new songs convey a more urgent sense of the tragic, and they are much more overtly pleas to bring the lost spirit of Apollo to life once again on the prairies. Reviewers rushed to compare the original and the new anthologies, but few critics noticed how *The New Spoon River* extended beyond an indebtedness to the *Greek Anthology* to a greater immersion in a larger classical vision.

In one of the epigraphs to *The New Spoon River* Masters quotes Milton, who updated Aristotle on the cathartic effects of tragedy. Even in physics, Milton says, "things of melancholic hue and quality are us'd against melancholy, sour against sour, salt to remove salt humour." The tragic spirit Masters invokes is also a clue to the deepening tones of his own vision as he transforms classical energy into a mystical stillness.

The new tombstone hymns still carry the dark tones, but the mood is now hopeful in the tough classical sense. Reason Robb's soul is still shattered by an electrolytic force; but there is also a warning from Sarah Dewitt that as soon as man presumes "to prison God," the Protean "magic" will resurface. The classical allusion is no coincidence for questers trapped by the symbols of a Judeo-Christian culture which inadequately replaces the classical gods. When the dreamer is willing to struggle with the Proteus-god, hope cut from a tough fabric can replace a too modern despair. "You never can catch Him," says Sarah Dewitt, because "the game of the soul" is always to follow and "never to find."

There is an overwhelming sadness in *The New Spoon River*, a pervasive note of what the cover blurb of the paperback edition calls "the chronicle of a small American town in the throes of a new and crushing modernism." But there is also the indestructible hope of endurance itself, the same kind of classical toughness that Masters invoked in songs to the Greek gods, celebrated in Reedy, and wanted to instill in future generations on the Illinois prairies. At least one character in *The New Spoon River*—Albert Husband—looked to the lost vision of Greece to keep alive the possibilities of soul-making:

> Never since Athens, never since charity
> Became the word for love, and the hydra-headed
> Beast of the snake and the dove took rule in the world
> Has friendship thriven between a man and a man:
> The vision and flame that binds two heads and hearts
> In a life of wooing the soul, and making the soul.

And Albert Husband was, of course, misunderstood. Masters' relentless pursuit of the lost vision surfaces again in Prof. John Scott's suggestion that "what made Christianity most beautiful" and "most imaginatively philosophical" was "the Jesus forbidden genius of the goat-footed Hellas." And Rev. Leonard Hash lists a catalog of misbeliefs, calling them "the worm eaten seed of Isaiah and Heine" and the "dwarfed and stunted stalks of the perfect flower." Again the norm is the classical vision of the spirit of Greece:

> You are small souls grunting under the heavy load
> Of great causes, visions and dreams,
> And you make only homilies of them,
> Distorting, and hiding and falsifying their reality.

The New Spoon River is about the consequences of such distortions, but there remains a hopeful alternative in the Beauty-making power of mystical Greece. Heraclitus Procrustes affirms it in his proclamation that "Fire is the soul of the universe." Peter Van Loon finally sees it but only after he is "exhausted by the battle for soul triumph." Nevill Hone finally dismisses "this Bible created and Bible dominated era" as "the most monstrous period of time, / Tangled, wounded, tortured, imprisoned / By a thousand falsehoods and slaveries." Again the beauty-making power replaces the guilt culture for Norris Kernan:

> There is a god more terrible than Jesus,
> To whom Heine, Shelley and Poe
> Gave everything of heart and brain,
> Of love and life,
> Amid dishonor, want, disease,
> Hatred, contempt of the world,
> And without hope—
> O merciless Apollo!

The New Spoon River is again a critique of a dislocated world and a plea to return to classical wholeness. It holds out hope for an American epic that will be able to interpret the times and answer the questions posed by Meredith Phyfe:

> What do you want for irony, satire or pathos?
> Is there not everything here, grotesque,
> Absurd, tragic and heroic?

Masters' own epic quest led him to celebrate, with Margaret Moynihan, "A new freedom, breaking with eager roots / The tough old sod of the past."

Classical Greece began to move into the background in the long narrative history of American life and letters in *The New World* (1937). This book will be discussed more fully in other chapters of this study, but Masters' purpose in the poem draws heavily from his unwavering devotion to the Greeks. The speaker refers frequently to the special hope of liberty offered in the New World and the role of the poet in making the freedom of the people a reality. "The New World cannot as a nation sing / By singing the nation," he warns, "it must sing the People, / An old theme in the annals of the world / Along the ways of Hesiod and of Langland" (*NW*, 267). Masters was fond of linking Whitman with Homer and Hesiod, but he offers evidence of how American culture goes beyond the old. Though Hesiod sang about the people, his songs were "never chosen for a nation's epos." The contrast Masters is driving at is centered in his crucial use of the concept of *epos*, and his view that the people must be the essence of nation building is central to the evolution he describes in the history poem:

> Yet never have the People been obscured
> To the eye discerning, whatever was the work.
> Amid the Sumerian kings they visibly swam,
> Around the building of the walls of Babylon;
> In ships that conquered the Aegean Isles,
> Doing the work of nobles, as it happened.
> So do they stand amid the fall of Athens
> Their work demolished, with new work to do.
> Around the fall of Sparta, Sparta ended;
> Swarming about the hopes of Alexander
> Forth to the East to Hellenize the world.

Masters doesn't want to bring Greek ideals to America; rather, he wants to capture the spirit of Greece to create America's own ideals. In the old soil the people were "never sung as kings were sung, / As captains and statesmen were sung, / But without whom kings and captains were nothing." The poem celebrates the possibility of a new song energized by the spirit but not the letter of the old. "Fitting it was," says the speaker, "that Dvorak / Composed his symphony of the New World / On the banks of Turkey Creek / In the village of Spillville, Iowa" (*NW*, 267–269).

The next year Masters pushed off further into the new music, recreated from the old. "Hymn to the Universes" (1938) uses the machinery of classical verse only to overturn the traditional invocations. The epic poet sings now not to Demeter, Pan, Earth, Apollo, not even to Uranus "called heaven, the husband of Earth, /Herself once called the most ancient of created things." The tone and energy of the Hellenic spirit dominate in this new hymn, but now the bard journeys out into new universes beyond our galaxy and the epic song is now in praise of "the spirit of man." Within the classical form, the music is becoming more solemn.[15]

Masters' total absorption in the spirit of Greece and the energy of Goethe affected all his reading. In Whitman and Emerson he found hope for re-creating the classical sense and the romantic quest in the new land. In Shelley and Browning he found passion and dramatic control. As he digested his wide reading in the Greek classics, German literature, and the Anglo-American tradition, Masters' own poetic vision took on the deeper tones and the intenser rhythm of the mystic. He held fast throughout his career to classical norms; the romanticism of his Faustian quest and his anti-romantic skepticism flourished side by side. His predisposition to the classics and to mysticism made Masters part of the paradox of modernism. His contribution to that paradox is only now coming clearly into our view.

4

"Awakened and Harmonized"

MASTERS AND EMERSON

On more than one occasion, Masters called Emerson "the most inspiring and formative influence in American life." He never wavered in that opinion—from his earliest days as a schoolboy in Illinois through the publication of his last books nearly six decades later. Emerson represented for Masters the American original of all that was best in the spirit of the classics. His lectures, essays, and poems provided nourishment for Masters' inventive powers. In addition, these same writings offered further advice for poets in the New World on the best ways to convert the riches of the past into their own unique culture. Emerson shaped Masters' attitudes toward the processes of invention and influence while he himself continued to be a major source of that influence. Emerson "awakened" Masters to enlarging forces in his own reading and experiences and helped him "harmonize" the riches of the past as he converted them to his own use. As a unifying force in Masters' thinking, Emerson also helped him synthesize the effects of his wide reading.

Emerson was a formidable influence on all American writers who came after him. A recent volume from the English Institute was devoted to the problems of influence in the light of Emerson's enjoyment of what he called "an original relation to the universe."[1] Ironically, Emerson's largest influence on American poets was his cry that they "never imitate," that they avoid being influenced and instead trust themselves. Harold Bloom refers to this phenomenon as "the only poetic influence that counsels against itself, and against the idea of influence." Bloom traces "the war of American poets against influence" through its long Emersonian heritage of self-reliance.[2] Comfortable with that heritage, Masters told a *New York Times* interviewer in 1942: "I believe in an America that is not imitative, that stands alone, that is strong, that leans on nothing outside itself and permits nothing to lean on it."[3] The Emerson in Masters helps explain apparent contradictions in his repeated allusions to sources while he insists, at the same time, on a fiercely self-reliant originality. To use Bloom's terms again, Masters "completed" Emerson by displacing his fierce self-reliance into the unique experiences of the midwestern plains and the small town not so different from Concord.

As Bloom has shown at considerable length, there is in Emerson's attitudes toward influence a "double sense." Always there is an emphasis on originality and self-reliance, an "insistence upon poetic priority" and "the freshness of transformation" in converting past riches. But Bloom also finds in Emerson a "peculiar dialectic" in which he asks the poet "to be at once wholly individual and wholly part of the commonal."[4] Emerson says "never imitate" and at the same time "we need not fear excessive influence." He advises writers to "trust thyself" only, and also to become one with the oversoul. This paradox of immersion in the larger flow while maintaining one's personal integrity was consistent with Masters' classical view of imitation with its emphasis on the process of converting the past to one's present use. Masters' knowledge of the classics diminished for him somewhat the all-out war against influence and the anxiety about imitation experienced by many of his contemporaries. Nonetheless, the Emersonian directives about self-sufficiency created an influence on Masters' career which interpreted itself as it unfolded. Emerson stimulated Masters' inventive powers as a poet by showing him how to be influenced and then himself providing limitless resources as an influence. A closer look first at Emerson on the process of influence and then at the Emersonian influence on Masters' career will reveal much about the deeper music of the *Spoon River* poet.

The chronology of Masters' awakening in Emerson reveals a long and steady exposure to his life and works. In *Across Spoon River*, he recalls that he read Emerson's *Essays* before graduating from Lewistown High School (*ASR*, 74). In "Autochton," in an early collection, he referred to Emerson's "pruning his slim wings / For flights into broad spaces" (*GV*, 34). Twenty years later in his biographies of Lindsay, Whitman, and Twain, Masters used Emerson as a measure of achievement. In the long narrative poem *The New World* (1937) Emerson turns up as "the noblest face that the New World has seen." In 1939, he included a glowing tribute to Emerson in *More People*; two years later he wrote "The Pasture Rose," a poem remarkably close to Emerson's "The Rhodora" which Masters referred to as "one of the most beautiful poems in the English language." These are only a few of the sustained allusions which culminated in *The Living Thoughts of Emerson* (1940), collected and edited by Masters for "The Living

67

Thoughts Library" series. His critical introduction "Presenting Emerson" is not only the culmination of a lifelong indebtedness to Emerson's thought but also a fitting conclusion to a highly productive and often overlooked decade in his own career. Whether exuberant or despondent, Masters found joy and consolation in Emerson. In rapture he would break through to the visions found in the "wild honey" of Emerson's poetry, and it was at Emerson's grave that Masters took a measure of brooding strength from the admission that life had "cornered" him.

Masters listened throughout his entire lifetime to Emerson's advice about how poets should or should not be influenced. From his high school days he knew the famous cry that great men have always vibrated to the "iron string" found within themselves. He knew that success demanded that he be a nonconformist, that the Eternal stirred within his own heart, that his giant would go with him wherever he went, and that in the end the only sacred space would be the integrity of his own mind. Yet Masters also read with great care Emerson's many lessons from history, and he studied the achievements of Emerson's heroes in *Representative Men*. In short, he absorbed Emerson's view that influence is a state of self-sufficiency learned through long reflection on the lessons of the past.

Emerson said much about literary influence in his essays, lectures, poems, journals, and other writings. Masters was familiar with most of his works, though his editorial decisions in compiling *The Living Thoughts of Emerson* are good indicators of what he knew best and considered most important in the large corpus. Following his introduction, Masters presented 125 pages from *Essays, Representative Men, English Traits, Poems, May Day and Other Pieces*, and *Various Notable Lectures*. He included passages from "History" about the perfection of "the Grecian State" wherein "spiritual nature unfolded in strict unity with the body"; he stressed Promethean skepticism and the realization that "every man is a divinity in disguise, a god playing the fool." Of course he also quoted the most famous passages from "Self-Reliance" about nonconformity and "foolish consistency" and other classic quotations that backed up his own tough-minded confidence in himself. He included also many descriptions of the relationship between spiritual and material laws, definitions of beauty and the oversoul, and strong beliefs on politics, education, and poetry. The sections on the poet as Sayer and on Emerson's opinions of others (including impressions after a trip to England) reinforced Masters' own developing visionary aesthetic. Most of what he included from *Representative Men* and from "The American Scholar" describes the inner power and "active soul" required for characters that "summed up eras, life-logics, masterful dealings with conditions, interpretations of the living of a given time."

The Living Thoughts of Emerson includes, not surprisingly, a wealth of insights about influence. Masters chose for the epigram a famous passage from "Circles" about the present uses of the past: "Life travels upward in spirals. He who takes pains to search the shadows of the past below us, then, can better judge the tiny arc which he climbs, more surely guess the dim curves of the future above him." That epigram becomes a keynote for the volume, and duplicate examples need not be produced to show Emerson searching the shadows and climbing the arc of tomorrow's curve.

The present use of those spirals from the past demands, for Emerson, an absorption and transformation of the thoughts and accomplishments of others. Masters was drawn to Emerson's metaphors from biology in "The Uses of Great Men" (*E*, 83–84). Each man becomes the interpreter of all nature, including those shadows from the past. "As plants convert the minerals into food for animals," Emerson declares, "each man converts some raw material in nature to human use." The example of great accomplishments from the past should become nourishment for new creation. "Great men are thus a colloquium," continues Emerson, "to clear our eyes from egotism, and enable us to see other people and their works." And he adds: "We keep each other in countenance, and exasperate by emulation the frenzy of the time." Masters might also have quoted the following Emersonian praise for being influenced (also from "The Uses of Great Men"): "We need not fear excessive influence. A more generous trust is permitted. Serve the great. . . . Compromise thy egotism. Who cares for that, so thou gain aught wider and nobler? Never mind the taunt of Boswellism: the devotion may easily be greater than the wretched pride which is guarding its own skirts." Here Emerson seems to relax his usual insistence on self-reliance. Instead, he appears to counsel against the excesses of originality for its own sake and at any costs. Emerson emphasizes for a moment his own classical heritage which in part kept Masters coming back for more: "Be another: not thyself, but a Platonist; not a soul, but a Christian; not a naturalist, but a Cartesian; not a poet, but a Shakespearian. In vain, the wheels of tendency will not stop, nor will all the forces of inertia, fear, or of love itself hold thee there. On, and forever onward!"[5] In these seemingly uncharacteristic remarks, Emerson solves the influence puzzle. One becomes all these other people in order to be more fully oneself. With Emerson, the paradox of classical imitation crossed the ocean. An individual can move forward by going through others, and the ultimate destination becomes a fuller possession of one's own self.

Emerson's metaphors for the uses of the riches of the past are essentially the language of nourishment through the conversion of raw material to new and usable energy. He applies these same metaphors repeatedly to the active, transforming powers demanded of a reader in the process of reading. In "Self-Reliance" he complains that "our reading is mendicant and sycophantic." Masters quotes also the famous passages from "The American Scholar" (*E*, 114) warning that books must be well used to be valuable: "Books are the best of things, well used; abused, among the worst. What is the right use? What is the one end, which all means go to effect? They are for nothing but to inspire. I had better never see a book, than to be warped by its attraction clean out of my own orbit and made a satellite instead of a system." Following his tribute to "the active soul" as "the only thing in the world of value," Emerson makes an astonishing statement on how the past can be a burden as well as a creative force: "The book, the college, the school of art, the institution of any kind stop with some past utterance of genius. This is good, say they, let us hold by this. They pin me down."

Masters believed with Emerson that the right use of books required a strenuous activity of the soul. Reading was to be a creative process very like the writing of poetry, and thus the reader must undergo training and discipline to enrich the experience. Emerson's friend Thoreau summed up the Emersonian heritage of active reading which masters embraced:

> The works of the great poets have never yet been read by mankind, for only great poets can read them. They have only been read as the multitude read the stars, at most astrologically, not astronomically. Most men have learned to read to serve a paltry convenience, as they have learned to cipher in order to keep accounts and not be cheated in trade; but of reading as a noble intellectual exercise they know little or nothing; yet this only is reading in a high sense, not that which lulls us as a luxury and suffers the nobler faculties to sleep the while, but what we have to stand on tip-toe to read and devote our most alert and wakeful hours to.[6]

For Emerson, the lessons of the past, all institutions, even the process of reading itself are valuable only insofar as they release the creativity of the individual human mind in the present moment. All resources and influences are creative to the extent that they feed an ever-renewing cycle of growth in the subjective self. Ultimately, then, literary influence is in the process in which the present individual chooses his or her own influences by re-creating the past through the transforming agency of an active soul. Emerson celebrated this process in the poem "History": "I am owner of the sphere, / Of the seven stars and the solar year, / Of Caesar's hand, and Plato's brain, / Of Lord Christ's heart, and Shakespeare's strain" (*E*, 162).

For Emerson, the active soul constantly brings into being the entire world and reshapes that world around itself. If he had had more space in the Living Thoughts volume Masters no doubt would have included the following on the uses of past resources (from "Experience"): "Thus inevitably does the universe wear our color, and every object fall successively into the subject itself. The subject exists, the subject enlarges; all things sooner or later fall into place. As I am, so I see; use what language we will, we can never say anything but what we are; Hermes, Cadmus, Columbus, Newton, Bonaparte are the mind's ministers." Masters followed Emerson in the belief that we can never say "but what we are." He acknowledged the subjective dimension of the reading process and the belief that precisely that subjectivity makes it possible for readers to transform the riches of the past to their own use. Here is Emerson again on how the great writers from the past serve as ministers to the present mind's new creation:

> Instead of feeling a poverty when we encounter a great man, let us treat the newcomer like a traveling geologist who passes through our estate and shows us a good slate, or limestone, or anthracite, in our brush pasture. The partial action of each strong mind in one direction is a telescope for the objects on which it is pointed. But every other part of knowledge is to be pushed to the same extravagance, ere the soul attains her due sphericity.[7]

Emerson's telescope to that sphericity is his answer to the intimidation one might feel on the presence of past achievement. No matter how great the past accomplishment, it will always be enlarged by the new "owner of the sphere."

That enlarging transformation of the past is clarified in more concrete terms again in Emerson's description of subjectivity in the reading process. Once more this emphasis is on the interaction between the self and the "mind's ministers" from the past: Consider the "sphericity" in the following well-known passage from "Self-Reliance": "A man should learn to detect and watch that gleam of light which flashes across his mind from within, more than the lustre of the firmaments of bards and sages. Yet he dismisses without notice his thought, because it is his. In every work of genius we recognize our own rejected thoughts; they come back to us with a certain alienated majesty." See your own ideas in what you read, Emerson appears to be saying. No longer simply "trust yourself," now it is discover yourself, create yourself, bring a new self into being through forceful, creative, self-directed reading. "Great works of art have no more affecting lesson for us than this," he continues. "They teach us to abide by our spontaneous impression with good-humored inflexibility then most when the whole cry of voices is on the other side." In other words, in the process of being influenced, one can become most secure in one's own beliefs. Failure to seek out influences which support one's own beliefs can have disastrous consequences: "Else tomorrow a stranger will say with masterly good sense precisely what we have thought and felt all the time, and we shall be forced to take with shame our own opinion from another."

Masters knew the famous Emersonian arguments that writers choose their own influences in order to discover, enlarge, and support their own ideas and talents. He knew that he was attracted to certain writers rather than others not only for what they offered him but also for what they drew forth out of his own subjective self. Masters actively sought influences that would become ministers to his own mind. He formed his ideas about traditions and his critical theories with no regard for a "foolish consistency" and little thought about whether and how he might be "misunderstood." Again "Self-Reliance" was his guide in striking the balance between classical imitations and the conversion of resources: "There is a time in every man's education when he arrives at the conviction that envy is ignorance; that imitation is suicide; that he must take himself for better or for worse as his portion; that though the wide universe is full of good, no kernel of nourishing corn can come to him but through his toil bestowed on that plot of ground which is given to him to till." Emerson's declaration of independence not only encouraged Masters to be self-confident but also supported his belief that sooner or later all strong readers revise as they read.

Perhaps the most revolutionary idea for which Masters found support in Emerson was the notion that writers must consciously choose and define their own influences. In his introduction to *The*

Living Thoughts of Emerson, Masters describes the influences on Emerson in exactly those terms. Emerson was most affected, Masters contends, by "men who furnished him with themes for the interpretation of his own point of view, for the solving and exposition of his own philosophy." Although this choosing of one's own influences might eventually lead to solipsism, the process is a more accurate account of taste than more idealized notions of sudden inspiration.

Masters' explanation of how Emerson selected material for *Representative Men* is also consistent with their shared commitment to self-reliance: "Its subject matter was what most interested Emerson, in that he treated of characters that most drew him, and best brought out his mind by a species of magnetism what was deepest and truest in it." Again that magnetism draws poets to "search the shadows" of the past, and in that search they learn more fully how to be themselves. In Masters' view Emerson found and shaped resources which could call forth his own "stored up conclusions about men" and help him understand more fully his own "analysis of spiritual properties." In his review of forces influencing Emerson, Masters sees a predictable, organic whole. He doesn't find any thunderbolts of inspiration. Instead he uses phrases such as "it was natural for his mind to turn to . . ." One way of describing the process would be to say that Emerson's mind was made up and he sought out influences that would further support what he already believed. Though a good corrective to simplistic notions of causality, that formulation is too extreme. A better image is Masters' metaphor of magnetism in which a self-confident mind is drawn to what naturally lures it. In the resulting interaction the influence and the source of the influence undergo a mutual change. Ultimately, the source itself is revised, and the self is better for having gone through the process.

Emerson gave Masters support in his thinking about what poets ought to read and how they ought to be influenced. Moreover, his liberating hymns to visionary insight helped in at least three other ways. First, Concord's most famous citizen strengthened Masters' celebration of the village in the midst of sardonic attacks. Repeatedly Masters describes how Emerson's energetic self-confidence gave new life to those struggling with "orthodoxy." Secondly, the visionary poet in Emerson provided a solid traditional basis for Masters' attempts to counter the modernism of the Eliot school. Finally, in Emerson's essays and poems and especially in *Representative Men*, Masters found an Americanized version of the heroism of magnanimity and the daemonic energy of Goethe, Nietzsche, and classical Greece. The best clues to the Emerson in Masters are found in "Presenting Emerson," the introduction to his Living Thoughts volume; in his selection and arrangement of Emerson's writings; and in his own prose works and poems of the thirties and early forties.

Above all else, Emerson helped the poet of small-town Illinois to find himself. Masters' recollections sound Emersonian self-reliance in epic tones. Initially, the effect was a loosening of insulation: "Out in middle Illinois when I was in high school we eager young found ourselves stifled by the parochial orthodoxy that surrounded us. The unsmoked sky was above us, the fields and woods were around us, yet we needed air. We could not be free without knowing what we were, and what we possibly could do. We could not then speculate, examine the evidence of things without being emancipated from the bandages that tied us in." In Emerson, Masters found an energetic Americanized rendition of Shelley's quests for the infinite and Browning's heroic self-exploration: "We needed someone to say that we had possibilities, and moreover in the encouraging doctrine of Emerson that we were potential geniuses, ready to expand wings and fly if we laid our hands upon the springs of courage that were within us and within the human breast everywhere." Back in the Midwest, he heard no condescending eastern tones in Emerson's counsel. He read Emerson's accounts of the courage needed to emerge from suffocation as descriptions of a universal malaise that was fatal to poetic creativity at any time and place. Faced with "the cramping influence of the village," Masters felt that Emerson "lifted and strengthened us, and gave us courage, and opened up to us fields of interest by which we escaped from the American conditions, which were the same in his youth in Boston and Concord" (E, 2, 4).

Liberation is the keynote of Masters' forty-one-page tribute to Emerson. From his high school days, he recalls the great delight at finding in the sage a "sportive and abandoned license" so untypical of the "lofty-minded Wordsworth," "the metaphysical Coleridge," or "the pious America of the last century." He also found in Emerson "strength and understanding which sang the American spirit, instead of patriotism, which stood for truth rather than regularity." Masters' examples were always to a point: "In the case of my girl schoolmate it did not make a genius of her, but she became an interesting mind, much beyond what she would have become without Emerson, and she had happiness in the circumstance of her self-confidence." From these concrete and often poignant reminiscences, Masters builds to a final assessment: "I can think of no other American that did so much for the general emancipation of the growing mind of America." And he adds: "Not even Whitman counts for so much, all things considered" (*E*, 4).

Emerson helped Masters celebrate the Midwest. In *The Small Town in American Literature*, Ima Honaker Herron has noted Emerson's attraction for "rural quiet" and "personal associations" found in the spirit of place in Concord.[8] His entries in his journals reflect his enthusiasm about the people and customs of the town, an enthusiasm that Masters must have found refreshing in the climate of criticism which seemed fixated on the cramping influences of midwestern life. Excessive romanticizing about the pastoral village had always been hard to dispel in American literature, and as Herron notes, *Spoon River Anthology* began what was to be a long demythologizing process in the works of the twenties. Alongside Masters' cynicism about small-town life there was always his strong identification with the land and with the basic goodness of people reflected in his populist politics. Emerson's harmonious vision of small-town life became a part of Masters' solid identification with the land which was often free of the romantic gloss created later by his critics.

Emerson's effects on Masters are manifest also in what Charles E. Burgess has called "village-based cultural influences." Emerson's influence ironically yet appropriately stimulated the fierceness of Masters' midwestern independence. "In the pragmatic Midwest of the 1880's and 1890's," Burgess notes, "there was no Brook Farm to combine their creative energies, no *Dial* to give them a convenient vehicle for expression. They were often judged eccentric or at least 'high-brow!'" Emerson fed what could be considered such eccentricity in Masters. In a lengthy passage worth quoting in its entirety, Burgess describes the midwestern intellectual landscape in which Masters grew:

> The Midwestern village of several thousand persons in the late nineteenth century cannot be compared intellectually to the moribund rural hamlets of today, culturally anesthetized by television, the *Reader's Digest*, and the outpourings of book clubs. True, the villages of Masters' time did know conformity, isolation, poverty, and ignorance—and how effectively he portrayed these shortcomings!—but a surprising number of villagers lived active, cosmopolitan lives of travel and of the mind. If they lacked continuous urban diversions and broadening, they escaped the city's inconveniences and petty distractions. In the quiet village milieu there was a comforting sense of civilized ease that came with the transition from a rough pioneer society to a stable community buttressed by traditions. Many minds there found excitement in

following and contributing to the courses of science and philosophy or in joining the effort toward mature American literature and criticism.[9]

Masters kept that mature Emersonian vision alive at a time in American letters when it was less than fashionable. Tough-minded as Masters always appeared in the thirties and forties, his critical insights are now appreciated in ways not imaginable then. Our age has given Emerson the place Masters wanted for him. Moreover, we are now recovering from the tyranny of many narrow poetics which long controlled judgments on the "modern" sensibility. Accordingly, the critic in Edgar Lee Masters will receive a good deal more study. Again Masters took solace in Emerson's push to go beyond influence: "Under his influence we felt that we were not hostile to the good life by free thinking about religion, or about anything else. . . . As he [Emerson] told an old theologian that he must go his way, and if he were a child of the devil it had to be so, we too could stand forth as children of the devil, if that was our role in life. We did this very thing and were happy and strong as we did it" (E, 2). In Masters, that strength became one midwestern rendition of Emerson's legacy for the moderns.

Masters' commentary on Emerson's style and major themes also anticipated later critics and revealed how like Emerson he was himself: "His essays are full of *nonsequiturs*, except where they are considered in their total effect. He was a mind of spiritual discernment in reference to man and society, moral, social and political wisdom. One of the pleasures in reading Emerson lies in the fact that he so often expresses what was in your own mind as something nebulous, but surely felt" (E, 5). On themes close to his own thinking in 1940, Masters used Emerson's own metaphors: "Emerson said that what draws men and women together was deciduous, or was the scaffolding by which the house was built, but the purification of the intellect and the heart, from year to year, is the real marriage, foreseen and prepared from the first, and wholly above their consciousness" (E, 21). The metaphors of "urge" and physical union are of course the same as Masters had developed in "Cleanthus Trilling" (*The New Spoon River*, 1924) and in "Amphimixis" (1938) (see chapter 6). Emerson's image of the "scaffolding" translated into the language of correspondences much of Masters' thinking at the time. It was another way in which Emerson told potential writers in Lewistown that they "had possibilities."

Many of Masters' selections from *Representative Men* (E, 83–114) are about self-sufficiency and the creation of soul through "love of the sexes." The "uses of great men" show that "each man is by secret liking connected with some district of nature, whose agent and interpretor he is." Through Plato's "Banquet" Masters finds in Emerson an explanation for "the passion of the soul for that immense lack of beauty it exists to seek." There follow the expected comments on the doctrine of correspondence, on the necessity for "wise skepticism," and the inevitability that "great believers are always reckoned infidels." And much of what Masters often referred to as his "Hellenism," set against America's "Cinderella complex," came through Emerson's assessments of Plato, Swedenborg, Shakespeare, and Goethe.

With Emerson, Masters believed that the poet is an "eternal man" who not only bears the torch but is of "the same divinity" as the fire itself. Emerson's view of the poet was surely linked up in Masters' mind with his selection from "Self-Reliance" on "mendicant" and "sycophantic" reading. The "imitative" must be replaced with "new thought" and "the world seems always waiting for its poet." Perhaps Masters thought of himself as that poet for which his age was or should have been waiting, that poet who could "tell us how it was with him" and who would thereby make all men "richer in his fortune." That this recognition had not come forth may be buried in the admission at Emerson's grave that he had been "cornered." But such thinking from a poet of some thirty years was not self-serving or pathetic. Later in the volume Masters quotes Emerson on why society mistreats its writers:

> The writer does not stand with us on any commanding ground. I think this to be his own fault. . . . How can he be honoured, when he does not honour himself; when he loses himself in the crowd; when he is no longer the lawgiver, but the sycophant, ducking to the giddy opinion of a reckless public; when he must sustain with shameless advocacy some bad government, or must bark all the year round in opposition; or write conventional criticism, or profligate novels; or at any rate, write without thought, and without recurrence, by day and by night, to the sources of inspiration? [E, 108–109]

Emerson on the abandonment of true poetry in his day sounds very much like Masters' conclusions about the moderns of his day: "They have no principles, no individuality, no moral code, and no roots."[10]

For Masters, Emerson's poetry was a way back from the wayward stuff of his own time, a way to "forget the machinations of merchants that have put us in the grip of monopolies and reduced the people to doles, and the whole land to distress and poverty." His poems have for Masters the "earthy smell" of "uncultivated blossoms" singing of "the oneness of things," "the feel of earth," and "daemonic and celestial love." The poems Masters called "the very wild honey of poetry" accomplished much of the casual, almost improvised techniques which he called gnomic—effects he wanted to create in his own works. He saw in Emerson's essays "poetry in the best sense of the word" and he pictured the Emersonian poet-sayer as "a fine seismograph that records the slightest trembling of the earth." Masters shared Emerson's attraction to scientific metaphors, and in his extended image of swarming flies their mystic hymns and scathing satire merge: "All through Emerson's works can be found his sensitive appreciation of what was going on in America. The pangs and trials of life are multiplied by growing and mounting evils and immoralities and injustices, as flies can propagate and swarm and bite, and at last life can show up as something regarded chemically as the environment of an homunculus, instead of something in which thinking and feeling spirits live and move" (*E*, 40–41). Again, Masters on Emerson provides a commentary on the poet's own beliefs and accomplishments in 1940, twenty-five years after *Spoon River Anthology*.

Of the twenty poems Masters selected from Emerson's small canon, several are well-known. "Fate," "The Snow Storm," and "Brahman" are reprinted often, as are "Merlin's Wisdom" and "Terminus." "Give All to Love," with its ascending bond of physical love, was one of Masters' favorites, and the magnitude of self-sufficiency in "History" supports many of Masters' own beliefs.

On closer examination, these twenty poems turn out to be a remarkably revealing selection. Several of the poems are about influence of one kind or another; all of them express themes and concerns which were urgent for Masters himself. In selecting poetry for this volume as well as in writing his own poems, Masters was drawn to a source he hoped would bring out the best in his own thinking.

Consider a few examples. "Fate" (*E*, 152–154) repeats the ambivalence between imitation and self-sufficiency. The rose is beautiful because it has an "untaught strain." The best music is "a melody born of melody" and "a music music-born." The goal is a self-sufficiency that refuses to "pine for another's gift." In the end, in what seems to be a rejection of any influence at all, pure vision only lasts: "Toil could never compass it; / Art its height could never hit; / It never came out of wit." In a burst of Emersonian transcendence, the vision "melts the world into a sea." This kind of mystical vision appealed to Masters, and he comes back to it immediately in his second selection "Good-Bye" (154–155). Here the merging back into Oneness takes place not in the sea but in the land which becomes the "sylvan home" for all at death. Emerson's imagery has magnetism for the Masters who, throughout the thirties, grew increasingly mystical about the hills and prairies of his native land.

Masters was also drawn to a sense of poetic madness Emerson described in "The Snow-Storm" (*E*, 155–156). The snow drives across the fields like the frenzy of inspiration trying to reach minds huddled around the fireplace, "enclosed / In a tumultuous privacy of storm." The image of the fierce mason at work celebrates visionary breakthrough and paints a picture of influence as a significant but harsh process:

> Come see the north wind's masonry.
> Out of an unseen quarry evermore
> Furnished with tile, the fierce artificer
> Curves his white bastions with projected roof
> Round every windward stake, or tree, or door.
> Speeding, the myriad-handed, his wild work
> So fanciful, so savage, nought cares he
> For number or proportion.

There is a theory of composition here and forceful interaction between source and recipient at the point of impact. It is not surprising that the self-confident and somewhat unorthodox modern sensibility in Masters was drawn to some of Emerson's most disquieting imagery:

> And when his hours are numbered, and the world
> Is all his own, retiring, as he were not,
> Leaves, when the sun appears, astonished Art
> To mimic in slow structures, stone by stone,
> Built in an age, the mad wind's night work,
> The frolic architecture of the snow.

Masters looked to Emerson's mad song for that same architecture of influence.

Several others among the twenty poems Masters selected are meditations on the process of influence. "Musketaquid" (*E*, 159–162) begins as a hymn to the rewards of a life in accord with nature, with fields and streams which grant "the freedom of their state." The speaker recalls that "in their secret senate" the partial wood gods "prevailed / With the dear, dangerous lords that rule our life, / Made moon and planets parties to their bond, / And through my rock-like, solitary want / Shot million rays of thought and tenderness." Influence as an influx of power takes the form of shooting rays and the ever-present creative power of nature's flow: "Then flows again / The surge of summer's beauty; dell and crag, / Hollow and lake, hill-side, and pine arcade, / Are touched with genius." The central image of the poem soon becomes the conversion of this natural flow of genius for human use. Influence at once is a shooting ray and an absorption of powers into a new creativity:

> The landscape is an armory of powers,
> Which, one by one, they knew to draw and use.
> They harness beast, bird, insect, to their work;
> They prove the virtues of each bed of rock,
> And, like the chemist 'mid his loaded jars,
> Draw from each stratum its adapted use
> To drug their crops or weapon their arts withal.

In Emerson's recurring metaphor, the landscape becomes a source of power which must be harnessed and adapted by the active soul. Meadow and forest are "transmuted" into a higher order.

"Musketaquid" is a nature hymn which no doubt helped Masters to recognize and use the flow of genius symbolized by the silence of the Illinois prairies. But the poem can be read as well as a startling commentary on literary influence and the process of poetic composition. The writing metaphors of the last stanza invite such a reading. "What these strong masters wrote at large in miles," the speaker states, "I followed in small copy in my acre." The poet took the first step in being influenced through a kind of imitation:

> The gentle deities
> Showed me the lore of colours and of sounds,
> The innumerable tenements of beauty,
> The miracle of generative force,
> Far-reaching concords of astronomy
> Felt in the plants, and in the punctual birds.

But no matter how awesome the lessons, the poet was not about to drown in a flood of influence. Self-reliance rallies even in the face of such miracles:

> For there's no road has not a star above it;
> The cordial quality of pear or plum

Ascends as gladly in a single tree
As in broad orchards resonant with bees;
And every atom poises for itself,
And for the whole.

In that single atom of the self, the poet converts the resources of the old and recreates the whole order. The lessons of influence are once again painful ("I am a willow of the wilderness / Loving the wind that beat me") and healing ("All my hurts my garden spade can heal"). The paradox of influence remains for Emerson, and for Masters after him, the interchange between self-reliance and absorption into the whole. Again the speaker expresses that recognition: "Chiefest prize, found I true Liberty / In the glad home plain-dealing nature gave." Yet the poem ends again with the incalculable puzzle:

Canst thou silent lie?
Canst thou, thy pride forgot, like nature pass
Into the winter night's extinguished mood?
Canst thou shine now, then darkle,
And being latent feel thyself no less?

"Musketaquid" suggests that one must answer such questions both "yes" and "no." It is no coincidence that Masters includes in a short volume this rather long and brooding meditation on the paradoxes of influence.

Nature's inner secrets become a symbol of the lessons of history, tradition, and influence in several other more familiar poems. In "Nature" (*E*, 162) the emphasis is on the mystery waiting to be discovered:

Though baffled seers cannot impart
The secret of its labouring heart,
Throb thine with Nature's throbbing breast,
And all is clear from east to west.
Spirit that lurks each form within
Beckons to spirit of its kin;
Self-kindled every atom glows,
And knits the future which it owes.

That inner spirit, central to all Emerson's thinking, is a part of the etymology of "influence" itself. Kindred spirits are joined by a magnetism, and a new creation emerges. But still there is the paradox in the joining of "kin," though all the while the new atom's glow is "self-kindled." That paradox is repeated in "History" (162) where "There is no great and no small / To the Soul that maketh all," and yet "where it cometh, all things are; / And it cometh everywhere." Again the self must receive the flow of nature's spirit even as it brings that spirit into being through the powers of its own active soul.

Emerson's last word on influence always comes down on the side of the self-reliant individual who remakes the past into a fresh vision. "Merlin's Wisdom" (*E*, 163) advises:

> Say not, the chiefs who first arrive
> Usurp the seats for which all strive,
> The forefathers this land who found
> Failed to plant the vantage-ground;
> Ever from one who comes tomorrow
> Men wait their good and truth to borrow.

That is simple enough counsel. Poets must look to the past not as a burden but as a vantage ground where they can borrow the resources to create tomorrow's truth. "The richest of all lords is Use," Merlin continues, "And ruddy Health the loftiest Muse." In order to create "the music that can deepest reach" he advises poets to convert the riches of the past by living to the fullest now: "Live in the sunshine, swim the sea, / Drink the wild air's salubrity." The same endurance and renewal through living is found in "The Test" (164–165), where "Sunshine cannot bleach the snow, / Nor time unmake what poets know." Self-reliance dominates also in "Terminus" (165–166), Emerson's "Ulysses" poem. "It is time to be old," a time when the poet can "no more invent." Still the self must "obey the voice at eve obeyed at prime" and celebrate "mature the unfallen fruit." In the end the recurring image in Emerson's nature poetry is the relentless and healing flow of old powers becoming new. The timeless stream is his final irreducible symbol of influence:

> Thou in thy narrow banks are pent:
> The stream I love unbounded goes
> Through flood and sea and firmament;
> Through light, through life, it forward flows.
>
> I see the inundation sweet,
> I hear the spending of the stream
> Through years, through men, through nature fleet,
> Through passion, thought, through power and dream.

Typical of Emerson, at the center of the life-giving flow is the ever-renewing creative power of the self-generating poet. The self-kindling atom which, nonetheless, needs the energizing flow is the puzzle of influence for Emerson as well as for Masters.

Of the twenty poems included in *The Living Thoughts of Emerson*, the poem most directly linked with Masters' own works is "The Rhodora" (*E*, 1955). In "An Unpublished Poem by Edgar Lee Masters" Charles E. Burgess has noted the "many references to Emerson" in Masters' poems of the thirties and examined in detail the parallels between "The Rhodora" and Masters' "The Pasture Rose" (1941).[11] What Masters called "a lifelong devotion to Emerson" shows up directly in his poems of the thirties. In "Beethoven's Ninth Symphony and the King Cobra" (1932), "Hymn to the Earth" (1935), and "Hymn to the Universes" and "Ode to America" (1938), Masters celebrated the fusing of nature and spirit, "Eternal essence" and "the intelligence of nature," and "the transcendent miracle" of "the spirit of man." Masters' poems of this time owe to Emerson their peculiar qualities of "lyrical chant" and "gnomic utterance"—terms Masters used to describe Emerson's poetry.

Emerson's Blakean chant "The Rhodora" and Masters' "The Pasture Rose" are striking parallels in celebration of the beauty of the solitary soul:

THE RHODORA
ON BEING ASKED, WHENCE IS THE FLOWER?

In May, when sea-winds pierced our solitudes,
I found the fresh Rhodora in the woods,
Spreading its leafless blooms in a damp nook,
To please the desert and the sluggish brook.
The purple petals, fallen in the pool,
Made the black water with their beauty gay;
Here might the red bird come his plumes to cool,
And court the flower that cheapens his array.
Rhodora! If the sages ask thee why
This charm is wasted on the earth and sky,
Tell them, dear, that if eyes were made for seeing,
Then beauty is its own excuse for being;
Why thou went there, rival of the rose!
I never thought to ask, I never knew;
But in my simple ignorance suppose
The self-same power that brought me there brought you.

Masters reworked this timeless essence into the soil of the Illinois prairie:

THE PASTURE ROSE
(Written For Edith L. Masters)

In barren places, meadow wastes,
Through which the breeze of sunset hastes,
By its lone self the pasture rose
In solitary beauty grows.

What is it there for? Can you ask
What does it do with life's brief task?
It makes the inquiring eye grow bright,
Its fragrance gives the heart delight.

How came it here? Was it intent
That beauty such as this was sent?
I dare to say it came to pass
Just to adorn the summer grass.

If everything must have a use
'Tis something to subserve the Muse.
What besides beauty can there be
Of such profound utility?

And just because it gives away
Its soul and is content to stay
Where it is chanced upon and known
By those who dream and walk alone,

And just because it does not seek
For admiration, and does not speak
Save with a breath that loves and gives,
And by that token solely lives,

I could stand by with misted eyes
And listen to the kildeer's cries,
Borne by the pasture wind afar,
That tries to tell us what we are.

The parallels are remarkable in the themes of these two poems,
though the mood and the spirit of place are very different. Emerson
catches the Blakean tone of prophecy, whereas Masters settles in for a
calm evening on the silent prairie. Emerson's rhodora is in the woods
near sea breezes; Masters' rose blows in the open meadows far from
the sea. Both emphasize solitude and the unlikely bloom in the desert
and waste. Both flowers thrive and in the process bring beauty out of
a barren state. And the pivotal questions are the same: why is there
such beauty in such an unlikely place? or, how and why is there

beauty at all? The answers, too, are the same. Emerson's "beauty is its own excuse for being" is more boldly prophetic, but the mystical vision on the prairie sends the same message and "tries to tell us what we are."

Masters arranged excerpts from Emerson's essays and lectures as well as poems and selections from *Representative Men* to demonstrate the strong links between Emerson's cultivation of the reflective life in Concord and his ability to break through trivialities to what was real. Masters saw that in Puritan New England, as anywhere, "repressed conditions" stimulated the need for self-reliance and led Emerson to the "rebellion that characterizes his philosophy." Masters understood that much of Emerson's sense of self-reliance grew from a rebellion against stifling forces similar to what he and his friends experienced in the Midwest. Emerson's counter to such restriction was a complex mix of rebellion and calm withdrawal, a paradoxical indignation (so typical in the scathing attacks found in his own and Thoreau's journals) tempered by an appreciation for the deep calm that allowed his mind to mature: "When he said goodbye to the proud world and took up his residence in Concord, in the Old Manse, he brought himself into a state of peace where he could reflect upon his country and its people, and draw out of the woods and the fields around that beautiful place the secrets of nature, the intimations of the Over-Soul, the laws and characters of compensation. Here too he could evolve the worlds of representative men."

Emerson's "representative men" often shocked his audiences in ways similar to the people of *Spoon River* or Masters' later characterizations. The ambivalence of struggling serenity and daemonic greatness in Emerson's portraits shows up later in Masters and helps explain some of the controversies surrounding his reputation. Masters the editor stressed the "audacious spirit" in Emerson's critiques of the values of his time: "He was writing and saying that life was halfness, shallowness. That will not do in an optimistic country like America, preaching success." Masters included poems about "the feel of earth, the richness of life in the country" and other selections that suited his own beliefs about the struggle to achieve greatness: "We can judge Emerson's reaction to the earth-scene and the lives of men upon it by casting up the types that he treated in *Representative Men.* There is no theologian, no divine in the list, and no reformer. . . . In fact, Emerson disliked reformers and professed philanthropists. He said once that they were an altogether odious set of people whom one would shun as the worst of bores and canters" (*E*, 22–23). This is typical of Masters' thinking about Emerson around 1940.

That nearly daemonic strength also contributed to Masters' Emersonian sense of "magnitude." One of Masters' chief reasons for editing the Living Thoughts volume was to dispel popular misconceptions that linked Emerson and "the quackery of mental healing" and other "rubbish of his day." His intent was not to produce another collection for intellectuals but a compact volume which people would read to experience the power of primary documents instead of "dilutes of Emerson" in which his thought was too often "reduced to quackery." The editorial opinions he expressed in 1940 were the result of over fifty years of reading and writing about Emerson. Throughout the immediately preceding decade Masters' Emersonian stance can be traced through the long narrative poem *The New World* (1937) and the literary biographies *Vachel Lindsay: A Poet in America* (1935), *Whitman* (1937), and *Mark Twain: A Portrait* (1938).

The New World (1937) was an energetic and controversial narrative poem of epic proportions. The story was a DeMille-like cinemascope production beginning with the early explorers of the New World and extending down through the revolutionary heroes, the Civil War, and Woodrow Wilson. The wide scope and often bitter tone made the book an interesting experiment, though the vitriolic attacks on the way democracy had been compromised by greed made its reception less than enthusiastic. The following capsule is a sample of the flavor:

> Out of this muck of money and falsehood
> Arose the false American histories,
> And the magnification of certain American characters.
> For if they were idealized, and the real facts lied away
> They gave support to the fatal spindles, the machines,
> And the dragon ships, and the counters of Midas.
>
> [*NW*, 127]

Naturally the book was roundly castigated for its narrowness, though the *Times Literary Supplement* cited it as Masters' most ambitious work to date.[12]

In his epic attempts to rewrite the "false American histories," Masters gave the highest place in his own new order to Emerson. He stood in awe at the "fierce accusations" which Emerson "hurled against his own day." He even coined a vigorous and precise new verb when he said that Emerson "said things that also charactered the New World." In Masters' view, Emerson was that solitary rhodora blooming in a desert:

O inscrutable nature that out of the New World
Of falsehood, hypocrisy and greed
Produced the spirit we call Emerson,
And clothed it in the most beautiful flesh of all American man,
Giving him the noblest face that the New World has seen!
What was it that grew this rock flower,
Scarcely to be told from the azure of heaven,
Growing amid boulders by pine trees
Springing to the eternal sails of clouds
Hastening across the sea of a sky?

[*NW*, 129]

Emerson's "bright visions" gave him the courage to say that the New World was "sick / Of conservation and cowardice." Masters emphasized how Emerson stood up against "manifold censorships / Growing out of theology and trade, / Which cowed independence of mind." Masters believed that such censorship through dogmatism and imposed ideologies "aborted" great writers in the New World. Here again the magnet drew him to Emerson:

How he was fearless to say that statecraft was base,
That the letters of the New World did not cheer,
That the New World distrusted Nature;
And New England distrusted the emotions;
That the whole land was a mass of cowards
Lacking nerve and daggers
Where there was no moral independence,
But only the slap of neighborly kindness.
How he cried out that the spirit of the New World
Sowing obedience, fear, imitation, and snobbery
Cropped gravity, pomp, and dumbness.
To flower in cities like New York, Boston, and Chicago.
How he showed that the New World hunted health
In pills, nostrums, and mental healing,
And sought cure of the ills flowing from the privileges
Grabbed by spindles, ships, and sweaters,
By applying local remedies to a present distress;
And that the sickness of the New World
Came from self-interest in statecraft, theology,
And in the exchanges.

[*NW*, 130]

Emerson said all these things and more, of course. He said enough to make Masters' critiques in *The New World* seem plausible and even tame. Philosophically, at this point the overlap between Masters and his New England mentor was substantial.

In the several biographies Masters published in the thirties he frequently used Emerson as a standard of greatness against which he measured Vachel Lindsay, Twain, and even Whitman. He chided Lindsay for failing to listen to Emerson's advice "to live after the infinite Law that was in them, and to keep company with the infinite Beauty which heaven and earth reflected to them in all lovely forms" (*L*, 193). Because he didn't listen with confidence to that inner law, Lindsay was "left in vacillation, in fear, and in distress of soul." A little later Masters identifies with the distress Lindsay felt and again credits Emerson for offering a way out:

> When I was a youth there [in Illinois] all of us who did not get jobs in the abstract office there to record real estate transfers, who did not become the manufacturers of cigars, or begin as clerks in the stores with the hope of one day owning the store, or take with alacrity to the practice of medicine or law, or raise chickens or vegetables, or in short do something else which made us permanent denizens of our villages, were in rebellion. The church choked us to death, the constant ringing of prayer-meeting bells filled us first with melancholy, then with resentment; the moral intermeddlers which broke up every dance and frowned upon every amateur dramatic venture set our nerves to bristling with pugnacity. We had nothing but each other, and we were few; and except for the sustaining voices of Whitman and Emerson we should have sunk to the dregs, worn out with the struggle against the prohibitionists and the Sunday-school workers. [*L*, 199]

That sustaining voice of Emerson helped Lindsay survive, but in Masters' final analysis Lindsay fell short by not listening enough to that voice. Whereas Lindsay was restless to the point of frenzy, Emerson referred to himself as a "delineator of occult harmonies and unpublished beauties." Whereas Lindsay was "all bard," Emerson was "the philosopher with Pythagorean verses" who "sang infrequently," but when he did brought down "gnomic secrets" (*L*, 299, 317).

In short, Masters zeroed in on Lindsay's tragic flaw as a writer: "He could study an Egyptian grammar in order to draw hieroglyphics; he failed to take to heart what Emerson said that 'the strength of the Egyptians is to sit still'" (*L*, 331).

Two years later in *Whitman* again Emerson was for Masters the logical measure of his subject's achievement. Though Whitman was himself a very significant influence on Masters (and deserving of further treatment in chapter 5, below), a comparison of the two reveals important insights. Masters spent a good deal of time in his study showing how each of the two men was favorably disposed to teach the other and he devotes considerable space to the famous split of their later years. Most interesting in a parallel study of two seminal figures are their remarks about each other and the peculiar nature of the counsel against influence that took hold in Whitman's consistent refusal to listen to Emerson's advice.

Masters quotes Emerson's remark that in *Song of Myself* Whitman produced the "Bhagavad Gita and the *New York Herald* combined" and adds his own assessment that the book contained "all the solipsism, errant spirituality, transcendentalism, Emersonism, socialism, and the stir of America of that day of 1855" (*W*, 92); Masters also offers Whitman's appraisal of Emerson for its penetrating summary of both minds. Emerson "may be obscure," Whitman admits, "but he is certain." Whitman said of Emerson: "He has what none else has; he does what none else does. He pierces the crusts that envelope the secrets of life. He joins on equal terms the few great sages and original seers. He represents the freeman, America, the individual" (*W*, 248–249).

Most of American culture got a good deal of its Emerson through Whitman. Just how true that was of Masters can be seen in the following challenge which Whitman issued and Masters spent a career striving to answer: Emerson's "words shed light to the best souls," contended Whitman. And he elaborated:

As a spring from the pine tree or a glimpse anywhere into the daylight belittles all artificial flower work and all the painted scenery of theatres, so are live words in a book compared to cunningly composed words. A few among men (soon perhaps to become many) will enter easily into Emerson's meanings; by those he will be well beloved. The flippant writer, the orthodox critic, the numbers of good or indifferent imitators, will not comprehend him; to them he will indeed be a transcendentalist, a writer of sunbeams and moonbeams, a strange and unapproachable person. [*W*, 249]

Here Whitman foresaw the problems Masters would face in his attempts to reassert the Emerson legacy against the indifference of his time.

The subject of how Whitman and Emerson influenced each

other is, of course, a gem for any literary historian. Their interaction was a great fascination for Masters in a career devoted to the pursuit of a uniquely American culture. The intricacies of how they affected each other had a special magnetic pull on Masters' concern with the dynamics of influence. Perhaps nowhere is the paradox between imitation and self-reliance more obvious than in Emerson's influence on Whitman. The debt is obvious and yet puzzling. Whitman's debt to Emerson is colossal—including his acceptance of Emerson's counsel against influence itself. Perhaps as much as any American poet, Whitman heard Emerson's grumbling against relying on sources of any kind and took him up on it. Masters quotes extensively from a conversation between the two men in which Whitman found himself roundly attacked by his friend. Following a list of scathing accusations, Emerson asked him "What have you to say then to such things?" Whitman's reply contains all the contradictions which he, Emerson, and Masters richly enjoyed. To the objection Whitman replied, "While I can't answer them at all, I feel more settled than ever to adhere to my own theory." Surely Emerson agreed with such independence as the two rivals went off and "had a good dinner at the American House." Masters' summation is to the point: "Thus the two wisest, most inspired and consecrated men of their times met and compared points of view, touched and took a soft rebound and parted in friendship" (W, 203–204). In that crucial experience of influence, the rebound taught each man how to be more deeply and securely his own self.

In his rather scathing *Portrait* of Mark Twain (1938), Masters again used Emerson as a measure of the greatness that strove to "emancipate the culture of America" (T, 83). Emerson knew the West, Masters noted, whereas Twain fled to the East. Emerson lived "simply and easily," whereas Twain desired prosperity too much (T, 78). Emerson spoke out vigorously against "the Courtly Muses of Europe," whereas Twain "was afraid to publish what he really thought about England" (T, 210). Consistently Masters used Emerson as a foil for Twain in his outspoken and controversial reassessment. Twain's restlessness was, for Masters, a symbol of deeper confusion. "One looks with great satisfaction," he notes, "at the life of Emerson lived out in his native country, there at Concord." Emerson settled into the "spiritual richness" that such stability affords. On the other hand, Masters felt that whenever Twain's "nervous stability was upset," he became "neurotic," and "he indulged his fancies to go where he pleased and to live where his inclination took him" (T, 165). Masters saw that kind of aimless wandering as the exact opposite of Emersonian self-reliance.

Among Masters' many allusions to Emerson, his tribute in *More People* (1939) is an epitome of Emersonian harmony. The poem stands for itself as a hymn to the "word that endures" in pursuit of the ultimately "elusive myth." The divination of the poet Masters called the "sweetest of all our singers" deserves full quotation and needs no commentary:

EMERSON

Creature of the pine forest,
But not with shaggy limbs,
Walking where light is hoarest,
With meadow gathered hymns;

With tang of mint and cone,
With sound of robin, thrush,
With music which has tone
Just as the wires hush.

Sweetest of all our singers,
Most equable, most wise,
America still lingers,
And harks your melodies.

All that was pastoral Greece,
All highest thoughts of saints
Became your beauty, peace,
Untouched by worldly taints.

America has no face
So noble, pure as yours,
No eyes with such a grace,
No word that so endures.

At Concord on a hill
Where sunshine, stars and clouds
Pass over where jaybirds shrill
There earth your body shrouds;

There drifts the scent of ferns,
And takes the silence with
The mood of storied urns,
The Sphinx's elusive myth.

But there above, enskied
Like Plato's spirit, soars
Your music, still allied
To Earth and Heaven's doors.

This is an altar where
America should kneel
In happiness, and prayer
To win our country's weal.

In Masters' poetry after 1940, the presence of Emerson can be found in the silence of the prairie where man's soul became a "Muse of distance eyeing the solitude." Consistently in the late poems, Emerson's "scaffolding" supports the primary symbol of the prairie as a force and spirit. "Influence" in *Along the Illinois* (1942) is no longer so "self-conscious" as it was in *Across Spoon River* six years earlier or in the poems of the late thirties. In many of the poems of the early forties (posthumously published), Masters transformed what he found earlier in Emerson into a "mystical Presence." "Influence" in the later poetry became a more somber brooding (see chapter 8).

In *The Litany of Washington Street* (1929), Vachel Lindsay described the mind of the Midwest as a mix of "the peculiar pride of the South" and "the iron mind of the Emersonian." The resulting hybrid created, according to Lindsay, "a standard of self-reliance and freedom and dignity which finds its ultimate hope in the tradition around Springfield, Illinois, and in the legends that haunt that place." [13] Lindsay published these attempts at a "Definition of the Middle West" about fifteen years after the initial impact of *Spoon River Anthology* and seven years before Masters' own autobiography. Masters' own mix of pride and self-reliance was strengthened by a fiercely self-critical sense for which he also found support in Emerson. As an epitome of American thought and poetics, Emerson showed Masters not only how to take pride in the midwestern prairies but—even more importantly—how to eternalize them by using the land he came from and his own experiences as an access to vision. Through Emerson, Masters realized his poetic ambitions by reinforcing what he had learned all his life through experience and wide reading. Masters' essay on Emerson was a ritual enactment of one poet's debts to another and a significant document on their major contributions to modern poetics.

In spite of his adulation for Emerson, Masters was capable of quarreling with the judgment of the man he had enshrined. When Emerson's reading of Goethe swerved from his own, Masters held to his own belief. "Emerson adjudged that Goethe had not ascended to the highest ground from which genius has spoken," Masters notes. And then he softly but firmly protests: "It may be that Goethe's earthiness, his erotic interests, his love of the good earth, of physical well being, affected the ascetic side of Emerson in the forming of his estimate" (E, 28). Emerson may not have agreed with Masters' opinion here, but he would like the self-reliant refusal to be influenced.

5

"The Natural Child of Walt Whitman"

BEYOND THE "*SPOON RIVER* POET"

In order to trace the peculiarly American sources of Masters' poetry, it is instructive to move from his comments on Emerson in 1940 back to some of the bizarre events which took place a quarter of a century earlier. In April 1915 the then-famous English critic John Cowper Powys delivered a series of lectures in New York in which he referred to Masters as "the aboriginal American poet" and the "natural child of Walt Whitman." That was high praise from the Cambridge man who thought of Whitman as "the only poet with true Americanism in his bones." Powys' stirring proclamations seconded the judgment of Ezra Pound who had announced only three months earlier that in the *Spoon River Anthology* "at last America has discovered a poet." [1]

Powys' appearance in New York received a good deal of press, and the heralding of Masters only increased the publicity. The *New York Times* assigned its Chicago correspondent to interview Masters at his home. Their exchange was published under the title "Spoon River Poet Called Great: Famous English Critic Lifts Edgar Lee Masters from Chicago Obscurity to the High Peak of Parnassus." [2] The interview was typical of the overnight fame and sensationalism which greeted "Webster Ford" now revealed as Edgar Lee Masters of Illinois. Macmillan was about to publish the anthology, which had made such a stir in piecemeal publication in the *St. Louis Mirror*. Reviews of the book later that year would prove equally enthusiastic, and the headlong rush toward becoming an overnight one-book "phenom" was underway.

During the thirty-five years after the publication of *Spoon River Anthology*, Masters wrote biographies and histories as well as poetry and fiction. His bibliography includes over fifty books which have been overlooked in later assessments of his contribution to American letters. Although the "*Spoon River* Poet" was well-known in 1915, his poetry of the twenties and thirties generally ran counter to the dominant views of his times and was seldom accorded the recognition it deserved. The general impression persists even today that, after the *Anthology*, Masters' powers gave out. The highest praise for his Spoon River characters is nearly always dampened by the disappointment that he never achieved further vision. Even the best criticism of *Spoon River Anthology* rarely survives the notion that Masters' lightning Muse struck hard—but only once. Even now, this oversimplification dies hard.

Critical response to the "one-book poet" was based on several misunderstandings from which Masters' reputation has yet to recover. Early reviewers of the *Anthology* heaped praise on its sensationalistic innovations and glossed over its place in the solid American tradition of Whitman and Emerson. From the start, Masters' reputation was built on the wrong foundation. For example, reviewers referred to his indebtedness to the *Greek Anthology* and overlooked his deeper foothold in the larger classical tradition; critics alluded to "echoes" of Browning in *Domesday Book* and elsewhere, only to overlook the richer dramatic tones he absorbed from the monologues; even the best commentators mentioned Masters' "devotion" to Shelley but didn't follow up on where that devotion led him; and for over sixty-five years students of American poetry have nodded to Powys' suggestion that Masters belongs in the Whitman tradition and neglected to explore the intricate relationships between the "aboriginal" child and his imposing literary ancestor. The sensationalism and oversimplification which dominated the reception of *Spoon River Anthology* have long stood in the way of an understanding of Masters' later accomplishments.

The coming and going of Masters' reputation over the last sixty years reflects the stops and starts of the American poetic tradition which he helped shape. In order to reassess his place in the tradition of Whitman and to begin a study of his accomplishments after *Spoon River*, this discussion will review briefly the meteoric rise as well as the subsequent collapse into obscurity. Reviewers, literary historians, and compilers of anthologies seemed generally to dislike *and* like the *Spoon River* poet for what are now beginning to look like equally wrong reasons. With the advantage of hindsight, we can see in Masters' variable reputation several clues about why many of his later poems have gone unread.

Criticism of *Spoon River Anthology* from its serialized publication in Reedy's *Mirror* through its many reprints is just now being sorted out. John T. Flanagan's survey of the critical reception makes lengthy summary unnecessary here.[3] Flanagan notes that Masters' first impact on American poets was comparable to "nothing since the appearance of Whitman's *Leaves of Grass*." Reviewers judged Masters in several marked stages. Initially, they were enraged over his characters and his portrayal of small-town midwestern life. Reviewers were also perturbed by his "cynicism" in creating "sordidness" and "perversion." At the same time—in 1915—there was lavish praise from Powys, Pound, Floyd Dell, and others—as well as unusually large and enthusiastic coverage in the popular press.

For the next several years, debates about *Spoon River Anthology* appeared everywhere, and the controversies raged. Foreign reviewers saw great significance in the work. Amy Lowell linked Masters to Strindberg and Dostoyevsky; Conrad Aiken and Louis Untermeyer contributed qualified and cautious praise. But in 1921, Untermeyer sounded the sour notes of criticism to come on Masters' poetry after the *Anthology*: "With *Spoon River Anthology*, Masters arrived and left." Amidst furor about his free verse forms, cynicism, and sexual explicitness, Masters' impact on contemporary poetry was hotly debated in alternately flowing and caustic reviews. *Domesday Book* (1920) was immensely popular with the public, but—in spite of praise from no less than Mencken and Braithwaite—the book has not received the place in American literature that it deserves.

With the publication of *The New Spoon River* in 1924, controversies stirred again. Most critics compared the later volume to its predecessor and found the sequel lacking. Estimates ranged from "candleflare of beauty" to "shop-stick prose." It is fair to say that most reviewers of the volumes of poetry Masters published in the thirties continued to look back to *Spoon River Anthology*. Many commentators continued to lament what they saw as the decline of a one-book author.[4]

Masters' works after *Spoon River Anthology* have seldom received the critical attention they should command. In spite of repeated popularity with the public, his work has been largely dismissed by critics with regrets that he wrote too much too quickly. He has been thought of as a popularizer, a writer of polite verse, a dabbler in fiction, an amateur historian whose training in law spilled over into chronicles about the land of his origins. Literary historians mention his work as part of either a "Chicago school" or a group engaged in a "revolt against the village." Until recently, most regionalist studies of midwestern literature have assigned Masters a place among local colorists who praise the prairie and satirize the narrowness of smalltown life.

Masters' accomplishments are much larger. Today's more enlightened approaches to midwestern literature are attempting to redefine the mind and culture of the Midwest. These redefinitions are likely to look to phenomena like *Spoon River Anthology* and place their achievement in the broader and richer traditions reflected in the literary sources and life experiences which fed them. As a result of more far-reaching regional studies, the later works of this "one-book author" should provide material especially suited for the kind of broader and more complete reassessment that Masters deserves.

Whitman's "child" absorbed much of the power and energy of his poetic ancestor. On more than one occasion, Masters explained how the spirit of Emerson and Whitman helped him in his earliest years. In relating the history of his career to a *New York Times* correspondent in 1915, Masters noted that his earliest "sketches" were inadequate. When he showed the drafts to Reedy, the *Mirror* editor told him that "they were not interpreting American life adequately—that they lacked the American punch." When he revised and resubmitted what grew into *Spoon River Anthology*, Reedy wrote back: "This is the stuff." Whitman's child had found the punch. Twenty-two years and over ten books later, Masters published an extended tribute in *Whitman* (1937). The book made a substantial impact in its time and was reissued in 1968 as part of a vastly underplayed centennial year.

Critical response to *Whitman* from 1937 to the present is a good measure of the ups and downs of Masters' position among the "moderns." Allen Tate's and Newton Arvin's reviews were typical of the quarrelsome response of 1937. Carl Van Doren, on the other hand, thought Masters' was the "best general account of the poet to date."[5] In our time renewed interest in Whitman is matched favorably with attempts to reexamine Masters' contributions after *Spoon River*. In one of the best recent studies of Masters, Cesare Pavese makes the logical connections:

> The sternest and most conscious poetry of Lee Masters inheres in this humiliated celebration of the energy and the youth of a great past. Not a lament for his own youth, for his own personal pride and pleasure, but a heroic dream of "the republic," of "giant hands [who] from the womb of the world tore the republic," the real "pioneers" who loved and fought with courage. To this dream Lee Masters gave a name, "Jeffersonian democracy," and in the course of his slow set of sun he wrote many historical and poetical books about its most memorable figures. In the second decade of the century, he thus originated a longing for, and a recollection of, the purest American tradition which so many writers were to take up again, a sure sign that the tradition was sinking to sunset, was already past history.[6]

That "purest American tradition" which Masters "longed for" throughout his entire career originated with Whitman. Though most of his formal education and reading emphasized the classics, the Greeks, and British poets, Masters' love of Whitman held out a special hope for his own writing. Whitman's accomplishments offered encouragement in the gloomiest times in the law office and an energizing reinforcement later on.

Above all else, Whitman taught Masters how to reread the roots of his own poetic tradition. Masters fed his own inventive powers with many of the same sources championed by Whitman. Much of *Whitman* is devoted to Whitman's reading as preparation for the "taste of poetry" (*W*, 73). Several chapters include lengthy quotations from Whitman's own prefaces as he celebrated Goethe, Homer, Hegel, Browning, Shelley, and, of course, the "star of the first magnitude"—Emerson (237–251). Masters collected quotations from Whitman on every major American writer and on most of the British and continental poets from Shakespeare to Ibsen. Masters called these passages "glimpses of Whitman's mind" and from these glimpses he became convinced that the poet must become a visionary singer of "cosmic consciousness."

Masters looked to Whitman for vision. He read the characteristic catalogs as "a way of presenting to the eye of imagination the content of a vision" (*W*, 60). He looked to the "poet of great vision" whose "prophetical power" was a "psychical stage" of "cosmic consciousness" which celebrated "the life forces that are never disrupted or reduced." A generation before Charles Olson or Allen Ginsberg, Masters recognized that Whitman "put into his long lines the rise and fall of his own spiritual diaphragm" (76, 84, 313, 81). Over three hundred pages reviewing Whitman's reading illustrate Masters' own astonishing insights on the whole range of the American tradition. Masters' treatment of Whitman is a good index of his own sensibility twenty years after *Spoon River Anthology*.

That vision which attracted Masters to Whitman is most succinctly stated in their reactions to the Hegelian dialectic which, Masters said, "appealed to Whitman's conception of a tumultuous democracy working itself into wisdom and good laws with government forces of spiritual evolution operating from within" (*W*, 69). In *Specimen Days*, Whitman saw Hegel's theories as the best reconciliation of the apparent contradictions that plagued him all his life:

> What is the fusing explanation and tie—what the relation
> between the (radical democrat) Me, the human identity of un-

derstanding, emotions, spirit, &c., on the one side of and with the (conservative) Not Me, the whole of the material objective universe and laws, with what is behind them in time and space on the other side? Immanuel Kant, though he explain'd or partially explain'd, as may be said, the laws of the human understanding, left this question an open one. . . . But G. F. Hegel's fuller statement of the matter probably remains the last best word that has been said upon it up to date. . . . According to Hegel the whole earth (an old nucleus thought, as in the Vedas, and no doubt before, but never hitherto brought so absolutely to the front, fully surcharged with modern scientism and facts and made the sole entrance to each and all), with its infinite variety, the past, the surroundings of today, or what may happen in the future, the contrarieties of material with spiritual and the natural with artificial, are all to the eye of the *ensemblist*, but necessary unfoldings, different steps or links in the endless process of Creative thought, which amid numberless failures and contradictions is held together by central and never broken unity. [*W*, 68–69]

Whitman elaborates on the place of Hegel in his own thinking in the famous passage that begins, "Only Hegel is fit for America—is large enough and free enough." Again Masters quotes the passage to explain the evolution of Whitman's cosmic poet:

Absorbing his speculations and imbued by his letter and spirit, we bring to the study of life here and the thought of hereafter, in all its mystery and vastness, an expansion and clearness of sense before unknown. As a face in a mirror we see the world of materials, nature with all its objects, processes, shows, reflecting the human spirit and by such reflection formulating, identifying, developing and proving it. Body and mind are one; an inexplicable paradox, yet no truth truer. The human soul stands in the centre, and all the universes minister to it, and serve it and revolve round it. They are one side of the whole and it is the other side. It escapes utterly from all limits, dogmatic standards and measurements and adjusts itself to the ideas of God, of space, and to eternity, and sails them at will as oceans, and fills them as beds of oceans. [*W*, 243–244]

Whitman taught Masters a lesson which he learned also from Shelley and Browning: that in the midst of the disparate and the ephemeral, only the deepest natural human urges could create unity and satisfy man's quest for the eternal. Love and sex as eternizing influences and unifiers of all experience became a major theme in Masters' poems after *Spoon River*. In "Cleanthus Trilling" in *The New*

Spoon River, Masters celebrated "the urge to unite"; twenty years later he devoted entire poems to that urge as in "Amphimixis," where the Shelleyan and Whitmanesque longings take on epic dimensions. This theme in Masters' poems of the thirties and forties will be a major concern in the following chapters.

Whitman is eminently quotable on "pulsating love and friendship," "terrible, irrepressible yearning," and the "never-satisfied appetite." Masters quotes phrases in Whitman such as "this old, eternal, yet ever-new interchange of adhesiveness, so fitly emblematic of America" and a "fervent, accepted development of comradeship" through which people are "most effectually welded together, intercalated, anneal'd into a living union." Masters selected not only representative passages but obviously also those in accord with his own thinking. Consider one example typical of Masters' own beliefs:

> The *irrepressible yearning* with which Whitman credited the human soul is nothing less than that lacuna at its center which sex, by some trick of nature, fills. It lifts human beings out of their soul loneliness while it stays, if only for a moment, the desolate gap of eternity which tortures the soul all through its earth pilgrimage. But it does not allay the pain of separation from eternal things. [W, 104–105]

Masters also traced Whitman's stress on the unifying force of love through a wide variety of his sources. Whitman admired, for example, the views of Socrates in the *Symposium*. He also cited lengthy passages from Shelley and Browning on love as the directing and binding force of society. Masters points to Shelley's "prophesies of a happier world based on love," and a "new day of earth happiness created by social love." Browning's philosophy, he says, begins with "love of men for women" and emerges into "general love, into ethical passion and social ideals" (144, 145). For Masters, Whitman was "hinting at those profound intimations of nature, of man and of love, which visit all deeply imaginative souls." Masters calls this need for union a "cosmic longing" which Whitman expressed even at the "risk of being mocked, of being grossly interpreted by the vulgarity of the world" (148–149). Whitman "spoke for sensuality, not the life of wayward and hedonistic indulgence, but for man's and woman's spirit playing through the body and thereby ministering to the spirit and finding itself" (323). When Masters translated this sensuality into his own terms, he wrote poems about the urge for two to become one and, through such a passionate merging, touch the infinite. The language is there again in his assessment of Whitman: "This is the love which divines the recapitulation of the urge of the life essences, blindly and powerfully, inevitably and swiftly seeking to be merged and to be one. Man as a lover repeats this passion and this process and finds in them, when he finds it, the secret of the mystery of life" (149).

The bard of Camden, New Jersey, and Manhattan also encouraged Masters to celebrate his midwestern roots. Masters reveled in Whitman's Jeffersonian democracy and his identification with "the good earth," with "Nature as the visible embodiment of creative thought and mind." In the kind of lyrics Whitman sang, Masters looked for technique that "extracts the essential from landscapes and the souls of men and women in their daily life and in heroic moments" (*W*, 324). Through Whitman, Masters didn't feel the need to look anywhere else but more deeply into where he already was. In America's epic poet and his philosophical friend from Concord, Masters found an expansive and flexible regionalism:

> It cannot be said too often that Whitman's great and really significant contribution to American poetry lies in the fact that he surveyed its future territory. When Texas has grown to twenty millions, when the country west of the Mississippi River is as populous as the Middle West is now, and when as accompaniments to such growth the thousand and one streams of American life and liberty are swept into national consciousness, what will be the significance of Robinson and his somber delineations, his word-splitting refinements, the near and thin utterance of Frost, and all mere Eastern schools of literature? It seems inconceivable that they can be anything but rocky headlands and peaks which a spiritual geology has deserted and left to their lonely sterility. Emerson will likely remain, since he was in his own way so American and so spiritually profound. [*W*, 298–299]

Masters also found in Whitman guidance on how to be inventive, how to be influenced. Again in the classical sense, Masters studied closely Whitman's elaborate preparations "for the task of poetry." He observed how Whitman "prepared himself as an athlete would do for a great contest of strength and endurance." The invention process extended to setting down "in writing the resolution to abstain from every weakening and corrupting indulgence the better to clarify and spiritualize his mind." That clarification included wide reading, and the contest often became a struggle with influential writers and monuments of past tradition. The study of Whitman's growth had an unmistakable impact on Masters' thinking: "There is no parallel to this preparation in any literature of which we have a record" (*W*, 73).

The attraction Whitman held for Masters was direct and simple. They shared a common theory of poetry and a set of motivations about what a poet ought to do to reach readers. Masters quoted extensively from Whitman's explanations of what he was trying to do in *Leaves of Grass*:

> I also sent out *Leaves of Grass* to arouse and set flowing in men's and women's hearts, young and old, endless streams of living, pulsating love and friendship, directly from them to myself, now and ever. To this terrible, irrepressible yearning (surely more or less down underneath in most human souls)—this never-satisfied appetite for sympathy, and this boundless offering of sympathy—this universal democratic comradeship—this old, eternal, yet ever-new interchange of adhesiveness, so fitly emblematic of America—I have given in that book, undisguisedly, declaredly, the openest expression. [*W*, 104]

They also shared common attitudes toward their own reputations and how they should feel about the critics. Masters approvingly quotes Whitman again:

> *Leaves of Grass* will finally make its way. The book is like the flukes of a whale—if not graceful at least effective; never super-refined or ashamed of the animal energy that imparts power to expression. . . . I do say with regard to myself that I must be judged elementally—that the Arnolds, the disciples of books as books, the second and third hand men, the scholars pure and simple, the lovers of art for art's sake, cannot understand me—cannot take me in—I elude their circumscriptions. [*W*, 268]

That "elemental" judgment describes the American tradition which Masters wanted to restore. Again he cites Whitman as the chief spokesman:

> Whitman in his day had to contend with those who claimed to speak with authority of the soul, those who somehow, whether they exactly meant to or not, always stood in the way of the new days, blocking the steps of wisdom and the muses with Bibles and with solemn orthodoxy. One of the absurd propositions of such thinkers, a proposition that contradicts such wise men as Goethe, is that something arises in the human mind by introspection and by books, by religion, so-called, too—which is superior to the flesh, to nature and to normal impulses. As if any inner check could possibly be superior to the natural life of the mind and the body! This cannot be, and Whitman is the great spokesman in

America of the impossibility of such a theory and for the life of freedom. [*W*, 302]

One of the principal subjects of *Whitman* is Masters' fascination with the interactions between Whitman and Emerson, the two voices offering him hope back in the village. In order to explain Whitman's motivations and achievements, Masters frequently dips into Emerson's essays and places their theories "side by side." The occasion of one such comparison goes to the core of Masters' own thinking about the origins of poetry and the renewed dedication to which he felt himself called. The passage in question is a well-known definition from Emerson's "The Poet":

> Here is the difference betwixt the poet and the mystic, that the last nails a symbol to one sense, which has a true sense for a moment, but soon becomes old and false. For all symbols are fluxional; all language is vehicular and transitive, and is good, as ferries and horses, for conveyance, not as farms and houses are, for homestead. Mysticism consists in the mistake of an accidental and individual symbol for a universal one. [*W*, 80]

For "mysticism" read "modernism," and you have Masters on the problems of being an American poet in the 1930s.

Petit the Poet would ask us to look a little deeper at Emerson and the Emerson fleshed out in *Whitman*. "Poetry was all written before time was," says Emerson in "The Poet," "and whenever we are so finely organized that we can penetrate into that region where the air is music, we hear those primal warblings and attempt to write them down, but we lose ever and anon a word or a verse and substitute something of our own and thus miswrite the poem." There we have Emerson on influence at his puzzling best. Poetic language is itself a revision, a falling away from the primal music. The strength of poetry is also, ironically, the point of its collapse, and all the best and worst that the poet can hope for is Petit's Whitmanesque roar.

Masters read Whitman through the Emersonian poet working through and yet beyond language:

> Though the origin of most of our words is forgotten, each word was at first a stroke of genius, and obtained currency because for the moment it symbolized the world to the first speaker and to the hearer. The etymologist finds the deadest words to have been once a brilliant picture. Language is fossil poetry. As the limestone of the continent consists of infinite masses of the shells of animalcules, so language is made up of image or tropes, which

now, in their secondary use, have long ceased to remind us of their poetic origin. But the poet names the thing because he sees it, or comes one step nearer to it than any other.[7]

Emerson's emphasis on literary origins revels in a world before the intrusion of fragmentation and literal meaning. He deals in the irreducible stuff of "sacred history" where "the birth of a poet is the principal event in chronology." The poet deals with "the one hidden stuff" from which all things are made; the poet "stands one step nearer to things, and sees the flowing or metamorphosis." The poet "perceives that thought is multiform; that within the form of every creature is a force impelling it to ascend to a higher form; and following with his eyes the life, uses the forms which express that life, and so his speech flows with the flowing of nature." And so poetry must abandon itself to its limitations and celebrate outlandish strength: "The poet knows that he speaks adequately, then, only when he speaks somewhat wildly, or 'with the flower of the mind'; not with the intellect used as an organ, but with the intellect released from all service and suffered to take its direction from its celestial life; or as the ancients were wont to express themselves, not with intellect alone but with the intellect inebriated by nectar."[8] For Emerson, this is what it means to be stuffed. Masters' Petit, the Poet, understood the horrible waste of time spent on "little iambics" while the much neglected "Homer and Whitman roared in the pines!" The roar Masters heard grew more intense on the brooding, silent prairies where the mystical visions created a deeper harmony. That deepening tone of silence was also a part of Whitman's plan as Masters read him. In *Democratic Vistas* Whitman described what he hoped might happen: "Alone, and silent thought and awe, and aspiration—and then the interior consciousness, like a hitherto unseen inscription, in magic ink, beams out its wondrous lines to the sense. Bibles may convey, and priests expound, but it is exclusively for the noiseless operation of one's isolated self, to enter the pure ether of veneration, reach the divine levels, and commune with the unutterable."

The mystery of Whitman's interior consciousness guided Masters throughout his entire career. When Whitman died, Masters wrote a tribute and published it in his earliest collection *A Book of Verses*. Long before *Spoon River Anthology*, he read a paper before the Fulton County Scientific Association. Later, he summarized the point of that paper: "I looked forward through Whitman to a republic in which equality and fraternity should bind all hearts with a culture of that profound nature which enabled an Athenian audience to sit in the Theater of Bacchus and follow with appreciative delight a tragedy by Sophocles. In that America Whitman would be the Hesiod and someone yet to arise the Homer" (*ASR*, 336). It seems safe to speculate that Masters wanted to be Whitman's Homer.

The chronology of Masters' career-long debts to Whitman is a revealing touchstone of his own ups and downs. The unreserved praise for *Spoon River Anthology* in 1914 and 1915 included frequent mention of Masters' lineage to Whitman. More recently Charles E. Burgess has summed up general opinion: "*Spoon River* was the culmination, to a considerable notorious extent, of Emerson's and Whitman's movements away from strict verse form." Burgess adds that Masters "added broad objectivity" to Whitman's "personalized stand for freedom in choice of a subject matter."[9] In the midst of the first waves of his sudden fame, Masters wrote that the poetry of the time "must acknowledge the paternity of Whitman." The problems begin when proponents of the "one-book author" approach lose sight of the Whitman tradition as it works itself out over the next thirty years. That tradition—which so many acknowledged and then discarded—must be reconstructed.

In 1916, Masters published *Songs and Satires*, a collection that suffered many of the problems of any follow-up to a big hit. Though the volume couldn't re-create the sensation of the *Anthology*, many of the individual poems were successful experiments in free verse and Whitmanesque catalogs. "Silence" is a typically sprawling probe with tones of *Song of Myself* and a hint of the poetic mysticism that transcends language. "The Loop" and "The City" suggest Whitman in the ways of Carl Sandburg. "In Michigan" extends Masters' efforts to transplant Whitman's songs into the soil of his own origins.

This celebration of the midlands continued in *The Great Valley* (1916) and expanded two years later in *Toward the Gulf* (1918). At that point Masters was eclipsed when Sandburg published *Chicago Poems* in the same year. Sandburg's volume renewed Masters' dedication to go beyond what he called "the poetical idiom, the stock imagery and often-repeated subject matter of the prominent poets then writing." In *Across Spoon River* he recalls his fascination for Whitman's "conception of America as the field of a new art and music in which the people would be celebrated instead of kings" and where "the liberty of Jefferson should be sung until it permeated the entire popular heart" (*ASR*, 336). In these early volumes perhaps his most typically Whitmanesque celebration of those people appears in an unlikely place—*Starved Rock* (1919), a collection known neither for unity nor distinction. "I Shall Go Down into This Land" captures the Whitmanesque energy and expanse which Masters wanted to make his own:

> I shall go down into this land
> Of the great Northwest:
> This land of the free ordinance,
> This land made free for the free
> By the patriarchs.
> . . . .
> Shall it be Michigan,
> Or Illinois,
> Or Indiana?
> These are my people,
> These are my lovers, my friends—
> Mingle my dust with theirs,
> Ye sacred powers!
> . . . .
> Clouds, like convoys on infinite missions,
> Bound for infinite harbors
> Float over the length of this land.
> And in the centuries to come
> The rocks and trees of this land will turn,
> These fields and hills will turn
> Under unending convoys of clouds—
> O ye clouds!
> Drench my dust and mingle it
> With the dust of the pioneers;
> My mates, my friends,
> Toilers and sufferers,
> Builders and dreamers,
> Lovers of freedom.
> . . . .
> O Earth that looks into space,
> As a man in sleep looks up,
> And is voiceless, at peace,
> Divining the secret—
> I shall know the secret
> When I go down into this land
> Of the great Northwest!
> .. . .
> Draw my dust
> With the dust of my beloved

Into the substance of a great rock,
Upon whose point a planet flames,
Nightly, in a thrilling moment
Of divine revelation
Through endless time!

[*SR*, 126–127]

That land became, for Masters, a symbol of unity, a mingling of lovers, of rocks and trees, of builders and dreamers. And in the years to come Whitman continued to show him one way to "the secret."

The deep influence of Whitman can be heard in everything Masters wrote, from the earliest apprentice poems to his last unpublished manuscripts. His comments about Whitman are among the most revealing in his autobiography (1936), in his published essays, and in biographies not only of Whitman (1937) but also of Vachel Lindsay (1935) and Mark Twain (1938). In the thirties, Masters' Whitman tradition developed primarily in five volumes of poems—from the offbeat *Lichee Nuts* (1930) to *Invisible Landscapes* (1935), the epic history *The New World* (1937), and finally two volumes celebrating the people—*Poems of People* (1936) and *More People* (1939).

Lichee Nuts (1930) is a seldom-read and never-discussed poetic experiment. The book didn't get much in the way of serious commentary in reviews, but Masters' skill in picking up on a vogue for Chinese witticisms was duly noted. In the guise of Oriental philosophy, however, Masters got a good deal of his own theories stated concisely and with a sharp sting. One of the "nuts" speaks of "Huang-ti" who "burned all books of critics" because "critics are worms who eat leaves / But make no silk." "Chinese Religion" strikes the note of Whitman who also wanted "To love Something, which is all pervading / Still, formless, unchanging, nameless":

To make the inner life full,
And to gain the center of Being.
To carry the lotus flower through boundless space;
To make the heart a clear pool
Which mirrors Nature;
To become a pine tree, a mountain, a river;
To ride moonbeams;
To adore the sun and to become a flame—
This is Chinese religion.

[*LN*, 117–118]

It is also the religion which came to Masters through Emerson and Whitman. Finally, Masters doesn't pass up the chance to nudge Whitman's theories just a little and at the same time elaborate his critique of the modern scene. The following is entitled "Great Audiences and Great Poets":

> Two Chinese students
> From University of Chicago,
> Go with Yet Wei to see Yuan Chang
> And have much talk about war,
> Confucius and at last Li Po.
> One Chinese student speak of Walt Whitman and America,
> And say to have great poets
> There must be great audiences too.
> Other Chinese student say:
> "To have great audiences
> "There must be fewer poets."
>
> [*LN*, 75]

In the last chapters of *Whitman*, Masters rhapsodized on Whitman's ability to see "in nature, beneath all shows and appearances, spirit and creative thought." Whitman taught him that life was "the law of the whole visible scheme of things" and that nature, in the end, was "the only absolute substance." Everything that happened was, as Masters read Whitman, an "interplay of waves" in "the life process." Only one year earlier Masters had published *Invisible Landscapes*, a collection of nature hymns which celebrated that same "spirit and creative thought" in the observable laws of the landscape. The volume continued Masters' typically Whitmanesque probe into the "laws" of visible nature, and it signalled a new emphasis on the invisible waves of the mystic. The poet's symbolic use of nature has long been a source of confusion in literary criticism. Masters tried to head off such confusion by quoting Whitman at length to explain the various meanings of nature in his own poetry of the time.

Masters quoted from Whitman's *Democratic Vistas* to explain his own expanded reading in the symbols in the landscape:

> Nature, true Nature, and the true idea of Nature, long absent, must above all become fully restored, enlarged, and must furnish the pervading atmosphere to poems, and the test of all high literary and esthetic compositions. I do not mean the smooth walks, trimmed hedges, posys and nightingales of the English poets, but the whole orb, with its geologic history, the cosmos, carrying fire

and snow, that rolls through the illimitable areas, light as a feather, though weighing billions of tons. Furthermore, as by what we now partially call Nature is intended, at most, only what is entertainable by the physical conscience, the sense of matter, and of good animal health—on these it must be distinctly accumulated, incorporated, that man, comprehending these, has in towering superaddition, the moral and spiritual consciences, indicating his destination beyond the ostensible, the mortal. To the heights of such estimate of Nature indeed ascending, we proceed to make observations for our Vistas, breathing rarest air. What is I believe called Idealism seems to me to suggest (guarding against extravagance, and ever modified even by its opposite) the course of inquiry and desert of favour for our New World metaphysics, their foundation of and in literature, giving hue to all. [*W*, 317]

Masters walked in that "rarest air" while forming his own "New World metaphysics," with its "towering superaddition."

In his poems about the Illinois prairies Masters wanted to extract "the essential from landscapes and the souls of men and women in their daily life and in heroic moments" (*W*, 324). *Invisible Landscapes* is a celebration of those landscapes and heroic moments. The title poem "Invisible Landscapes" introduces "the life force" in a man which "keeps moulding him afresh" and "the landscape" which "follows the plan / That shapes a life of flesh." In "Hymn to Nature" the "Universal Power" of nature's laws provides access to the "mystery" beyond mortality. "Invocation" is a plea for a restored oneness in the midst of fragmentation. "Hymn to the Earth" celebrates a Whitmanesque "earth stuff." "Sandridge" turns to the "brooding spirit" for witness to the "landscape's secret mood." And "Give Us Back Our Country" laments the passing of that same vision.

In the long tradition of nature poetry which Masters knew, he went most often to Whitman. He didn't especially like "idyllic" verse—even Virgil's. Masters found that the English way of translating the Eclogues and Georgics, though "sensuous and musical," did not "touch the inner heart of nature." In a list including Keats, Wordsworth, and Bryant, Masters still found that Whitman "passed them all by." The poet of *Invisible Landscapes* was drawn especially to Whitman's combination of mystical awareness and authentic descriptions. Again Masters' list of Whitman's accomplishments is a good index of what he hoped to achieve himself:

He looked with fresh eyes upon Nature. He didn't live in the city and celebrate the country. Rather he studied the country by actual contact with it, around Brooklyn, in upper New York, near Washington and Camden, and through the Far West. He was in the country when he was in the city, and his youthful days were so impregnated with the hills and the sea that wherever he was in later years the country was with him. He was not a recluse singing of nature in his study. He roamed the streets and went riding in busses. But while he loved the stir of New York he spent hours alone in the Battery looking at the ships. He wandered away from the thoroughfares to walk like Chyrses by the shore of the many-voiced sea. People were to him but one more phase of nature, and Nature to him was the mother of people. He gathered together enough material for lyrics and sonnets to nature for the hands of a hundred lesser poets. [*W*, 316]

Whitman's love for the city and the country and his life dedicated to a fullness of experiences received Masters' unwavering admiration.

In the middle thirties, Masters' nature symbolism began to take on deeper tones. The prairies and hills were still beautiful in themselves, but increasingly they carried mystical messages beyond language. The landscapes became invisible and silence itself sounded what one posthumously published poem calls "the harmony of deeper music." Again Masters' reading of Whitman nourished that new growth in Masters' consciousness. Consider the following passage which Masters quotes in *Whitman* alongside his own nature poems of the mid-thirties:

Lo! *Nature* (the only complete, actual poem) existing calmly in the divine scheme, containing all, content, careless of the criticisms of a day, or these endless and wordy chatterers. And lo! to the consciousness of the soul, the permanent identity, the thought, the something, before which the magnitude even of Democracy, art, literature, etc., dwindles, becomes partial, measurable— something that fully satisfies (which those do not). That something is the *All* and the idea of *All*, with the accompanying idea of eternity, and of itself, the soul, buoyant, indestructible, sailing Space forever, visiting every region, as a ship the sea. And again lo! the pulsations in all matter, all spirit, throbbing forever—the eternal beats, eternal systole and dyastole of life in things— wherefrom I feel and know that death is not the ending, as we thought, but rather the real beginning—and that nothing ever is or can be lost, nor even die, nor soul nor matter. [*W*, 315]

That same "idea of All" was prominent also in the writings of Goethe, Melville, and Hawthorne, among many. It comes through repeatedly in *Invisible Landscapes*. "Hymn to the Earth" is a rhapsody to a "seeming lifelessness" which is really "deeper life." "Ultimate Selection" is a more somber poem about the life forces expressed through biological union. From protoplasm to new sexual union and through the eternal cycle, mind and matter unite to express energy, and genius, and new growth. Accordingly, the expression of "The All" is also calmer:

And the infant spider unerringly spins its web,
Even as man by the mind which rises in him
Spins steel across a river, or measures the sky.
Mind is a flame which trims the wick and brightens
The flame of life, forever upturning the wick.
Mind is the cause, the force of evolution.
The mind in the germinal cell is the mind of the All,
And that is mind discerned in slime of the sea,
In plants, in micromites, in beasts and man.
The Mind that uses the wind to fertilize
The spores of oak trees, spinach, dock and nettles,
Which have no beauty or scent to offer insects,
Gives bright hues to the flower to lure the bees,
And brings compelling passions, and wonder dreams
To the heart of man to win the desirable mate.

[*IL*, 55]

The achievement of vision and a new wholeness through physical union remained a major theme of Masters' poems of the thirties.

Masters published *Poems of People* in 1936 and three years later a sequel, *More People*. The portraits heed Whitman's advice to look to ordinary people, though the dramatic tone Masters developed owes more to Browning. The two volumes will receive fuller treatment, therefore, in a later chapter. Though he published two volumes of poems in the early forties, Masters' last direct tribute to Whitman is found in his epic history *The New World* (1937). Like Emerson, "ample and Homeric Whitman" is one of the unheeded prophets who dream of "numberless individuals" living "petty grotesques, phantoms and malformations." Whitman helped Masters see that "the real soul of the New World / Could never be satisfied with railroads, shops, and banks, / But needed Merchants of the Light." Whitman also reinforced Masters' Emersonian view that American poetry needed emancipation:

How he saw that England was no model for the New World
For its poems, histories and tales;
That after all the letters of England

Were moody and melancholy, like Hamlet
Moping, sick, inconstant and uncertain;
And that Shakespeare was inferior to Aeschylus and Homer!

[*NW*, 131]

While English letters sang of kings and feudalism, Whitman maintained that the People were "the source / Of all letters, all art, all victories, / And at last the support of all fames!" Whitman's diagnosis matched Masters' about the diseases of "counting rooms," "mad theologies," and the "worship of profitless pasts." They also concurred that American literature had not yet matured, that "the poems of the New World / Came from pens apt at reproducing English excellence, / At raising flowers with seed grown by others, / In soil not earned by them" (131–132). Masters' peroration in Book VIII of *The New World* returns to the image of nourishment on a bitter note typical of the whole work:

The New World was being remade
By men who did not keep it new.
Slow was the effect of great words by Emerson and Whitman,
For the maggot mass neither hears nor sees,
But squirms on itself and looks for food.

[*NW*, 133]

Whitman never failed to give Masters confidence in himself. His bacchic statements about poetry energized Masters' own critical theories and increased his determination to revive the American debt to Whitman. In attempting to restore a wavering tradition, Masters attempted to clarify his own place in the poetic movements of his time. Writing in *The American Mercury* he traced what he called "the poetry revival of 1914." He went back as far as Stedman's *American Anthology* of 1900, noting the advice given in that book that America's poets would do well to return to Emerson, Poe, and Whitman for inner inspiration. He applauds this judgment, adding that "for some time before American verse was largely derivative and warmed over." The problem of origins reached to the source of creativity itself for Masters: "My own opinion is that there was no progenitor of the movement, because there was no single movement, but on the contrary there were many schools, ranging from imagists to realists, and from those who were innovating to those who were holding on to the traditions in form and theme of the past."

Masters frequently objected to the imposition of "the academic mind" and the mere "power of thinking" which were quickly gaining a strangle-hold on the poetic establishment of the times:

> No one can say that Robinson has not a brain, for he has; and a very sound and subtle one, and well adapted to the kind of fastidious psychology in which he indulges. But brains do not make poetry necessarily; they only back up poetry with authentic thoughts without which poetry is but words, unless it happens to be that peculiar thing known as magic, in which men like Coleridge and Blake excelled. Shelley, with all his ethereal fancy, had more depth and strength of mind than either Byron or Keats and his great odes.[10]

In the middle of the various "revivals," Masters never strayed from Whitman who said that "it takes both a man and a book to make a book."

Masters' devotion to Whitman caused him to tangle with most of the accepted poetic norms of his time. In Whitman he found a counter to everything he didn't like about the modern scene. Ernest Earnest has drawn the lines sharply between *Spoon River* with its Whitmanesque symbols and its celebratory tone and the tradition of Eliot in which poetry was "learned, filled with literary allusion and abstruse symbols." Earnest blames the decline of the reputation of *Spoon River* on the appearance of *The Waste Land* after which "the pervasive influence of Whitman was displaced by the courtly muses of Europe."[11] When Eliot's "sophistication" ran Emerson in reverse, Masters and everybody like him got in trouble with the poets and critics then in vogue. Any re-evaluation of Masters will profit from a close look at the links between what happened to Whitman and the strangle-hold on poetry exerted by Eliot. From the more favorable position Whitman now holds in our eyes, Masters' plainer and more robust songs are not so easily eclipsed by poetry with esoteric symbols.

Perhaps the most famous reassessment of the Whitman tradition in our time was Karl Shapiro's *In Defense of Ignorance*, an irreverent attack on "the dictatorship of intellectual modernism," "the sanctimonious ministry of the Tradition," and "the ugly programmatic quality of twentieth-century criticism." Shapiro blames what he calls "the death of literary judgment" on Pound's and Eliot's attempts to "correct taste." Masters' discussion of Whitman was often squelched by something akin to what Shapiro calls "junior executives in the international culture conference of ideology."

Just how much Shapiro's defense of "ignorance" resembles Masters' attempts to swim upstream forty years ago can be seen in striking parallels in their comments on Whitman. First, Shapiro:

> The power of Whitman in the world is incalculable. In literature it has long been calculated as nothing. It is because of poets like Whitman that literature exists but it is always literature that determines to exterminate its Whitmans, its Blakes, its Lawrences, its Henry Millers. The probability is that Whitman will never be "accepted" as one of the great writers of mankind; acceptance is always a function of the writers who assume the power of literature, for whatever reasons, and who make literature one of the arms of the law.

Again, the poet-critic Shapiro is fully sympathetic to the atmosphere in which the Whitman in Masters tried to break out:

> Whitman is not a complicated case of poor manners, confusions and paradoxes; of philosophical muddle and literary naiveté; of good intentions, high passages and bad dreary bogs. He is the one and only poet of America who has ever attempted to adumbrate the meaning of America. The twentieth-century American poet avoids this commitment, by and large: he considers it fitting and proper to take refuge in History against the horrors of progress; or in pure dialectic; or in the catacombs of established faith; or failing that, in what is a thing called the Language; that is, the American Language, the natural nonhieratic language out of which a mythos might germinate. But Whitman contended that the mythos was at hand. He defined it; he sang it; he poured it out. To no avail.[12]

Alongside Shapiro's revisionist comments, consider Masters' struggle against the conventional theories he was forced to live through:

> Whitman had the right idea, namely, that poetry, the real written word, must come out of life—not out of books or erudition. It must come out of the earth. When it speaks for a land and celebrates a tribe it has done the greatest work that poetry can do. Without invention, as that word is understood in poetry, he relied upon realities. It is no wonder that a man as sincere as Whitman, whose sincerity chose prosody without rhyme, meter or ornament, had to endure the sneers and the chatter of New York critics in magazines and newspaper columns. These are educated and traditional minds who expatiate upon the workovers, the repaintings of descents from the cross, the ephemeral and well-worded stuff, and often miss the important, the real and truly American art. [W, 307]

For Masters, what was "real" and "truly American" in Whitman's art helped him counter what he found lacking in "modern" poetry. Masters stuffed himself with Whitman's poems and what he digested became his own creative use of a more powerful American past. Whitman helped Masters look to nature for poetic vision, taught him that sex and love were the unifiers of disparate elements of experience, and led him to celebrate the unique elements of his own vibrant midwestern heritage.

6

Hymns on the Midwestern Prairie

SHELLEY AND MASTERS

Despite the range of his reading and his absorption of all that he read, Masters never ceased to come back to Shelley, with whom he went "aloft on wings of flame," where he learned to celebrate the "Awful Shadow of an Unseen Power" through "exquisite music in words" and "ethereal imagery" (*ASR*, 77).

Masters consistently found in Shelley an enlarging influence. Faced with what he summarily called "the cramping influence of the village," he looked to Shelley for liberation. Not surprisingly, Shelley's presence is foremost in Masters' densely poetic celebration of the prairie:

> As a boy on the Masters farm the silence of the prairie had seemed to me to be the silence of my own heart. And in the stillness of evenings when the sun set beyond the farthest farmhouses I walked about the pasture where I flew kites with something choking in my breast, with a longing that I could not understand. When I found Shelley and read such lines as "I thirst for the music that is divine" I saw that eternity and the mystery about life beckon sensitive souls to realms that lie below life's horizon. At last I understood that my passion for beauty in women, and my attempts to realize myself through erotic love, were just futile searches to fill the void in my heart. [*ASR*, 284–285]

The first part of the passage contains some of the best of Masters' poetry; the second part is Masters at his best on poetic influence. Also startling is his celebration of his midwestern identity in the emblem of "the silence of the prairie." In repeated allusions to the prairie he often interprets its silent broodings in Shelleyan terms: "All through my boyhood there are the pastoral scenes of the Masters farm . . . here arose my own longings and griefs for something that seemed far off in life when I should be mature; but that something was more distant than that—it is distant now, and will ever be so" (*ASR*, 403).

What will ever remain "distant" provides clues to Masters' understanding not only of his midwestern sensibility but also of his development as a poet and his need to go beyond what restricted him in his personal and literary "environment." What he later said about Emerson also describes his reactions to Shelley: "We needed someone to say that we had possibilities . . . that we were potential geniuses, ready to expand wings and fly if we laid our hands upon the springs of courage that were within us and within the human breast everywhere."

Masters read Shelley for the first time as a young man at home in Lewistown. Later he often analyzed his reading of those years. In "The Genesis of Spoon River" he recalled the special attraction he felt for Shelley from the first: "The only books we had at home in Lewistown at this time, and for long years, were these: a copy of Virgil, Macaulay's History, the poems of Burns, a few plays of Shakespeare, and Bryant's 'Library of Poetry and Song,' which I absorbed, Crabbe's poems and a large illustrated book called 'Album of Authors,' which I read to tatters. I studied constantly the faces of these notables, picking Goethe and Shelley as the best of all."[1]

During his high school years, this interest in Shelley deepened. He later recalls that while waiting for a train he looked in the window of a bookstore where he saw "a book bound in red with golden scrolls and decorations, and the words 'Shelley's Poems.'" He had often read "The Skylark" and liked it. His pleasure in that poem and "the beauty of the book" prompted him to buy it. He remembers having "gone through Burns over and over" and reading Bryant and "much of Poe." But Shelley quickly began to affect him as none of the others had. In short, Masters found Shelley exhilarating and expansive: "Shelley took me aloft on wings of flame. This passion for humanity, this adoration for the beautiful, this celebration of the Awful Shadow of an Unseen Power, this exquisite music in words, this ethereal imagery!" (*ASR*, 77).

Masters continued to read Shelley throughout the early days of his legal career. The tensions he experienced in those years between the workaday world and his poetic impulse are a matter of record. Often he was forced to read the literature he loved at night after the day's work. The portion of his autobiography covering these early years reviews the tortures of his greatly divided attention and answers his ever-recurring question as an artist: "Why was I not obliterated?" (*ASR*, 402). The poetry of Shelley is one significant and complex answer to that question. *Across Spoon River* is an odyssey of Masters' developing imagination; the path in which Shelleyan expanse helped his poetry to overcome "negative" influences provides an illuminating map.

In the midst of myriad influences as a student, in the law offices, and in his reading, Masters was stimulated by Shelley to search for the influx of new powers that would expand his potential. The search not only introduced him to new approaches but also turned him away from some of his favorite writers to that point: "I was carried out of myself. I began to see that I, too, had a passion for humanity, and that my father's democracy and integrity were the roots out of which this devotion to Shelley's poetry took immediate nourishment. And to what ends Shelley led me! To more metaphysics, to Plato, to the Greek writers. Poe and Burns fled back out of my interest" (*ASR*, 77). As Masters' sensitivity to his own "sources" deepened, he began to think of himself as a kind of "romantic" in the Shelleyan sense which he contrasted with "lushness." The opposition he felt, as he later reported, was identified with Poe and Shelley. His later description of his opposition stressed the creative impulse in physical beauty and hinted at the emphasis on sexual relationships that would emerge in poems indebted to Shelley:

> There is an apostrophe to woman in Poe's "The Poetic Principle," where he rhapsodizes on the grace of her step, the luster of her eye, the melody of her voice, her soft laughter and the angelic rustling of her robes. That sort of lush romanticism was not mine. I saw my divinities through the poetry of Shelley, clothed in woven wind, and innocently walking before me in their immaculate nudeness, willing to yield their loveliness in obedience to unashamed passion. [*ASR*, 250]

In Shelley Masters found what he liked to see in himself as well: "a poet who expressed the ideal phases of the erotic impulses" (251).

Though Shelley's influence thrived throughout Masters' career, it was strongest in the mid-thirties when its dominant metaphor was sexual and its major theme the creative union of two becoming one. At this time Masters self-consciously explored these influences on his poetic development in *Across Spoon River* (1936) and expressed his most Shelleyan themes and forms in several volumes—notably *Invisible Landscapes* (1935) and *The Serpent in the Wilderness* (1938)—and in the posthumously published "Amphimixis" (1938).[2] "Amphimixis" was dated by Masters June 28, 1938, and is one of the many poems he wrote while living at the Chelsea Hotel in New York, where—as he said—"all I have to do is close my eyes and I can look at the Mason County Hills and see my kite high among the clouds" (*ASR*, 397). The poem expands the "urge to unite" of "Cleanthus Trilling" and is thoroughly Shelleyan in allusion, style, and theme. "Amphimixis" is a poetic embodiment two years later of some of the major concerns of *Across Spoon River*. I shall first present the poem in its entirety and examine how Masters emphasizes the primacy of Shelley's "Unseen Power." The poem is ultimately about the creativity of sexual union and poetic influence. "Amphimixis" is, in short, Masters' tightly wrought poetic commentary on his own autobiography, published two years previously. The poem is not only influenced *by* Shelley, but is also in many ways *about* poetic influence *itself*—particularly, but not exclusively, that of Shelley. Masters used this metaphor "urge to unite" in poems from *Spoon River Anthology* and the volumes of 1916–1924 to the poems throughout the thirties, and in the later reworking of Shelley's collapse of vision in *The Serpent in the Wilderness* (1933) and "The Triumph of Earth" (1940).

AMPHIMIXIS

Everywhere in creation is the urge
To enter in another, fuse and merge.
Roots turn toward the earth; the church's wall
Attracts the vine; the electric current draws
Steel filings and arranges them by laws
In patterns, star-rayed, geometrical.
There is response to touch, to earth, to light.
The chromosomes of cells detect the might
Hidden in heaven and in earth, arrange their poles
10 Centered in fibrous stars: So flesh and souls.

Creatures at first bi-sexed—sponges and snails,
Volvox and flat worms—long for severance
That life may be increased, that heads and tails
Of the sperm may grow, the ovum's waiting trance.
But being severed then, they seek and long
For union; they divine that they must win
Oneness again, and by that fate begin
A life more individual and strong.
The Genius of Creation which made them two,
20 Divided their hermaphroditic state,
Drives them together then and makes them mate,
That greater life, more perfect, may ensue.

Think you of That—call it the Secret Power,
Or call it God—which hour by endless hour
Stirs plasm and awakes it, which conceived
Sex as the way for life to be retrieved
From floating jelly! Think of That which made
The sperm and ovum severally incomplete,
Then formed the great perfection by the aid
30 Of fusion through desire that scorns defeat.
Oneness, autogamy, would divide, be free
For selfhood, then for union by ecstasy.
Oneness is loneliness at first, and then
A solace, consummation for plants and men.
Whether it be in lifting from the mist,
From water, by a passion none resist,
Or whether it be at last, the cycle done,
Of sinking to the source and entering in
The ocean where all living things begin,
40 Life's passion would be two, and then be one.

The hypae of black mold on common bread
Are intertwined; the cells of ulothrix
Swim round until the ovum feels the head
Of the sperm, and then their substance starts to mix.
Marine life listens to the summoning sea
Which calls them by a wedding symphony.
So from the alga swarm the restless sperm
Seeking the egg, and so the rockweed's eggs
Are hunted by its male gametes which worm
50 An entrance, then their life no longer lags.
Malarial cells which touch and conjugate
Themselves shape like a swastika, and then
Find head and tails; so it is, too, with men
Emitting life love-driven to penetrate
The waiting ovum, and enter and be lost
In whirling change for life exchanged and crossed.

For with an entrance made begins the toil
Of larger being; the plasm starts to boil,
To froth with destiny and secret dreams.
60 Granules are threaded; there are stars, spiremes,
And radiate lines, and spindles which in turn
Enter the spireme; union further thus
Wins an achievement, is victorious;

For union, oneness, do these creatures yearn.
Then there are splitting, halving, stars and poles,
As even later there are in our souls.
On higher levels everything repeats
The self-same story; union and life more deep
Flowers till the consummation finds defeats;
70   The cycle being run, then there is sleep,
Or energies so fine the microscope
With their invisible movements scarce can cope.

Man grown to fullest stature, in mind complete,
Is nothing but a world-enclosed gamete.
Shelley and Shakespeare, larger than the swarm
Of human gametes, and of clearer form,
Prove that a man from microscopic life
Arises to a level where he feels
The frothing, boiling, and the surging strife
80   Which stirred in him when he was coils and reels.
And so he swarms, and swims, and dives and darts,
And seeks to enter mysteries and hearts,
Along the way of finding the high ovule
By which he may a greater being rule.
Is it heaven, is it God that he would find,
And enter in, and first if used and blind,
And then devoured, then by that union stirred
Gather more life? The truth is, everything—
Whether it be amoeba or man—is spurred
90   To seek more life, whatever by the sting,
The tragedy of transition: That's the Word
Which was at the beginning, and never rests
In plants and animals and human breasts.

June 28, 1938.

I have quoted the poem exactly as it appears in manuscript, though I have numbered lines for convenience. I shall provide just enough summary and explication to clarify what I take to be its central subjects: literary influence and the origins of creativity expressed through the metaphor of sexual union, or "amphimixis." The opening ten lines celebrate the impulse within nature to unify disparates through a merging of separate identities. Though the direction is toward patterns of fusion, the language and imagery preserve the duality of interlocking opposites. All this culminates in the extended metaphor "So flesh and souls," a Platonic language which Masters quickly juxtaposes with the intricate biological jargon of the next stanza. The gist of lines 11–22 is that while "at first" creatures "long for severance," once "severed" they then seek the more perfect state of union once more. The ambivalence is preserved throughout the poem. The "Genius of Creation" oversees the mating so that "greater life, more perfect, may ensue." This image of personal relationships is remarkably similar to Masters' observations on women as well as his shattered idealism about Shelley and Mary Godwin. Again, in *Across Spoon River*, he located his personal and literary influences in his early reading of Shelley's "Epipsychidion": "In these days of my adolescence with Dr. Strode and the studies I have mentioned I longed for a woman who was beautiful of person and gifted in mind. I expected to find such a woman finally, and I dreamed of her. That was the love I sought. Somehow I believed that Shelley had found such a mate in Mary Godwin, in the face of his poems revealing that he had not found such a mate, and that this dream of the highly organized masculine nature is a false lure" (*ASR*, 87–88). In his autobiography as well as in "Amphimixis," Masters explored and reworked Shelley's views on the imaginative liberation of fulfilled relationships.

In a series of flashbacks, Masters is not so much interpreting "Epipsychidion" as describing his own expectations and the reasons for his attraction to the poem. Shelley's masterful creation of the unity achieved in physical relationships underlies much of the quest of "Amphimixis." The most famous passages of "Epipsychidion" deserve extended quotation:

> And we will talk, until thought's melody
> Become too sweet for utterance, and it die
> In words, to live again in looks, which dart
> With thrilling tone into the voiceless heart,
> Harmonizing silence with a sound.
> Our breath shall intermix, our bosoms bound,
> And our veins beat together; and our lips
> With other eloquence than words, eclipse
> The soul that burns between them, and the walls
> Which boil under our being's inmost calls,
> The fountains of our deepest life, shall be
> Confused in Passion's golden purity,
> As mountain-springs under the morning sun.

[560–572][3]

Of course the vision wanes; and though Masters never surrendered Shelleyan expanse, he later at least hinted at identification with the finality of Shelley's "annihilation":

> We shall become the same, we shall be one
> Spirit within two frames, oh! wherefore two?
> One passion in twin-hearts, which grows and grew,
> Till like two meteors of expanding flame,
> Those spheres instinct with it become the same,
> Touch, mingle, are transfigured; ever still
> Burning, yet ever inconsumable:
> In one another's substance finding food,
> Like flames too pure and light and unimbued
> To nourish their bright lives with baser prey,
> Which point to Heaven and cannot pass away:
> One hope within two wills, one will beneath
> Two overshadowing minds, one life, one death,
> One Heaven, one Hell, one immortality,
> And one annihilation.
>
> ["Epipsychidion," 573–587]

The direct parallels between "Amphimixis" and "Epipsychidion" need little elaboration here.

"Think you of That," Masters stresses in lines worth requoting because they go to the core of his thinking: "call it the Secret Power, / Or call it God—which hour by endless hour / Stirs plasm and awakes it, which conceived / Sex as the way for life to be retrieved / From floating jelly!" From the "severally incomplete" through "fusion" comes "perfection." All this "urge" is created by— in perhaps the poem's most crucial line—"desire that scorns defeat." Oneness must divide to be free and then recombine and reach a consummation in the Shelleyan "mist," a "passion none resist," a "sinking to the source and entering in / The ocean where all living things begin" (and though the poem doesn't say so, presumably end as well).

This second stanza (11–40) reproduces Masters' large philosophical exegeses in *Across Spoon River* by focusing his arguments on the single image of sexual union. Though distractingly clinical at times, his language echoes passages of his autobiography almost verbatim. Again the closest points of intersection are in his comments on Shelley. Following one of his many lengthy discussions of his reading in English literature, Masters concluded "I do not find in Shakespeare, in Goethe, in Byron, in Browning, in Keats the same attitude toward passional love that I have felt almost from boyhood. Perhaps Shelley is nearest to me." After several distinctions between the different attitudes toward love that he found in his reading, Masters continues, "For myself I divine the operation of the cosmic mind in the love of men and women, and hence I have identified a beloved woman with the mysteries of creative beauty, with influences and magnetisms, with summons from afar" (*ASR*, 407–408).

Masters returned to all of what follows in "Amphimixis," and one more lengthy passage outlines illuminating parallels:

> I dreamed what Shelley dreamed when writing "Epipsychidion," and perhaps at times I awoke in a heart what Shelley awoke in the heart of Emilia Viviani, to whom that ecstatic poem was addressed. She had said to him, "The soul of him who loves launches itself out of the created, and creates in the infinite a world for itself alone, how different from this obscure and fearful den." These words Shelley took for the text of his poem. They show that she understood, and, understanding, she and Shelley grasped the secret together. Having stood thus together on the sunlit peak of youth and great divination, it cannot have been amiss for his own heart that he descended into the valley and then disappeared into the sea. [*ASR*, 408–409]

In "Amphimixis" Masters captured this same kind of ideal relationship. In "Epipsychidion" it is, of course, not the biographical details but the poetic embodiment of "the secret" that matters most. Harold Bloom has long ago shown that Shelley's poem "celebrates love more than it does a particular love for Emily, a single epipsyche. Shelley is not affirming his immediate passion over his marriage so much as he affirms the continual and open possibility of love over either." Bloom also notes how the ideal in Shelley's poem must fail: "Love unites in act, not in essence. The counter myth demands union in essence, and so destroys the poem, in the movement to 'one annihilation.' The attempt both to extend and to realize the limits of relationship and expression fails, yet the poem remains."[4] Though he was not so critically analytical, Masters felt this necessary collapse of the myth in his description of the descent into the sea. His sensing of the contraries of ecstasy and descent suggests at least one further brooding passage in his autobiography: "I still wonder about the fate of the human heart that can burn with such longings and such dreams and still have no power either in itself or in the circumstances of life to realize them" (*ASR*, 406). Yet even when the tone is somber, the emphasis in the poem is on the Shelleyan "desire that scorns defeat" rather than Poe's achieved union in death. This urge—as much as anything—prompted Masters to conclude: "It was Shelley who kept me away from Poe" (*ASR*, 90).

The poem's middle stanza (41–72) catalogs images of biological mergings and culminates in a "So it is, too, with men" followed by images of swimming which overlap but also partially diminish the impact of the previous stanza's intensity. The locus of the images is entirely water, swimming, and swarming in a "wedding symphony" in the sea. The lines describing such union in humans tighten considerably as the images interlock: "Emitting life love-driven to penetrate / The waiting ovum, and enter and be lost / In whirling change for life exchanged and crossed" (54–56). The tropes are massively complex here, though they basically repeat "desire that scorns defeat" once more. The union becomes one of a "toil" into "larger being" and "dreams" become "victorious" in the yearning for oneness. But unity is ever forced to split again, creating a cycle which "On higher levels everything repeats." With the cycle complete, "consummation finds defeats," and there remains only "sleep, / Or energies so fine the microscope / With their invisible movements scarce can cope" (71–72). It is worth noting that Masters' imagery for this state of "larger being" is that of ongoing process and interlocking networks ("boil," "froth," "threaded"), rather than transcendence to another realm.

In the final stanza the underlying subject of poetic creativity surfaces in the image of Shelley and Shakespeare as "larger than the swarm / Of human gametes, and of clearer form." Theirs is a frothing and boiling and a surging that "seeks to enter mysteries and hearts" in order to give birth to "a greater being." The consistent imagery and exact repetition of terms carry through the poem's biological and philosophical tropes, building to the conclusion that everything struggles to a union that enables it to "gather more life." The poem thus builds to a conclusion that is not so much an achieved end as an ongoing state, a process rather than a product:

> The truth is, everything—
> Whether it be amoeba or man—is spurred
> To seek more life, whatever be the sting,
> The tragedy of transition: That's the Word
> Which was at the beginning, and never rests
> In plants and animals and human breasts.
>
> [88–93]

The spurring and the seeking, the "sting" and the "tragedy of transition" are Masters in his most Shelleyan temper. Masters' "severance" parallels Shelley's "to divide is not to take away" ("Epipsychidion," 161) and suggests—as does all of "Amphimixis"—Shelley's views on love and human interaction. Similar direct echoes of Shelley can be found in many of Masters' poems of the thirties and forties as well as in his autobiography.

But "Amphimixis" may also be read as a comment on the creative tensions of literary influence and the individual poetic impulse. The "Word" is actually the poem talking about itself as much as "Man grown to his fullest stature" is the poet referring to himself and to his "influence"—specifically here, Shelley. "The Genius of Creation" is surely the poetic impulse, and "the severance / That life may be increased" is the individual poet's creativity as distinct from the higher mind. Similarly, "the urge / To enter in another" is the throwing open of oneself to literary ancestors in an effort to absorb and grow—in the poem's language to "mate" so that in union "greater life, more perfect, may ensue." In *Across Spoon River*, the terms Masters uses to describe similar processes are "influence," "digestion," and "nourishment." Paradoxically the artist and his literary ancestors are joined in patterns, then "severed" so that "life may be increased," then joined into "oneness again" so as to by "fate begin / A life more individual and strong." The inevitable mixing and loss of identity attendant upon literary influence are reflected in the images "enter and be lost / In whirling change for life exchanged and crossed." The "toil," "achievement," "splitting," and endless repetition of "the self-same story" depict the quagmire that is literary history. The last stanza may then be Masters' most definitive statement on the nature of poetry itself: "Larger than the swarm of human gametes," the poet proclaims "the Word" and in so doing speaks "the truth" and shows man the way "By which he may a greater being rule."

Masters' at best ambivalent attitudes toward his legal career might prompt him to look askance at Shelley's image of poets as "unacknowledged legislators / Of the world." But he is everywhere in sympathy with the critical views and the language of Shelley's *A Defence of Poetry*. Though space does not permit it here, a comparison of the Epilogue to *Across Spoon River* and Shelley's *Defence* would show just how close they are in their views on the nature of poetry. Masters sums up his goals:

What poetry is is set forth in Aristotle's *Poetics*; what it is in its purest form is shown in the works of Aeschylus, in Homer, in the

Greeks in a word. There is the poetry of fancy and of the imagination, and the poetry that lulls and lifts, and soothes with music and pictures. But the greatest poetry is that which founds itself upon the truth which is the beautiful, and the beautiful which is the truth. It is the poetry which proves the laws of the spirit of man, and how they work to punish and to repay and always work, and how even in love, but misdirected love, the heart must pay; and how in sacrifice and good intentions gone wrong punishment comes—but how in love in the heart in defeat and in sorrow there is reward. This is the poetry to which I have devoted myself, and which I have tried to write, using all my powers at their heightened energies to write, and putting aside success in money or in any other way to write. [ASR, 413–414]

This same tension between the expansive and what is often joyless is central to a famous passage in the *Defence* on the poetics of sorrow:

Sorrow, terror, anguish, despair itself, are often the chosen expressions of an approximation to the highest good. Our sympathy in tragic fiction depends on this principle; tragedy delights by affording a shadow of the pleasure which exists in pain. This is the source also of the melancholy which is inseparable from the sweetest melody. The pleasure that is in sorrow is sweeter than the pleasure of pleasure itself. And hence the saying, "It is better to go to the house of mourning, than to the house of mirth"—not that this highest species of pleasure is necessarily linked with pain. The delight of love and friendship, the ecstasy of the admiration of nature, the joy of the perception and still more of the creation of poetry is often wholly unallowed.[5]

Similar parallels can be found easily throughout Shelley's treatise and Masters' autobiography. Though more detailed comparison is beyond this study, some allusions would, in closing, seem in order. For Shelley, poetry is "at once the center and circumference of knowledge; it is that which comprehends all science and that to which all science must be referred. It is at the same time the root and blossom of all other systems of thought; it is that from which all spring, and that which adorns all." Shelley is, of course, prolific on the clashes between utility and imagination:

Undoubtedly the promoters of utility, in this limited sense, have their appointed office in society. They follow the footsteps of poets, and copy the sketches of their creations into the book of common life. They make space, and give time. Their exertions are of the highest value, so long as they confine their administration of the concerns of the inferior powers of our nature within the limits due to the superiour ones. But while the sceptic destroys gross superstitions, let him spare to deface, as some of the French writers have defaced, the eternal truths charactered upon the imaginations of men. While the mechanist abridges and the political economist combines labor, let them beware that their speculations, for want of correspondence with those first principles which belong to the imagination, do not tend, as they have in modern England, to exasperate at once the extremes of luxury and want.[6]

Masters consistently felt—and sometimes bitterly so—the seemingly irreconcilable conflicts between his genius and what always threatened to "poison" it: "And this brings me to say that I have lived in the imagination. Perhaps this is the deepest secret of my nature, namely, that imagination has been the controlling influence of my life; and that I have not lived among facts of economics, among buildings of brick and mortar, among the concrete matters of worldly success. I feel that I twisted my genius, my nature when I went into the law" (*ASR*, 398).

In several famous passages, Shelley analyzed how the imagination illumines the otherwise familiar: "Poetry lifts the veil from the hidden beauty of the world, and makes familiar objects be as if they were not familiar; it reproduces all that it represents, and the impersonations clothed in its Elysian lights stand thence-forward in the minds of those who have once contemplated them as memorials of that gentle and exalted content which extends itself over all thoughts and actions with which it coexists." And in an image that anticipates M. H. Abrams' famous discussion of the romantic poets in *The Mirror and the Lamp*, Masters gives us a thoroughly Shelleyan "flashlight" of imagination: "For myself, I cannot rid my mind of the colorations which my imagination throws upon human life and the earth scene; indeed, my thinking seems to be lighted along the dark corridors of thought by the circling and the holding aloft of the flashlight of imagination. Some secrets seem thereby revealed; but often that light has blinded me to pitfalls right beneath my feet" (*ASR*, 398). Shelley's celebration of imagination as an instrument of love and "moral good" was what Masters meant when he called Shelley one of the "best of men":

The great secret of morals is love; or a going out of our own nature, and an identification of ourselves with the beautiful which exists in thought, action, or person, not our own. A man, to be greatly good, must imagine intensely and comprehensively;

he must put himself in the place of another and of many others; the pains and pleasures of his species must become his own. The great instrument of moral good is the imagination; and poetry administers to the effect by acting upon the cause. Poetry enlarges the circumference of the imagination by replenishing it with thoughts of ever new delight, which have the power of attracting and assimilating to their own nature all other thoughts, and which form new intervals and interstices whose void for ever craves fresh food.[7]

Across Spoon River and its epitome in "Amphimixis" contribute significantly to an understanding of Masters' Shelleyan poetry and consequently to a reexamination of his views on literary influence and the growth of poetic creativity. Read with particular attention to the influx of Shelley, Masters emerges as a poet-critic who is significantly more expansive and complex than commentaries on the "*Spoon River* Poet" have allowed.

As his often rhapsodic comments suggest, Masters was consciously drawn most to the exuberant optimism he saw in Shelley's depiction of erotic relationships. Generally, he sought and found in Shelley a soaring into ecstasy, a harmonizing music, a championing of democratic and humanistic values, and an expanding of his own ability to understand the potential of imaginative vision. In referring to Shelley's "power," Masters no doubt had in mind the "power, which like the truth / Of nature on my passive youth / Descended" in "Hymn to Intellectual Beauty" or "The still and solemn power of many sights, / And many sounds, and much of life and death" and "The secret strength of things / Which governs thought" in "Mont Blanc." He also understood the unresolved tensions of *Prometheus Unbound* and "Adonais." In the "Shadow" there is, no doubt, some of the "shadow of the tomb" of "Adonais" and echoes of Shelley's haunting "What Adonais is, why fear we to become?" But even when reading Shelley at his most paradoxical, Masters consistently emphasized the joyful and expansive. In *Whitman*, published only one year after *Across Spoon River*, he lauded Shelley's transformations of present reality through glorious hymns to new worlds: "The wonderful choruses of *Prometheus Unbound* with their prophecies of a happier world based on love; a new day of earth happiness created by social love, are things which Shelley looked forward to and sang in many poems and fragments" (*W*, 144). Again he emphasized the positive forces of love and human relationships.

But Shelley was not always uninterrupted exuberance for Masters throughout his career. For most readers of Shelley, the sadness and collapse of vision in "The Triumph of Life" vitiate much of the rhapsodic celebration of freedom usually taken to be the essence of his vision. Though Masters never stressed the bittersweet Shelley in his prose comments, the waning of beauty and the crumpling of the vision found their way into his later poems. In October, 1932, he published the haunting "Beethoven's Ninth Symphony and the King Cobra,"[8] a poem which reworks many of the Shelleyan strivings and entrapments most concentrated in "The Triumph of Life." And in 1940 he circulated in a private printing "The Triumph of Earth,"[9] a poem in which his self-consciousness, his broodings on influence, and his devotion to Shelley converged in a quest for new universes through mythic hymns.

Masters' interest in Shelley and his reworking of Shelleyan themes can be found throughout his poems from his earliest apprentice works to the lesser-known titles of the late thirties. Even some of the most famous portraits from *Spoon River* reveal the meditative brooding and the language of biological merging and separation. Sarah Brown achieved "the blest Nirvana of eternal light": "Through the flesh / I am spent, and through spirit, peace. / There is no marriage in heaven, / But there is love." Fiddler Jones' realization is similar: "The earth keeps some vibration going / There in your heart, and that is you." "William and Emily" repeats the epic experiences of "Amphimixis," and shared death becomes an ultimate "power of unison between souls / Like love itself!" Isaiah Beethoven conquered time itself when his soul merged with "the soul of the river." The Village Atheist's famous challenge to the "debaters over the doctrine" of immortality expresses Masters' astonishing meshing of Shelleyan despair and exultation. His conclusion is, of course, that immortality is "not a gift" but the "achievement" of those who "strive mightily."

In a series of volumes from 1916 to 1924 Masters returned frequently to the themes of separation and the urge to achieve an ultimate, harmonious whole. In *The Great Valley* (1916), "The Desplaines Forest" (129–130) "stills the clamor of the world" to reveal "the pangs / That each soul is alone, and that all friends / Gentle and wise and good can never soothe / The ache of that subconsciousness which is / Something unfathomed and unmedicined." "John Cowper Powys" (231–233) later in the volume pays tribute to the critic who is also "chemical analyst and microscopist, / Observer of men's involuted shells." In pursuit of the Protean "human secret," the poem runs into wrestling, change, and "rapturous thought."

Toward the Gulf (1918) picks up on the same pursuit of ultimates. In an astonishing interior monologue, "The Letter" (178–182), Masters explores death through an exploration of the horrors that remain behind. In a long Whitmanesque catalog, "soul possession" is found to reside not in the daily course of life on earth but rather in the process of "freeing / The soul from trammels on essential being." Union is consummate not in togetherness but in separation where two souls are one by "Communing as two memories with each other." Paradoxically, the clinician in "Dr. Scudder's Clinical Lecture" moves slowly through scientific analysis to soul "illuminations," and again the metaphors of merging and separation explain his madness and breakthrough to vision.

Two volumes in the early twenties continue the Shelleyan quest. Though most of *The Open Sea* (1921) is a series of powerful characterizations, several shorter poems use biological imagery to develop the striving for unity. "Pentheus in These States" is a sweeping historical and geographical panorama of flames and dreams and "swarming sallies." In *The New Spoon River* (1924), Rev. John Onstott characterizes the history of philosophy, art, and religion as an organic evolution moving to "further sublimate life." Sylvester Wilson's scathing critique of a people "trampling delight" is balanced by Cleanthus Trilling's celebration of the series of urges leading from the seed through life cycles to God.

In "Evolution in the Graveyard," Henry Hahn traces Masters' indebtedness to the graveyard poets who taught him the creative dimensions of solitude and the beauty of that special kind of naturalistic scenery. Hahn sees Masters attempting "to capture a living, changing 'scientific' concept of man" and then breaking through the "soulless world" to a purposive concept of soul via the graveyard vision. What emerges can be traced as well to the English romantics—and again particularly to Shelley—for, in Hahn's terms, "an unceasing flow of all experience" and a "living life to the fullest" are the activities whereby "the soul substantiates itself." This unending quest for fullness takes shape in the soul-flowing of many lesser known but significant works from 1932 to 1940—some published by Mencken in *The American Mercury* and others which are collected in privately circulated volumes.

"Beethoven's Ninth Symphony and the King Cobra" (1932) is a narrative description of exactly that kind of soul substantiation. In a highly ambitious epic pattern, the poem traces the urge for unity through its stages of separation and the struggle of pure energy to reclaim ecstatic harmony. The poem begins *in illo tempore* "when life was fermenting and crackling, and trying to escape / The trances of Nature, and get beyond itself." From "footless creatures" came "the bread which fathered Beethoven" through a restless, brooding, yet harmonious evolution. Out of "the sleeping spirit" or "trance" of nature man "soared up" and broke through to consciousness: "This same power awakes in the cobra; / It awakes in Beethoven. / It awakes when anything separates itself from Nature, / And becomes two instead of one."

Hence the awful secret that human consciousness begins in separation, in a twoness which is at once a power and a trap. Like the English romantics, Masters finds the meaning of human experience in the intrinsic pain which is restrictive while it is educative and liberating. The awakening brings "a head that knows pain is in the flesh" and that "pain brings something into existence / Which is an advance upon a mere state."

However, their common "births of consciousness" torment each other in the separation "between Nature the creator" and "any mind created." The cobra in his "glass cage" and Beethoven "through oboes" tell of "sorrows and sufferings." Each is "trapped by being fated to be constantly aware of its venom genius." A catalog of "traps" follows, describing a hell of loneliness and separation, culminating in "a trap of contemplation"

> Where all the traps are contemplated dimly
> It is trapped to the life of sensuous particulars,
> While the whole teases and is never known,
> The whole is a slowed-down film.

The traps are at once an awareness of genius and the hateful death of "the Dual Thing"—until at last Beethoven and the cobra struggle to merge into each other. Thus through the hypnotic enchantment of his music Beethoven "entered the cage of the cobra," and "Beethoven's soul stepped from darkness to brilliant light."

The salvation is a complex return to "steaming swamps" and above all an "ecstatic storm of harmony." In the reunification of primal energy and the life forces, all of human history repeats a pattern of collapse and regrowth symbolized finally by "the song of infinite chants / Lifting worlds into their orbits." Masters' rendering of the epic fall and rebirth deserves closer reading than space permits here. But the spiraling into the trap of isolation and separation followed by the inevitable struggle to reunite are central to the dominant theme of "urge" in all his poems. In this startling narrative, the images of urge describe not only the characteristic flames of sexual union but also the apocalyptic Shelleyan aesthetic which energizes his vision. The transformation to an eternal landscape is complete, and human consciousness has passed from the "trance of Nature" through the "traps" of experience finally to "spirals of Infinitude" where man is a "dweller with Eternity."

Masters' mystical apocalypse is nonetheless midwestern in its continued adherence to concrete particulars, the landscape, and the alternating rhythms of entrapment and liberation, separation and the achievement of new harmonies. That landscape becomes increasingly less visible as the harmonies deepen and turn inward to the mystical. Again the force of Shelley can be found in the themes of another volume of this time, *Invisible Landscapes* (1935). One poem particularly in that collection, "Ultimate Selection" (52–59), matches the Shelleyan style and energy and the visionary themes of "Amphimixis."

"Ultimate Selection" is a study of evolution and a struggle to define the fundamental interactions between matter, energy, and mind which create life itself. Like many of Shelley's metaphysical pieces, the poem begins in chemistry, moves through vast philosophical speculations, and ends in soul striving and the nonreducible unity achieved through love. The search for ultimates begins looking through "the eye of science" which sees into "the depths of plasm" and finds a "primal sparkle." That eye moves through various life forms until it climbs to man. Working from the "slime-stuff" which is the "basis of life," the ascent is energized by "an invisible element / Which toils within" and which "shows in protoplasm as a twinkle / But like the sun glows in the soul of man." This "life power" works within leaves as well as man. Each living thing shares the power of selection whereby it "achieves expression for itself as life."

In *The New World* (1937) that ascent is made more explicit. In this long narrative poem Masters chronicles the cobra-like process in which "the New World can come to an awakening." Again the images are biological as the speaker reviews the history of the westward movement, of political strife, and of the birth of American consciousness. Dvořák replaces Beethoven and "the symphony of the New World" shows none of the intensity and furor of the earlier poem. But the same impulse to reunite into the whole "magnanimous man" dominates the epic sweep across the prairies to "enduring words" and that same eternal landscape. The tone throughout describes "the vast indifference" of a "ruined age." But here the Shelleyan quest pours through Whitman, and the throbbing of "the People" unites the cobra of these shores and the Beethovens of the New World. Again the celebration of a mystical vision comes through a Shelleyan poet-prophet who "must sing the People."

Perhaps nowhere are the growth rhythms of "Amphimixis" and "Cleanthus Trilling" repeated so exactly as in the privately circulated and numbered volume *The Serpent in the Wilderness* (1933). The images are again genetic: "What we know of a former life lies in the germ plasm; / What we know about paradise can be seen in enzymes." And again biological rhythms embody the whole of human experience:

> Everything is in a flux,
> Everything is sundered and brought together by turns,
> Whether it be by magnetism in particles as cohesions and
> explosions,
> Or in human beings by love and hate, resulting in strife and
> war.
> These correspondences recur forever, and what they prove is
> limitless.
>
> [*Serpent*, 36]

The most intriguing poem in the collection is almost a continuation of "Amphimixis" and the epic of Beethoven and the cobra. Again the biological language of the life forces pervades the celebration of "Ode on America":

> There is but one story for everything, with no exception.
> The founding of the United States obeyed all these urges:
> Immigrants of many races swarmed here as sperm, and not
> only
> Brought forth children, but also impregnated the days
> So that they produced something inheritable out of a new soil.
> For the written word, music, religion, arts and laws
> Are inheritable, not as objects only, but as influences of mitosis.
> And here again, are correspondence and recapitulation.
>
> [*Serpent*, 33]

For Masters, the "urges" that became America combine Whitman's celebration of the people with Shelley's mystical breakthrough to achieve an inevitable unity. In "Ode on America" the push is to "the Purposive Whole" or "the Harmonious Whole"—each another name for the Shelleyan "shadow of an unseen power." Again the struggle is to overcome the death of separation through a transformation to soul:

> There is everywhere a uniting, as in the cells of obelia.
> What makes them unite is the secret. A man is nothing
> But oxygen, hydrogen, carbon and nitrogen—
> Nothing but the principle that made them become flesh.
>
> [*Serpent*, 39]

The images of the struggle are again biological, and the vehicle is the poet-prophet who creates "what might be called Des Moines or Indianapolis / Liquified to words—smelling and tasting of the trivial and factual." Through that swelling midwestern landscape there persisted

> The Purposive Whole throwing sperm all over the land
> From which millions rise faster than men did from the rocks of
>   Deucalion,
> Lift themselves to ideas through the harmonious activity of
>   generative electrons,
> So that there shall be music heard everywhere in America.

Here the sexual metaphor embodies the Whitmanesque and Shelleyan hymns which begin to dominate the songs of Masters' later years.

Shelley's presence in *The Serpent in the Wilderness* is most obvious in Masters' version of "Prometheus." Of course Masters knew Aeschylus and the long Promethean tradition of romantic poetry in the Goetheian and Anglo-American traditions. But his special debt is the fierce energy of Shelley's hero. In *Across Spoon River* he describes his mood when he wrote the poem as a "renascence of feeling and thinking," a time when he concluded that "there is no other God to seek but that one which is present in all beings, and in nature" (*ASR*, 416).

Masters shared what Shelley called in himself a "passion for reforming the world" (Preface, *Prometheus Unbound*). His "Prometheus" was also an attempt to capture—again in Shelley's words—"the uncommunicated lightning" of the human mind. In his hero, Shelley sought "the type of the highest perfection of moral and intellectual nature, impelled by the purest and truest motives to the best and noblest ends." The defiance which dominates Masters' poem matches Demogorgon's famous lyric which closes Shelley's play:

To suffer woes which Hope thinks infinite;
To forgive wrongs darker than death or night;
   To defy Power, which seems omnipotent;
To love, and bear; to hope till Hope creates
From its own Wreck the thing it contemplates;
   Neither to change, nor falter, nor repent;
This, like the glory, Titan, is to be
Good, great, and joyous, beautiful and free;
This is alone Life, Joy, Empire, and Victory.[10]

Masters' Titan sings the same hymn to the "immaculate fire" of the mind that lights the way to will:

I will endure, I do not repent,
I do not pray, nor ask for mercy,
Nor bow myself to any God.

[*Serpent,* 77]

The defiance of Masters' "Prometheus" is a celebration of the "awakener of mind," dedicated to the struggle through which "man will grow stronger than any God."

In Masters' later verse, as in Shelley's, not everything was "harmonious activity" or "generative electrons." In 1940 "The Triumph of Earth," published and circulated in a limited number by Masters, described the near despair of "Prometheus in chains" nearly defeated by the isolate separation that is earth's "triumph" over man.

"The Triumph of Earth" is a catalog of unspeakable horrors, each intensified by Whitmanesque expanse and midwestern particularity. At the core of each ironic "triumph" is a deep longing answered only by deception and separation:

In this earth life which envelops man in darkness,
But keeps urging him toward the light;
This earth life which makes men dependent upon earth,
But rouses him to struggle for heaven
Through the dark side of earth, through the light side of earth.
We cannot prove whether life be good or evil—
That is earth's triumph. What shall we do?

What to do is inevitably the question, and the onslaught of a life "falling short of the soul's vision and desire" is ever the despair of felt existence.

The urges toward despair are balanced all the while by intimations of eternal truth, and again the tight pattern of contrasts is Masters' reworking of the Shelleyan vision on the midwestern prairie. First there is the despair:

> O blue heaven of white clouds,
> And you the stars numberless in the measureless sky,
> Seen from the darkness of the cistern through the door of the
>   cistern,
> It is you that divide our thought, and when we weary for the
>   daily ebb and flow
> Of human folly, always like senseless and aimless waves;
> When symbols are around us and reveal a whole that we cannot
>   see,
> When we doubt that our visions and intimations
> Are responses to a reality, and the whispering of leaves
> Bring no peace against the restlessness of earth;

To be answered only by the uneasy victory of Prometheus' struggle:

> And we console ourselves with fields and hills,
> With meadows rimmed with white clouds,
> With rivers and mountains, and pastures of cattle,
> And with sheep by the flags of fresh water.
> We thus console ourselves, we the sons of Sisyphus,
> Who forever roll the stone up the steep,
> And forever see it roll down again until it catches and crushes
>   us.
> We, the sons of Prometheus endure the chains and bolts,
> Hoping against the shouts of those who brought the undying
>   worm to earth,
> We hope to the last against the triumph of earth.

As it is in Shelley, the final verdict is always in doubt. Vision must ever remain irresolute, ever searching. Masters' Prometheus understands this tension when he sings "I will endure" and again "I quest forever." But somehow Masters finds hope beyond mere endurance in the land. Just as in "The Prairie: Sandridge" (*AI*, 34–36)

> These prairies here,
> Surviving the death of hope, of liberty
> Will brood upon the centuries year by year.
> And tell of plenty, peace, domestic joy
> . . . .
> In this beneficent land of Illinois,

so also earth's "triumph" must contend with man's ultimate urge to make it until

> The idiocies, ill woes of earth
> Seem at least as the annual weeds which come and go,
> And leave the oak forests standing.

The richness of Shelley's energetic quest and his mesh of hope and despair provided Masters with rich sources for his own writing. The later works of the "*Spoon River* poet" should be read as what Cesare Pavese has called "a kind of Shelleyan hymn to the liberated world."[11] In 1944 Masters was presented the Shelley Memorial Award by John Hall Wheelock of the Poetry Society. In accepting the award, Masters recalled how he began to read and "cherish" Shelley over sixty years earlier in his high school days. He never wavered in his pursuit of lyrical passion and Promethean energy. The poems of the thirties are dominated by his shaping and reshaping of bittersweet hymns to liberation.

Shelley and Masters shared a total commitment to the beauty and energy of Greek culture. They also shared a classical view of literary influence as a delicate interaction between imitation and the originality of one's own vision. Shelley summarized his use of Greek mythology in his poems in his preface to *Prometheus Unbound*. Masters knew that preface well; in his biography of Lindsay he remarked "Shelley knew that Aeschylus shaped his vision of the mystery of life out of a titanic dedication to the hope of uplifting the human race" (*L*, 183–184). In Shelley's own words: "A poet is the combined product of such internal powers as modify the nature of others; and of such external influences as execute and sustain these powers; he is not one, but both." Shelley was exactly that kind of external influence which sustained Masters' powers throughout a long and productive career.

7

Intense and Subtle

PARLEYINGS WITH BROWNING

Masters criticized Mark Twain for creating characters who were "merely externally realized in terms of everyday incidents, not dramatically conceived deeply and at the core." His foil to Twain's "puppets" was the authentic dramatic power he found in Browning:

> That imagination was not Twain's which reminds one of human heroism and reassures one concerning it; which leads hope as it led Browning to the unbelievable, and there sublimates the emotion; which sustained Whitman to the last in superb confidence in the cosmic scheme, as it did Spinoza. This is imagination, a greatness of mind which creates a life beyond itself, and thus lives what is thus created by itself for itself. [*T*, 231]

That kind of heroism and its sublimation in carefully conceived dramatic structure attracted Masters to the possibilities of the dramatic monologue.

Browning's influence on Masters is difficult, even confusing, to trace. While he praised the control and dramatic energy of the standard monologues, Masters never thought of Browning with the same enthusiasm and adulation he held for Goethe, Emerson, Whitman, or Shelley. He often alluded to Browning's contributions to the Anglo-American tradition, but he seldom elaborated on his own reactions as a reader. Clearly, the presence of Browning in Masters' poetry is not the exuberance of converting classical riches as much as what Harold Bloom refers to as a brooding defense against the flood of the giant precursor.[1] Browning had often visited the regions which Masters most wanted to reach as a poet. Masters looked over his shoulder at the giant shadow with due respect; but above all he wanted to clear space for himself.

In his autobiography Masters took pains to point out that he wrote *Domesday Book*—which has often been linked directly to Browning—before he "ever read a line" of *The Ring and the Book*. His anxiety shows in the afterthought: "and perhaps before I ever heard of it" (*ASR*, 369). In "I Smell the Blood of a Christian Man" (*Invisible Landscapes*, 1935) the speaker takes off against the misguided vision of Browning's "Childe Roland to the Dark Tower Came." Masters' widow, Ellen Coyne Masters, recalls that her husband enjoyed "The Last Ride Together" but adds: "the idiocy of the thought in 'Rabbi Ben Ezra' seemed to kill Browning for him. I remember him scoffing at that poem."[2]

Browning served as an energizer of Masters' inventive powers even when he turned away from some of the well-known idealism. The Browning in Masters is not so much a classical absorption of past riches as a troubled anxiety defense. Again, Harold Bloom's definitions will clarify:

> Poetic influence, in the sense I give to it, has almost nothing to do with the verbal resemblances between one poet and another. Hardy, on the surface, scarcely resembles Shelley, his prime precursor, but then Browning, who resembles Shelley even less, was yet more fully Shelley's ephebe than even Hardy was. The same observation can be made of Swinburne and of Yeats in relation to Shelley. What Blake called the Spiritual Form, at once the aboriginal poetical self and the True Subject, is what the ephebe is so dangerously obliged to the precursor for even possessing. Poets need not *look* like their fathers, and the anxiety of influence more frequently than not is quite distinct from the anxiety of style. Since poetic influence is necessarily misprision, a taking or doing amiss of one's burden, it is to be expected that such a process of malformation and misinterpretation will, at the very least, produce deviations in style between strong poets.

Influence in this sense is not resemblance but struggle and transformation. As the later poet or ephebe of Browning, Masters was "obliged" to his precursor even while he was compelled to push off from him. And again, as Bloom notes, Masters' way of unburdening himself was typically American:

> American poets, far more than British, have rebelled overtly against ancestral voices, partly because of Whitman's example, and also because of Emerson's polemic against the very idea of influence, his insistence that going alone must mean refusing even the good models, and so entails reading primarily as an inventor. Our greater emphasis upon originality has produced inversely a more malevolent anxiety of influence, and our poets

consequently misinterpret their precursors more radically than do the British.[3]

Nowhere was Masters' Emersonian sense of originality seen in practical application more than in his struggle with Browning. As an inventive reader of the Browning tradition in Anglo-American letters, Masters remained an admirer and a combatant throughout his career.

Browning hovers over Masters' handling of drama in *Spoon River Anthology* (1915) and *The New Spoon River* (1924) as well as *Domesday Book* (1920) and its sequel *The Fate of the Jury* (1929). As early as 1916 in "When Life is Real" he wrote a lyric after "The Last Ride Together" and created a Browningesque quest for ultimates in "The Star" (*Songs and Satires*). Similarly, in *Toward the Gulf* (1918) and *Starved Rock* (1919), Masters' dramatic monologues were modeled on Browning's artists, writers, and bishops. His character sketches also followed on that path—with *The Open Sea* (1921), *Poems of People* (1936), and *More People* (1939). Direct allusions to Browning continued also in *Vachel Lindsay* (1935), *Invisible Landscapes* (1935), *Whitman* (1937), and *Mark Twain* (1938). Much of the Shelleyan intensity of his quest for vision was fed in these years also by the Shelley in Browning. The lyrics were localized and tightened by his reading of dramatic monologues, parleyings, and mystery stories in verse. In Browning, Masters found poetic forms which sharpened and intensified his presentation of character.

Masters always held Whitman's opinions in high esteem, and his remarks on Browning's "roominess" were no exception. Masters also studied carefully "one of the ablest critics of Whitman," George Santayana, who compared Browning and Whitman "as poets of barbarism, as poets who ignored the past and did not accept life as an art, and history as a record of life's experiments." Masters quarreled with Santayana's view that Whitman sacrificed "underlying structure" to a phantasmagoric concern with "the surface" of things. But Masters went on to make his own comparison between Whitman and Browning: "I admit that Whitman did not penetrate into secrets as Browning did; for his mind was not as subtle as Browning's—but for that matter neither was Homer's." That is high praise, indeed, from the "Hellenist" who worshipped Whitman's vision. Masters was fascinated by this comparison of two very different poets, and he extended his remarks a bit further: "Whitman's points of view, his wisdoms, his philosophical verses, are less gnomic than Emerson's and less lyrical. They are more matter-of-fact. They are roots and stems, not flowers. Whitman's 'Eidolons' is quite inferior to Emerson's 'The Sphinx.' Whitman is to Browning and Tennyson as roots, stalks, leaves, to fruit—as all these are to apples or pomegranates" (*W*, 302–304, 306). Perhaps a variant of the old adage applies here, and in the end apples and pomegranates might not be compared. But Masters renews the contest one more time, and—in spite of his "subtle" mind—Browning loses:

> This will do as answer to the question whether Browning and Tennyson are superior to Whitman. Neither of these English poets had a national vision, or perhaps any definite vision for the betterment of their country or the world. Neither celebrated the tribe. Whitman was the tribal prophet and poet. In some aspects of a full appraisement this makes Whitman more important than his English compeers—always supposing that his vision is realized and that he is himself uplifted by that fact. [306]

Masters rated the "tribal prophet" in Whitman higher than the "apostle of individualism" in Browning. He wanted to keep striving for the "natural vision," but he continued to believe that the Browning subtlety was one way to get there.

Reviewers have frequently mentioned Browning as a source of Masters' dramatic monologues and as a direct influence on *Domesday Book*. In *Edgar Lee Masters: The Spoon River Poet and His Critics* John T. Flanagan has summarized the major reviews in which Browning and Masters have been compared. The parallels cited are usually only the obvious, and few critiques mention the deeper similarities in thematic intensity or dramatic structure.

The whole mood of *Spoon River Anthology* conveys what Masters referred to as Browning's sense of the "deeply conceived dramatic incident" which goes to "the core." As often as the Spoon River characters have been analyzed, the peculiarly Browningesque cast of Masters' ability to sublimate heroism in dramatic structure has not been recognized. Of recent commentators, only Pavese emphasizes the "powerful objectivity" and the "spirit of inquiry" which link the people of Spoon River to Browning. Pavese sees that Masters' chief accomplishment in the *Anthology* is the creation of "the answer never definitely given, but forever renewed through each person, the conviction, sorrowfully felt on every page, that however satisfactory and final any solution of life may seem, there will always be other people who remain outside it." What Pavese calls Masters' "spirit of inquiry continuously renewed" dominates in the famous tombstone monologues.[4]

Reread *Spoon River Anthology* the way Masters read Browning, and a sense of "roominess," "subtlety," and powerfully sublimated emotions breaks through. The deep repression of sleep sets the tone in "The Hill," and the restless quest is defined for Robert Fulton Tanner who must "work out" his soul. Each of the *Spoon River* characters struggles with what Serepta Mason calls "the unseen forces / That govern the processes of life." Each is dedicated to Jacob Goodpasture's "love of larger truth." The themes, too, often follow where Browning had been. Herbert Marshall believes that "one can be happy only where two are," and George Gray broods on his hunger for meaning and his fear to venture forth. Consider Mary McNeely's "To love is to find your own soul / Through the soul of the beloved one" or Penniwit the Artist's desire to "catch the soul" in his camera. Browning's heroes can be seen in Ernest Hyde's thoughts on sorrow as "the birth of the soul" or Ezra Bartlett's speculation that "the aspiring soul" might "By its own sheer power / Find the divine / By resting upon itself" or Jonathan Swift Somers' proclamations about soul enrichment, divination, and prophecy. And Davis Matleck sounds like the reincarnation of Browning's heroic doubters: "You must bear the burden of life, / As well as the urge from your spirit's excess— / Well, I say to live it out like a god / Sure of immortal life, though you are in doubt, / Is the way to live it." Add to this the Village Atheist's insistence that immortality is a pain-bought achievement, and you have the full force of Browning hovering over the Spoon River country.

Critics began to compare Masters to Browning in earnest upon the publication of *Domesday Book* in 1920. A summary reading of the reviews shows a typical pattern. *The Ring and the Book* is cited repeatedly as the source of Masters' narrative, and most reviewers conclude that Browning did a better job. Very little follow-up can be found. There is no extended comparison of the two books, no analysis of what Masters did or didn't take from Browning, no discussion of how he adopted earlier material, not even much detail on why he "fell short" of the alleged model.[5] In short, what the reviewers seem to see as an obvious influence turns up very little insight into how Masters responded to Browning for his own use.

Masters' contention in his autobiography that he wrote *Domesday Book* before he read *The Ring and the Book* seems convincing for several reasons. First, he enjoyed talking about his reading and speculating on how earlier writers enriched his own writing. He had no reason to deny a source, though the constant mention of Browning in reviews no doubt became annoying. Secondly, the two works show none of the typical kinds of parallels which could be expected in an over-the-shoulder influence. The indebtedness is a broader, more pervasive conversion of Browning's dramatic sense—an influence not dependent on lists of parallels. Thirdly, it seems likely that Masters' legal training would have drawn him to the courtroom narrative frame of *Domesday Book*—whether or not Browning had provided the model. Both *Domesday Book* and its sequel *The Fate of the Jury* (1929) grew out of Masters' education and experience as a lawyer. Recently, Charles E. Burgess has initiated a much needed study of how "the law contributed not only source material" for Masters' poems "but also the inquiring frame of mind and self-discipline that enabled him to bring forth steadily a vast amount of poetry and prose." Particularly instructive on Masters' attraction to Browning is Burgess' observation that he became "in large measure through the practice of law, an interpreter of human behavior who could portray a vast range of it with inclusive universality."[6] For over thirty years, Masters' character sketches and dramatic monologues were dedicated to that kind of incisiveness.

Masters' explanation of how he wrote *Domesday Book* underscores the interrelatedness of his two careers as lawyer and poet. During a month in New York following the publication of *Spoon River Anthology* in 1916 he spent days being "interviewed and pictured and entertained" at dinners and parties. Through all the celebration he thought there were "too much entertainment" and "too many interesting people" for him "to withdraw for composition." In spite of "all this happiness and diversion which poured around," the mood was on him for a different kind of project. "My psyche seemed to be dwelling in infinity," he noted, "I was far off, and it was with an effort that I was bringing myself back to earth. I had wandered to some galactic sphere so distant and alien to human life and its creative passion that I was returning only by slow degrees." On his return to the real world of everyday events, the new idea hit:

> On this bus ride quite suddenly as I was looking at the scene on Fifth Avenue I thought of the scheme by which I might use the material for what later became *Domesday Book*. Back in Lewistown when Will and Reese and I spent our evenings in my father's law office talking logic and philosophy, the idea of a story came to me which I wrote at the time, but never published. . . . I imagined a group of four or five young men similarly engaged as we were in discussion and study. One of them, a skeptic and misanthrope, committed suicide. The others came into the room and looked at the tragic scene. When they took in hand to report what they saw they differed from one another in many details,

some important, some trivial, just as I had seen witnesses do in the cases that I saw my father try. They also gave varying and contradictory analyses of the suicide's character, and even of his physical appearance. . . . That story which came back to me on this bus ride after that long lapse of twenty-five years or more was the germ of *Domesday Book*. [*ASR*, 366–369]

The disclaimer about *The Ring and the Book* follows to emphasize the long germination and practical courtroom experience which went into the making of the testimonies of *Domesday Book*. This account of how he translated his courtroom observations into narrative technique provides a significant clue to what Masters looked for in his reading of Browning. Again, the handling of varying points of view in contradictory testimony was a major attraction of all the well-known dramatic monologues.

Domesday Book and *The Fate of the Jury* show two dominant traits which Masters found in Browning. Both volumes capture the uniquely personal point of view which brings to life on the printed page an individual human mind. That subjective angle of vision can be felt in each of a succession of testimonies directed toward either the reader or an auditor in the dramatic setting. That special perspective from which each person perceives the world gives the language of the poems authenticity and energy. Masters' monologues also share with Browning's the quest in each speaker to achieve an intensity of experience. That intensity is prodded on by a restless urge for full participation in day-to-day experience. The heroes of Masters' monologues share what Browning called the "principle of restlessness / Which would be all, have, see, know, taste, feel, all."[7]

Masters' experience with courtroom testimony sharpened his sensitivity to the poetic possibilities in a montage of different perspectives on the same event. In *Domesday Book* the event is the death of Elenor Murray; the conflicting points of view unfold in a lengthy coroner's inquest about the circumstances of that death. In the midst of the testimony witnesses reveal as much about themselves as the events they recall, and the life and character of Elenor Murray become symbols of the "riches, poverty, and weakness" as well as the "strength / Of this our country."

The opening of *Domesday Book* is a commentary on itself. Here is the purpose of the drama:

Take any life you choose and study it:
It gladdens, troubles, changes many lives.

> The life goes out, how many things result?
> Fate drops a stone, and to the utmost shores
> The circles spread.

>   Now, such a book were endless,
> If every circle, riffle should be traced
> Of any life—and so of Elenor Murray,
> Whose life was humble and whose death was tragic.
> And yet behold the riffles spread, the lives
> That are affected, and the secrets gained
> Of lives she never knew of, as for that.
> For even the world could not contain the books
> That should be written, if all deeds were traced,
> Effects, results, gains, losses, of her life,
> And of her death.

And the method used:

>   I have made a book
> Called *Domesday Book*, a census spiritual
> Taken of our America, or in part
> Taken, not wholly taken, it may be.
> For William Merival, the coroner,
> Who probed the death of Elenor Murray goes
> As far as may be, and beyond his power,
> In diagnosis of America,
> While finding out the cause of death.

as well as a lawyer's brief on the evidence used:

> We take up Elenor Murray, show her birth;
> Then skip all time between and show her death;
> Then take up Coroner Merival—who was he?
> Then trace the life of Elenor Murray through
> The witnesses at the inquest on the body
> Of Elenor Murray;—also letters written,
> And essays written, conversations heard,
> But all evoked by Elenor Murray's death.
> And by the way trace riffles here and there. . . .

and even some advice to the reader on how to proceed:

> Read how the human secrets are exposed
> In many lives because she died—not all

146

Lives, by her death affected, written here.
The reader may trace out such other riffles
As come to him—this book must have an end.

The coroner's investigation sets the scene for a murder trial as well as a larger symbolic probe of American culture on the whole. The dramatic frame allows Masters to explore the intensely personal attitudes and beliefs of representative people from that larger culture.

Impassioned testimony from several witnesses forms the second link between Masters and Browning. The statement of each speaker in *Domesday Book* arises from the unique perspective of intensely felt experiences and represents at the same time a philosophy which explores deeply one phase of the human condition. In each instance, full exploration of the subjective viewpoint provides an access to truths not available from a less personal perspective. The "transcripts" from the testimony of *Domesday Book* are important monologues in their own right and serve as a testing ground for the concerns of Masters' later poems.

The same courtroom structure can be found in *The Fate of the Jury* (1929). Again the occasion elicits intense personal testimonies about "the stir of life, the mystic drone / Of peoples massed as cultures, or as breeds / And with the heat of life secreting wax / With which to build the future" (*FJ*, 9). *Fate* takes another look at Elenor Murray's death as the coroner and jury decide to probe their own lives in order to track down the "central clew" of their lives. In a combination of oral and written testimony the book develops a curiously modern dramatic and confessional probe into the depths of human personality. The testimony of Winston Marion, the newspaper editor, captures the mood of the new inquest. First, Marion defines the skill a poet must possess:

> It's having courage, resolution, will,
> A judgment true, a passion for the good,
> The beautiful in life, the love of justice,
> And rational thoughts that weigh with finest scales
> All logics, inner cores of the real
> That make a poet.

Marion's self-assessment also captures the mood of the whole:

> But I had courage of a sort,
> And will and resolution; though in truth
> There is the flash of powder in the pan

> And the burning flame which never fails, and I
> Was flashing, going black and flashing up,
> Until the mere explosive of my soul
> Was burned away. So had I for the good
> A passion, and that lasted me to prose,
> That's the ironic taunt against my life!

Marion begins to sound like one of Browning's artist-villains in his boastful self-indictment:

> I loved the beautiful with a love betrayed,
> Or else misguided by the encroaching lusts
> Which crawl upon a man who lets himself
> Fall into weak despairs; and so at last
> I walked all spotted from this evil world
> Whose enmity a poet must perceive
> In time to avoid its touch. And that's to say
> I lackèd the delicate scales of rationality
> Which weigh invisible logics.

> [*FJ*, 143–144]

The climax of *The Fate of the Jury* is also its most Browningesque moment. Summing up his achievement in taking the "census spiritual," Coroner Merival finds himself buried in depression as "magnanimous vastness" swallows all. Still his ultimate optimism is triumphant:

> But my hope
> Established me at last in peace with self,
> And made me tuned with vastness which demands
> Hope, love, truth, beauty, which I see as laws
> Eternal like the laws of gravity,
> Of energy. Then why this universe?
> Why mind of man which the great scene explores,
> If it be not for him to know, as part
> Of its inherent reason that it is?
> If it be not his mind was made to grow,
> As it has grown there twenty thousand years—
> As it must grow in the million years to come
> To a wisdom millions greater than to-day's?
> This is my faith, all reasonable, while doubt,
> Which sees a universe in defeat, and man
> Defeated as a mind for that defeat

Is all insane. No, I believe, and ride
By this belief vast wings from star to star,
From which I look on death beneath as a shadow
Thrown from a mountain by the rising sun;
And if night come as blotted consciousness,
The law conducts it; with what good compared
Is this law rendered bad? Were there not days
And nights before me and shall there not be days
And nights long after me?

[*FJ*, 170]

Nowhere in Masters' poetry is there a more fitting tribute to Browning's trust in the mind's ability to create and then live a fullness of life beyond all apparent limitations.

Masters greatly admired what he called the "greatness of mind" portrayed in Browning's heroes and villains. With intensity and subtlety, Browning's characters explored a full range of experiences and raised the ultimate metaphysical and aesthetic questions which Masters found absorbing. Masters' attraction to philosophical debate and courtroom dramatics drew him in a special way to the theories and counter-theories of Browning's famous artists. Critics write at great length about Browning's "optimism," the exuberance and intensity of his life-force, his "philosophy of the imperfect," his creation of fierce individualists who celebrate life's unexplainable contraries. In each new reading of Browning's monologues, further dimensions appear. His heroes are often evil, and his daemonic poets and artists never fail to penetrate to the core-stuff that energizes and excites readers. They traffic in ultimates. They almost always push poetry, painting, or religion to their limits. At the point when theory runs dry and the worst despair is about to engulf everything, the sheer intensity and energy of Browning's characters pull them through. From Pauline's sun-treading zest for ultimates to Childe Roland's dauntless blow on the slug horn, Browning's questers appealed to Masters' own special kind of optimism as it moved toward the determination and quiet assurance of mystical vision.

Browning influenced in some way everyone who has written dramatic monologues after him. The standard modern "confessional" formula can be traced in part to the relentless self-analysis of Browning's artists. Typically, the speaker begins in a reflective mood, builds to lengthy and pointed self-analysis, descends to seemingly hopeless despair, and then triumphs in a new realization which brings a less

149

exuberant but tougher hope. That pattern is especially convincing in the monologues which feature painters, musicians, and poets.

The poet's struggle with the power of art is one subject of "Cleon."[8] Throughout the monologue, Cleon is referred to as a poet, though he is more exactly a critic. Though it is said that his song "gives life its joy," his preoccupation with analytics brings him to the brink of despair. "I have written three books on the soul," he says, "proving absurd all written hitherto, / And putting us to ignorance again." Cleon stuffs his critical inquiries with sweeping quests that necessarily become clogged. "All arts are mine," he contends: "For music,—why, I have combined the moods, / Inventing one." His piercing self-awareness exhibits Browning's intense inner probings. But the more Cleon accomplishes, the less point he sees in it all. He feels burdened by the achievements of his ancestors and suffers the anxiety of "the small part of a man of us" alongside "some whole man of the heroic age."

Masters admired that same wholeness in the heroic figures of Greece, in the magnitude of Emerson's *Representative Men*, and in the visions of the Shelleyan prophet. His fascination with the processes of influence occasionally prompted him to feel intimidation alongside that "whole man" at the same time in which he sought to absorb the power and riches of that past accomplishment. Almost always Masters learned something about how to be influenced from the very influences he valued most. That kind of lesson from Browning is found in Cleon's anxieties about his own relationship to the riches of the past:

> And ours is greater, had we skill to know:
> For, what we call this life of men on earth,
> This sequence of the soul's achievements here
> Being, as I find much reason to conceive,
> Intended to be viewed eventually
> As a great whole, not analyzed to parts,
> But each part having reference to all,—
> How shall a certain part, pronounced complete,
> Endure effacement by another part?
> Was the thing done?—Then, what's to do again?

Cleon's questions have, of course, shattering implications for the very study of literature as well as for the creation of any *new* literature. He means what he says, yet he is being ironic and maybe even flippant in his "what's to do again."

Above all else, Cleon knows what's *for him* to "do again." He is a "synthesizer." He deals in new combinations for what has already been "done," else he contends—"where had been a progress, otherwise?" But he knows also that a synthesizer must learn to face collapse, for the synthesis can occur only when he pushes to necessary and inevitable, though painful, limits. He repeatedly protests: "Who can do more than reach?" And "Why stay we on earth unless to grow?" Tormented by his inability to be a new Homer or Phidias, or Terander, he cries out "Is it nothing that I knew them all?"

Cleon sees at least simply the massive accomplishment of reaching the point of collapse. Ultimately he revels in failure because he knows that in the reaching to limits, art triumphs in the process of its own collapse. In building toward his startling realizations, he describes the cycles of nature as an inevitable clogging:

> The shell sucks fast the rock, the fish strikes through the sea,
> The snake both swims and slides, forth range the beasts,
> The birds take flight till life's mechanics can no further go—
> And all this joy in natural life is put
> Like fire from off thy finger into each,
> So exquisitely perfect is the same.

His eloquent description of the force and beauty of "animal life" is famous, as is his passionate plea "but is there nothing more?" Beyond all the interacting realizations possible in the world of nature lies the "world of capability / For joy" where "still the soul craves all." Pushing toward an ever-widening expanse where, as a poet, he becomes stuffed, Cleon is the one "Who sees the wider but to sigh the more." His saving failure is his Browningesque rendering of the end of literature: "Most progress in most failure."

Cleon's intent to "seek which the joy-hunger forces us" ends in the sorrows that accompany any poet's facing up to the end of literature. As he grows into visions that his poetry cannot hold, the achievement of failure wears him down even as it becomes consummate. The result is a Tithonus-like death-in-life central to the simultaneous fulfillment and collapse of language arts:

> Thou diest while I survive?
> Say rather that my fate is deadlier still,
> In this, that every day my sense of joy
> Grows more acute, my soul (intensified
> In power and insight) more enlarged, more keen;
> While every day my hairs fall more and more,
> My hand shakes, and the heavy years increase—

> The horror quickening still from year to year,
> The consummation coming past escape
> When I shall know most, and yet least enjoy—
> When all my works wherein I prove my worth,
> Being present still to mock me in men's mouths,
> Alive still, in the praise of such as thou,
> I, I the feeling, thinking, acting man,
> The man who loved his life so over-much,
> Sleep in my urn. It is so horrible . . .

"Cleon" is one of Browning's most pessimistic works, despite its typical zest for the life forces. The concluding "live long and happy" and "Glad for what was! Farewell" are not convincing. The celebration of despair is close to the bitterness of Shelley's "Triumph of Life."

Of Browning's best-known heroic questers, Childe Roland held a special fascination for Masters. In *Invisible Landscapes* (1935) he responded directly to "Childe Roland to the Dark Tower Came" in "I Smell the Blood of a Christian Man." Four years later he returned to the same theme in "Lands End," the concluding poem in the collection *More People* (1939). These two poems display Masters' struggles with the liberating frustrations Browning regularly posed for him.

In recent years Harold Bloom has given us extensive commentary on what he calls "the willfully ruined quester" in Childe Roland.[9] Bloom's thesis is, in short, that the special appeal of Browning's "phantasmagoria" results from Roland's function as "a deforming and breaking agent" who confronts meaninglessness and futility and yet triumphs through assertion of his own will. Roland's endurance together with his discovery that his ruin is of his own making turn his despair into a hornblast of poetic prophecy. At first Roland sets out on the path where all others have failed. And through 26 stanzas of grisly landscape and intricate rhetorical tropes, Roland's "internalized quest" becomes increasingly more complex. His "darkening path" continues to worsen, and—in a horrifying inversion of traditional quests—by stanza 27 he is "just as far as ever from the end." But Roland breaks through to a triumphant vision at his moment of deepest despair.

In "I Smell the Blood of a Christian Man" (*IL*, 60–68), Masters' version of the eternal quester follows along the darkening path with Childe Roland. Along the way he experiences many of the same horrors but reaches very different conclusions. Browning's hero sets out with high purpose to achieve the vision symbolized by the tower. He is

a fiercely determined quester whose whole life has been "spent training for the sight." He has "long suffered," and generations from the
band of questers have warned him about inevitable failure. In spite
of such warnings, Roland's only hesitation is "Should I be fit?" Then
the courage to face despair becomes his triumph when he becomes
trapped along the way.

Masters' quester takes the same journey but turns Roland's assumptions upside down. He accepts neither Roland's craving for the
certainty that the Tower will bring nor the despair that accompanies
his massive disappointments. The "Christian blood" which the new
quester smells is for him a clue to the perverted world view which
tortures the misguided Roland. The speaker of Masters' poem thus
reinterprets the purpose, meaning, and outcome of Browning's famous searchers. He voices Masters' lifelong attack on the Judeo-
Christian ethic for what it did to the beauties of Hellenism. The
monologue is a sharp critique of Browning's poem and ultimately an
attack on the limitations of his world view.

According to Masters' poem, Childe Roland's anxiety, despair,
and triumphant "failure" are all a result of sublimated guilt, negativ-
ism, and other abuses of internalized religion. Masters' speaker begins with a critique of the earlier band of questers and an assessment
of why they failed. Dante, he says, was consumed by a hate taught to
him by "a starved desire" for "a heaven of candles / And altar furni-
ture!" His search for the tower was from the start "a spangled cha-
rade" in which "he made a hell / On earth." Even his "love" for Bea-
trice was concocted by a spell of "spiritual drugs" which only
increased his hunger and gave no satisfaction: "Dante, I say, call him
to me no lover— / (He was not half of Rabelais as lover)."

The speaker next calls upon Shelley for help in his evaluation of
what went wrong in the earlier quests. "The Triumph of Life," says
the speaker, was a vision of earlier "seekers for truth and love" whose
roots were "distorted" and who therefore were deceived in their
search. Only Plato, and the energy of Greek culture, he says, held the
conviction and strength to pursue true "soul beauty." Such visions of
"a higher world" were beyond the capacity of the "faith-man" who
preferred phantoms and superstitions and then sank into despair
when the superstitions couldn't stand up to truth. The "bad dream"
the speaker attributes to Browning is the result of repressed yearn-
ings for ultimates beyond the capacity of the religious machinery
which sets Roland on his way. Displaced religious concepts led
Browning to give "idiot voices / To hope, belief, to courage" con-

cluding that life's triumph could be "cow dung, and ditch dogs." Change your initial assumptions, argues Masters, and much of the anguish and despair of the dark path disappear.

From midway to the end of his monologue, Masters' speaker comments on how Roland went wrong. First, the dilemma they share with all other questers:

> What other faith-man following his belief,
> No matter how drear the country, following
> With courage which never slacked, yet found himself
> At the end of a land, as in a nightmare too,
> Caught as the trap goes click upon the rat,
> Making the soul a rat-thing to be caught,
> Caught with a click where at the right were hills,
> And at the left were mountains—thus the trap!
> Caught in the very place prevised in dreams,
> Foreseen in intuitions along the years;
> Caught after years of training to avoid
> This very trap of the soul!
> Caught following the memory divine
> Of truth and beauty in some higher world,
> Seen mid the shadows of this world by those
> Who love and seek.

Then the attempt to understand what moved all those who "strayed likewise to the idiot hovel" only to fail:

> To see these conquered souls all ranged
> Along the hillsides waiting to view the end
> Of Browning dauntless to the last, who blew
> His slug horn with the words of idiot Tom,
> And drank the cup, it seems, that's all, but still
> Made it not blithe hemlock, but the draught
> Of studied resolution, as who should say,
> He that endureth to the end is saved.
> But saved from what? Not from the trap, that's sure.
> And saved for what? Plato's imagined sphere!

Masters' Hellenist metaphysic makes the answer just that simple. Take away the petrified symbols of a repressed religious mission and the anguish of the journey becomes merely a part of human experience itself rather than an imposed metaphysic.

Like Roland, he realizes that endurance is all, but for quite other reasons and with very different consequences:

What else to do? What but to endure?
What but to say that I am saved to feed
The Giant Spider, making for his guts
Stuff for more spinning of betraying webs,
Who see in Browning, Jesus, and their kind
The genius for spiritual lies, and all awake,
And keyed beside with the caffeine of clear eyes
Cannot be anaesthetized by that poetry
Which would make Homer laugh, Lucretius mock.
Saved! But not saved in life from agony;
Saved! to whom truth has always been a chase;
Saved! In a world where wrong begets its kind,
And transient justice is a womb for wrong.
Saved! But how saved out of the haunted wood?
How saved who never have been heaven led,
But only dream enticed, whose counterpart
In earth reality was always stripped?
What care has been for me to find the truth?
What care has been save that I still should search?
What care has been save care to give me hope
Here in the wood where climbing serpents catch
The robin's wing, and where the rule is chance.

This is the serpent-world of modern despair, a world self-induced by an internalized guilt-culture and the residue of discarded religious machinery.

Masters thought Browning was attuned to that world, but the anguish Roland endures is less modern nihilism than the lingering effects of that Christian blood. His own lengthy critique of how the Judeo-Christian culture had replaced the heroism of Greece with superstition and magic speaks to the entrapment Browning devised for Roland in the famous "click" scene. Even Roland's final blast is less a release than a still-anguished cry. Masters' quester is also forced to confront his own fears and visions of horror at the tower:

But heroes ranged about the old Dark Tower
Saw nothing eviler than the thing I saw;
For in the wood I saw a hunting dog
Urged by the master's voice somewhere afar

To speed, to hunt, to nose the game, to find;
Urged to the thickets where the game might be;
Urged to the swamp alive with ticks and flies
To scare the quarry up for murderous guns,
Urged and so racing here and there with joy
Sniffing old logs, old roots of trees, earth holes,
And ruddy leaves which lay in innocent drifts,
Or so they looked to me and to the dog;
Wherein unnoticed for the mimetic hue
Was coiled the copperhead with steady eyes.
Then quick his nose stung, and he knew his fate.
He howled for pain, knowing his fate had come,
Knowing beside that there was game somewhere,
Which he had missed, only to find the snake.
He whined then, curling down upon the earth,
He howled, but the listless master did not befriend,
Nor come anear to help him. Did he accuse
That master of a malice, did he bark out
Accusals for that master's disloyalty?

These questions are, of course, a further attack on the "spiritual lies" and the "heaven hunger" which "anaesthetize" so many along the path. The dog is also trapped, but Masters offers his reactions as a counterexample of what the Hellenist would do and what Browning's Childe Roland should have done:

No more than any human soul, lying enraged,
Did he do this, a soul entrapped and killed,
Hunting for truth and love, and fooled at last,
But still believing there is truth and love,
Yet stayed from saying there is no truth, no love,
Lest there be such; so stayed and to the last
Loyal to the soul's desire for truth,
And hazarding no denial lest the soul
Speak out a lie in its last desperate throes.

The quest becomes internalized as the traditional heaven-bound urge turns inward. Homer laughs, and the agony is still there. But delusions of "dream enticement" are set aside in favor of a tough and enduring self-sufficiency.

That same toughness is the subject four years later of "Lands End" (*MP*, 189–192)—a narrative of a similar quest that finds the same strength free from illusions. The "End" of the title is the sea, the point "farthest West" on a crosscountry journey. It is the "tower" counterpart in the American landscape, the point "which stays all going forward," the shoreline that "permits but pacing back and forth" before massive cliffs and dark "eternal tides." At that ominous point of no return, the refreshing hope found in the landscape itself runs out. No "Springtime pastures" or "rambles in the hills" or "rapture days in cities" will stay the confrontation. Again the tower scene demands unshakable self-sufficiency:

> Strength is still left to face these walls of granite,
> And say the little that remains is little,
> Accept the prison rocks that bar retracing
> The meadow lands of summer winds and suns.
> Here the sea drifts, and here there is a murmur
> Of zephyrs in invisible sails, the whisper
> Of waves that wash a hull concealed by mists.
> But he who has marched hither, never shrinking,
> And labored as a gleaner in harvest seasons,
> May walk this shore with unaffrighted will.
>
> [*MP*, 189]

Roland's horror appears to tease "the heart's deep hunger," but now instead of despairing, the heart "ever grows / Larger with understanding and with longing / As life shrinks down and narrows along the way, / And leaves the soul through losses so much the greater." The lesson at land's end is found in the whispering sea winds: "Endure." The "tumult of humanity" is answered by "stilled music." "Depth of thought" is the antidote to the "world-ache." Roland's quest is free of displaced religious symbols. The dark tower is a calmer, more soothing place when it catches the breezes of the sea.

In the eternal quests of Browning's heroes and villains, Masters found intriguing models for the character sketches of his own monologues. His deepest debt to Browning was the use of dramatic technique to achieve objectified intensity of feeling. Masters knew the standard dramatic monologues, parleyings, and character pieces which Browning conceived. These tight, polished forms helped him to present his own controversial themes with impact and precision. Again the chronology of Masters' poetry shows the considerable impact made by Browning's sense of drama.

Of course in *Spoon River Anthology* (1915) Masters' form was the terse, graveyard reflection rather than the fully developed dramatic monologue. But even in the tight structures which recall the *Greek Anthology*, the "intensity" and "roominess" of Browning's more expansive form is already in evidence. Robert Fulton Tanner's advice on how to "work out your soul" (*SRA*, 6) suggests the similar quests of Browning's heroes. Frank Drummer spoke about that same kind of inner stirring toward "a high and urgent purpose in my soul" (29). Browning's love poems are recalled by Herbert Marshall's belief that "one can be happy only where two are" (64) as well as the conviction of William and Emily about the "power of unison between souls" (74). The anguish and intensity experienced by many of Browning's heroes and villains is caught in Robert Davidson's "Keen exhilaration of soul gymnastics" (113). The intrigues of the monologues are echoed in Editon Whedon's reflections on the "clandestine soul" (131); the religious zeal of the famous bishops can be heard in Oaks Tutt's "wings of flame" (168); the ever-present reaching for the beyond energizes Davis Matlock's advice that man must learn to "bear the burden" of the "urge" from the "spirit's excess" (230). Further examples would only belabor a point already noted in the sensation which the *Anthology* stirred in the press. From the haunting melodies of "The Hill" to Mr. Jonathan Swift Somers' monologue "The Spooniad," Masters displays a clear affinity with the poet who was to become an even more significant influence in his later development.

The next year in *Songs and Satires* (1916), Masters showed a genuine liking for Browning's lyrics. "When Life is Real" (*SS*, 76–77) nearly parallels "The Last Ride Together," a poem Masters read frequently. Browning's famous ride is a metaphor for the ongoing process of experience, an affirmation of striving itself as an achievement equal to the attainment of one's goal. Masters' own version of the metaphoric ride into eternity gathers to itself the labors, hopes, and desires of the ages. The love journeys are also mythic quests which particularize the scene in stunning detail and generalize the quest in epic tones. The parallel endings crystallize the eternal shared moment. Compare Browning's well-known climax:

> What if we still ride on, we two
> With life for ever old yet new,
> Changed not in Kind but in degree,
> The instant made eternity,—
> And heaven just prove that I and she
>   Ride, ride together, forever ride?

and Masters' version of the same theme:

You were as quiet as the sky.
Your eyes were liquid as the sea.
And in that hour that passed us by
We lived eternally.

[*SS*, 76]

Another early collection—*Toward the Gulf* (1918)—combines Masters' Shelleyan quests with a mastery of dramatic frame typical of Browning. "Victor Rafolski on Art" (82–90) recalls Browning's artists. Rafolski speaks from prison after he is arrested for satisfying his will to take forcibly the woman of his desire. The poem is a statement on art as much as on hunger, repression, and a type of vicarious living.

Rafolski maintains that his crime is only "hunger for more life" in a world where "beauty, rapture, love / Are walled in and locked up like coal or food / And only may be had by purchasers / From whose fat fingers slip the unheeded gold." He finds that "beauty lies in waste" as men deny themselves. He likens freedom and art to war which "lets loose desires, / Emotions long repressed." In that letting loose of desire, "the artist lived his work." Art must necessarily fall short because "You cannot live his life who love his work." Those who hope to "live through art" are, Rafolski says, like "the thrush that pecks at painted cherries."

All this Rafolski offers as an explanation for his "crime" of passion. And all this he says he "learned / While painting pictures no one ever bought." So he quits painting to become a butler because art was "vicarious life" rather than living: "I was not living while I painted pictures." In place of what is vicarious in art he offers at once his own life aesthetic and his defense for taking the woman. In boredom, fatigue, or strength he finds always the same secret:

> what the human heart
> Dreams of and hopes for till the aspiring flame
> Flaps in the guttered candle and goes out,
> Is love for body and for spirit, love
> To satisfy their hunger.

In "To-Morrow Is My Birthday" (*Gulf*, 99–114) William Shakespeare talks to Michael Drayton and Ben Jonson about his life and works and voices one of Masters' favorite themes: physical love is a way to overcome the painful sense of aloneness that comes with human loss and too keen a sense of physical limitation. The poem is a different version of the Shelleyan "Amphimixis," as it reworks into a dramatic frame that Shelleyan lyrical quest. In its theme, language, and tone the monologue recalls "Fra Lippo Lippi," "Cleon," and "Andrea delSarto."

"To-Morrow" is Masters' "Waste Land" poem, with an objectified sense of time and place providing the description for which Eliot looked to the Fisher King and other obscure symbols. A day before his 52nd birthday, the speaker faces a cruel April in a "habit of grief" wherein "the soul / Grows sick." He is afraid of death yet trapped also in the going on. Shelley's "West Wind" thorns serve his meaning: "twixt the fear of ceasing / And weariness of going on we lie / Upon these thorns!" Typically Shelleyan images of the growth of a seed with the fragmentation of imprisonment in consciousness give way to the unity of new creation—symbolized again by physical love. The soul-sickness, weariness, and broken images of existence itself finally give way to a sexual fire, an urge to unite, and a mixing which is mystical but again always achieved through the physical. These are the themes of the lyrical Masters of the thirties as they pass through Shelley and Browning to become a part of his own solid dramatic sense.

In sum the poem is an aging author's lament. "This poor machine is racing to its wreck," he announces and then presents a new rendition of the Ages of Man—along these lines: "in early youth / The life is in the loins." But what begins to look like an X-rated poem soon turns to a clinical discussion of the urges coded in germ plasm and the seed in spring. Like Browning's heroes, artists, and lovers, the making and unmaking of creation are found in intense emotion:

> Give me a woman, Ben, and I will pick
> Out of this April, by this larger art
> Of fifty-two, such songs as we have heard,
> Both you and I, when weltering in the clouds
> Of that eternity which comes in sleep,
> Or in the viewless spinning of the soul
> When most intense.

This birthday poem on growing old poses the essential problem succinctly: "What strength in place of sex shall steady me?" At least there are still the "visions" in a "restless ecstasy" from a soul which "beats up its prisoned wings / Against the ceiling of a vaster whorl / And would break through and enter." Again like many of Browning's heroes, the speaker raises his glass throughout--pausing to thank

God for "anodynes." Always anxious to recapture his youth, he seeks "virgins in their teens." His admission breaks off, however, with the qualification "I want them not, I want the love which springs / Like flame which blots the sun."

Following this definition of his desire, the speaker transforms his earlier "loin" lust into a more abstract pursuit of mystical union:

> No soul as mine has lived, felt, suffered, dreamed,
> Broke open spirit secrets, followed trails
> Of passions curious, countless lives explored
> As I have done.

After various interpolations, the quest becomes visionary before it once again breaks off:

> Bethink you also
> How I have felt, seen, known the mystic process
> Working in man's soul from the woman soul
> As part thereof in essence, spirit and flesh,
> Even as a malady may be, while this thing
> Is health and growth, and growing draws all life,
> All goodness, wisdom for its nutriment.
> Till it become a vision paradisic,
> And a ladder of fire for climbing, from its topmost
> Rung a place for stepping into heaven. . . .

In contrast with the turmoil throughout the scene, the ending is a peaceful acceptance of sleep and the song of the lark. The urge to unite seems at least momentarily fulfilled in the mystic union of spirit and flesh.

"Dr. Scudder's Clinical Lecture" (*Gulf*, 215–234) repeats Masters' recurring theme of soul-hungering and awakening into vision, again using the Shelleyan imagery of the seed and a Browningesque controlled dramatic structure.

Setting and story in the poem are somewhat grotesque, and Masters uses a double plot to heighten the horror. Dr. Scudder is lecturing on some more clinical phases of anatomy and physiology when he pauses over a laboratory brain and skull to tell its life story in the person of one Jacob Groesbell. Before getting to his digression, Dr. Scudder describes at great length the life of seeds and plants and soil and pauses to point out—rather unclinically—that "We are but plants, and all we are and do / Depends upon the seed and on the soil."

Groesbell's monologue (recorded secretly by Scudder) leaves the lecture room for a good two-thirds of the poem. In an impassioned account, Groesbell describes how he lived a simple life in a search for simple things until he experienced a "soul awakening" and was by others "counted mad." In a religious vision of eternity, he glimpses "one harmonious / Whole of universal life all blended / And interfused with universal love." He senses his own power as a "hungering soul" who is "chosen to . . . re-create the race." Mad with his vision, he learns that human misery results from separate urges—away from "the harmonious." His "soul's illumination" triumphs over death itself and Groesbell's monologue ends with a catalog of visionaries who burn through "The sun of fire, a sun of love and truth." A startling contrast, the conclusion of Dr. Scudder's lecture closes the poem: "Students who desire / To examine the skull and brain may do so now / At their convenience in the laboratory."

In addition to modeling his work on Browning's monologue structure, Masters began at this point in his career to match the dramatic form to the typical themes suited to it. Again in "Lord Byron to Doctor Polidori" (*Starved Rock*, 22–28) the speaker frequently breaks out of the setting into a rapturous confessional outpouring of his philosophy:

> A man's soul up to heights too rare to live in.
> I have not risen, therefore, will not rise
> Where thinking stops, because the blood leaves brain
> Therefore have had no falls, and no recoils
> Chasing the Plato vision, the star, the wonder,
> The beauty and the terror, harmony
> Of nature's art; the passion that would make
> The loved one of the self-same womb with me,
> A sister, spouse or angel, daemon, pilot
> Of life and fate.

The chase after nearly unreachable ultimates is well suited to the typical hero-questers of both poets. The Browning formula simply helped Masters fit that outpouring into a pattern which made it controlled and emphatic. Here Byron speaks again:

> Dreams seen most vividly by Petrarch, Dante,
> Who loved without achievement, balking nature,
> Till Passion, like an involute, pressed in
> Harder and harder on its starving leaves,
> Becomes a fragrance—sublimate of self

Sucked out of sorrow's earth, at last becomes
A meditative madness. All is written
Fairly across my page.

That deep repression is typical of Browning's heroes, and the monologue formula establishes the balance between emotion and meditation that is essential to all sublimation.

For the next twenty years, Masters' commitment to a variety of
dramatic forms increased. In the late thirties he turned to extended
character sketches in volumes such as *Poems of People* (1936) and *More
People* (1939).

Poems of People (1936) was a fuller objectification of sublimated
emotions using techniques which Masters learned from Browning.
"Catullus" (4–10) is a poem about poetry, the expression of "a soul
who never became becoming, / And starved in separateness with
hopes of merging." Catullus' unrequited love becomes the symbol
again of frustrated unity and death in separateness. His hope is that
"Lesbia and Catullus / Should merge together in the peace of
love, / And find thereby a higher universe." In momentary embraces
they "became a part / Of something universal and entire." But finally
he must settle for the separation which is worse than death: "To lose
you was defeat / Of all that leads the soul forever seeking / To be at
one with Something above itself." The theme is again Masters' Shelleyan mixing into a mystic union: "This is the analogue of life's conception: / Our souls become a higher form of life / When they have
mingled, even as the child / Arises swan-like from the stream of life."

In *More People* (1939) Masters presents a series of character
sketches, a few striking dramatic monologues and dialogues, a series
of poems in the form of letters or diaries, and a number of tone
poems. The result is a loosely constructed but fascinating collection
of people-watching.

Masters also uses skillfully several hybrid dramatic forms. "Ly-
dia's Diaries" blends the confessional graveyard speeches of *Spoon
River*, the dramatic monologue, and the detective probing of *Domesday Book*. Each line in the poem is a quoted fragment from a diary
entry. "Transfusion" is a more typically lyric drama. "Confucius and
Tsze'Lu" is a dialogue pitting Confucianism against Taoism and
culminating in the basic challenge to prove the value of inaction for
everyone. Inaction itself, it turns out, is "the secret of Tao," and the
bantering of the dialogue form brings home the full meaning of that
letting go.

What Browning's sense of dramatic intensity does for *More People* can be illustrated in three other short dramas. In "Philosopher in Love" (87–91), the speaker tells his "Secret / Round which my being whirls" to an "old friend" in the form of a letter. His problems are many. He is growing old: "age locks up the heart and gives it crystals, / Strange geometrics fanciful, even weird." His career has reached its peak in his "last book" which he hopes will tell "all the story in one book / Of what the greatest men have thought of mind." But this distillation of "fifty years of study" can't measure up to his real desire:

> I have reached sixty-five, and here's the rub:
> All this is nothing to me, nothing compared
> To one consuming thought, one great desire,
> One face, Virginia's.

The rest of the poem plays that "desire" and these "longings" against the "life-time spent on metaphysic." His anguish suggests Browning's tortured artist-lovers who lament their loss with great intensity:

> Though I speak with tongues of Plato and Plotinus,
> With Aristotle and with Schopenhauer,
> And know the world as idea and as will,
> And what the reason is, and what religion,
> Though all of this, if love no more is mine
> I am but sounding brass, the creaking cranks
> Of that old engine with its boiler full
> Of steam—and what's to do but let it hiss?
> Nothing but the fire out once for all
> With drink or poison. What else but sit and hear
> The cogs crunch, and the belts flap, and pretend
> The engine is in order, that is to say,
> Pretend there is no gray hair, fight the thought
> Of my unfitting person hers beside.

Much of what follows in the poem recalls Virginia's "one grand passionate affair" which did not include the philosopher. Again his remembrance of that horror easily displaces his lifetime of philosophical exploration.

Also in *More People*, "Peter Van Zuylen" (141–143) is another death song from a mystic whose "vision" comes forth like "wavering Zephyrs," though "all of it pieced together if you were alert." He wishes that young men be "told" (though he insists his telling is "no sermon") about the daemonic power of man's soul:

> Over and over he said, from whence come the rivers
> Thither again they return, yet the sea is not full:
> God is the sea, and the soul of a man is a little
> Stream of water forever seeking the depths.

The way to the power of God is through "the ocean's lure"—another urge that must be indulged if a vision of unity is to be achieved:

> When you have moments of fearless peace, ecstatic
> With feelings that nothing, not even powers of daemonic,
> Can disturb at all, for that time the Supreme is visioned,
> As a mountain brook rejoices at sight of the shore.

And again:

> God may be defined as the rivers twist with delaying,
> But what is akin must join together at last.
> And what can be better than water that finds the ocean,
> With wanderings ended, water in water at last?

That theme is again the typical Shelley in Masters but now more objectified in sublimated emotion released in the dramatic frame.

In collections not devoted exclusively to poems about Illinois, Masters also left memorable characterizations and landscapes of the region of his origins. The portraits of midwesterners in *More People* are significant documents along the way between Masters' earliest interpretations of his origins and his later retrospective tributes.

In 1939 Masters was one of the first quiet celebrators of native Americans in mainstream literature. "Black Hawk," for example, is a sketch of the plains warrior who "wandered" for years

> from Iowa to Illinois, south and north,
> East and west
> Trying to ease the pain in his breast,
> While Illinois shot up with spire and dome
> Dreaming a glorious goal;
> While melancholy settled on his soul,
> Facing it as he aged, facing it dumb—
>
> [*MP*, 3]

Or consider "George Rogers Clark," the "dreamer who was driven in his quest" until "Death came and found him with oblivion around him / In a cabin in the Valley of the West" (*MP*, 21). Or "Bill Dill," portrait of a midwesterner with "a mind as of earth things" and who "understood Nirvana as much / As a snake knows water by the touch" (22–23). In "A Kansas Cottage" "growths flourish in obscurity and face like human hearts in villages / . . . living from day to day, with no requests, / Save work thereby to keep the little house, / Go on from youth and strength to age and death" (33).

Dozens of examples could be cited of the vitality and endurance shown by these people living everyday lives on the land. One such "tiller" of "historic soil" was Ilya Rastuptchin whose descendants worked every inch of his "inviolate ground" and wreaked the dream of "eternity on the Hills." After many portraits of valley people there is "Milwaukee Avenue," which follows the famous Chicago Street through "a part of Norway, Germany, / Where markets, stores and local advocates / Where restaurants and stove-heated flats / Remain much as they used to be" (125). And the tributes are rounded with "Song in Late August," a hymn of praise to an inner strength that withstands the passing of time and experience:

> The lulling whisper of spent oak leaves
> Day and night make monodies:
> Vain the memory that grieves
> When the prairie is at peace.

> [*MP*, 132]

More People is rounded out with a series of character sketches and tone poems about the mystical prairie—from Nathaniel Page's "Awful Power, which ever brooded / Over the prairie" to the "world-ache" of the "interior country" in "Return to the Lost Orchard" and "Land's End." That power and that ache are central in the paradoxes of Masters' vision—a vision he was drawn to in Whitman, Shelley, and Emerson and which became more objectified in the dramatic structure he found in Browning. Above all else, Browning's influence gave Masters a sense of control over that power and a way of rendering in dramatic settings the lyrical expanse of the prairie and the people on it.

Among Masters' posthumously published works is a series of monologues entitled "Vignettes from Vermont." One after the other, a succession of old-timers addresses a poet who serves as the auditor in the standard format. Each speaks directly to the author who functions as a reporter seeking out his or her story. Mrs. Malatesta Meyerbaum describes herself as "one of the pioneers in the back-to-the-land trek." Charley the Hermit responds to questions with his life story, concluding "I make a good livin' / Sellin' bouquets and baskets which

I weave." Old Mrs. Comstock who is "breakin' up" her house and auctioning her goods, tells the poet "there's a few books there you can have / At your own price." That is the kind of detail which drew Masters to Browning and which enabled him to frame his quests for the infinite in a highly concrete and particularized narrative with the force of the real.

8

Invisible Landscapes and New Universes

"REGIONALISM" REVISITED

In his autobiography Masters describes how, in 1934 and 1935, he found himself "resting in one of those valleys of thought and reflection that come after climbing hills, and before the next hill is attempted." In this meditative mood, he described what he hoped to do in his later verse. Based on his understanding of the Emersonian view that "everything in one's spiritual life is the counterpart of the external world," his poetry of the thirties and forties found in nature symbols the invisible landscapes of mind and spirit. From his earliest days, Masters believed that the deepest truths are found in the brooding of the countryside: "The city is facts, is hard reality, is lifeless stone. The country is the haunt of something universal and deathless and infinite which broods upon the earth and reflects itself in it. In communion with nature we can wrest from the gods ideas identifying life with eternity" (*ASR*, 414, 415–416). Several late volumes and posthumous works reflect this wresting of mystical awareness from the intimations in the landscape.

From *The Great Valley* (1916) to *The Sangamon* (1942), Masters celebrated the land and people of the Midwest. In a very early poem, "Autochthon" (*GV*, 33–42) he sketched the primal origins of "one who springs from the land." Over a quarter of a century later (1942) he described the prairie in a hymn to eternal energy: "To contemplate the prairies is / To fathom time, to guess at infinite space, / To find the Earth spirit in a dreaming mood" (*Along the Illinois*, 34).

As his career progressed, Masters' celebration of the land deepened and expanded until he gradually internalized the landscape. Particular places and people became larger symbols of mythic quests and mystical visions. Slowly his "regionalism" broke out of a sense of place and into hymns to new universes. Throughout the thirties, Masters' symbols of the land came to speak what he called "a silent language of past generations, of the young who laughed and made marriages and grew old, and of the old who looked over this same scene and wondered, as we do, what the earth and the sky mean" (*The Sangamon*, 16). A closer look at how that silent language of the landscape developed over the years reveals a "regionalism" that is more celebratory, meditative, and expansive than commentaries have so far allowed.

Beginning with the sensational impact of *Spoon River Anthology*, critics looked to Masters as a spokesman for midwestern life. At its best, this approach has given him at least some place in modern American poetry; at its worst, some regionalist analyses have severely limited the scope of discussion about his works. John T. Flanagan has recently reviewed commentary on Masters in the form of "regional literary history," and his overview makes lengthy discussion unnecessary here. Flanagan finds that in such critiques "the emphasis fell not on aesthetic values but on his representation of a given area and cultural environment or on his influence upon other writers."[1] These early attempts to explain the "cultural environment" deserve another look in line with a recent, broader approach to midwestern life and literature.

In *The Small Town in American Literature*—one of the best of the standard regionalist studies—Ima Honaker Herron traces the long history of excessive romanticizing about the "pastoral village." Herron argues that *Spoon River Anthology* began, in 1915, to dispel such stereotypes—a process which continued in demythologized fictional accounts over the next five or ten years. Herron offers a methodical, insightful probing of everything from town meetings to border towns, as well as an in-depth review of "crusaders and skeptics" who comment on "the literature of the local." While Masters' later poetry is beyond the scope of her study, Herron mounts an attack on "the sentimentalists who had long praised the simple, satisfying life of the town" and in the process overlooked more universal themes. This clears the way for an expanded reading of Masters: "They failed to see that Masters, while ever aware of the unpleasantness of village life, also acknowledged the presence of loyalty, love, and spirituality in the average town and that some of his characters are the happy conquerors of circumstances."[2]

The standard regionalist approaches to Masters are valuable, though limited. In *The Chicago Renaissance in American Letters*, Bernard Duffey recognized Shelley as the "galvanizing force" who spoke to Masters of a "new glory" and who "gave him the hope that such glory was within his own reach." But Duffey doesn't find a Shelleyan awakening in the poetry after the *Anthology*, as this harsh estimate reveals: "With the exception of a few individual poems, perhaps a dozen in all, Masters' work was dull, tremendously garrulous, and wholly unenlightened by the imaginative and dramatic resilience which had marked *Spoon River*."[3] Twelve years later, Dale Kramer chronicled the personal lives of "six poor boys in search of themselves." Of special interest is Kramer's history of response to *Spoon River* and the demise of Masters' reputation. Much of the criticism from the regionalists is like Kramer's journalistic and biographical research—valuable background for study of the works but often not very helpful on the literary achievements.[4] Michael Yatron bases his study of midwestern life in the politics of Masters, Lindsay, and Sandburg. With emphasis on Masters' populism and his "revision of history," Yatron portrays "a frustrated agrarian sympathizer, who, though he personally could brook neither the village nor the city, fervently wished that America had remained a country of small Jeffersonian villages inhabited by a life-loving, homogeneous, farmer population."[5]

Regionalism is gaining renewed attention among today's critics of American life and literature. Recently the Society for the Study of Midwestern Literature has developed a Center for Midwestern Literature at Michigan State University and publishes a yearbook of research in the field (*Mid America*). Several new journals such as *The Great Lakes Review*, *The Old Northwest*, and *Western Illinois Regional Studies* are thriving.

Such institutionalized scholarly interest testifies to a new rigor in attempts to define and criticize a uniquely middlewestern literature. Masters' place in that literature is, of course, unquestionable—from the shocking characters of Spoon River country to his abiding concern with the people and attitudes of the Sangamon Valley long after he had left the area. But the deepest significance of Masters' Midwest has never been captured by the standard critical works. Masters' identification with the land is more complex than traditional approaches will allow. In "Notes Toward a Definition of the Mind of the Midwest," David D. Anderson finds the "mind of the midwest" in its "variety," "unpredictability," and "paradox," in its "rejection of orthodoxy," in a reality that is "alive, dynamic, and perverse." The Midwest of Masters' poetry supports Anderson's description of "regionalist" literature as "its own best and most eloquent refutation of whatever stereotypes have been imposed on it."[6]

In his own comments on what he called "localism," Masters described the land, the prairies, the towns and their people as the source of poetic strength that broke beyond itself into mystical vision.

The Sangamon, the most revealing prose account of Masters' Midwest, is a probe of "the genius that defines men and spots of earth, and chooses them for memory" (*S*, 240). His philosophizing about the Sangamon Valley emphasizes the "magic in that soil, in the plains, the borders of forest, the oak trees on the hills" (6). He watches "something float out of that soil" and rhapsodizes on "the silence of the grass" and the language it has spoken to generations of dreamers.

But Masters never let himself get caught up in excessive sentimentalism about the land; his record of observations made by Charles Dickens during a visit in 1842 reflects his own paradoxical responses. Likening the prairies to "a tranquil sea or lake without water," Dickens found "solitude and silence reigning paramount around." Yet "its very flatness and extent," he continued, "which left nothing to the imagination, tamed it down and cramped its interest." The strangely somber and eerie feelings Dickens experienced on the midwestern plains are quoted by Masters, a kindred spirit in these strong yet mixed emotions:

> It was lonely and wild, but oppressive in its barren monotony. I felt that in traversing the prairies I could never abandon myself to the scene, forgetful of all else; as I should do instinctively were the heather under my feet, or an iron-bound crest beyond; but should often glance towards the distant and frequently receding line of horizon, and wish it gained and past. It is a scene not to be forgotten, but it is scarcely one, I think, at all events as I saw it, to remember with much pleasure, or to covet the looking on again in after life. [*S*, 17–20]

Perhaps Dickens was just homesick, but Masters pauses over the sense of disappointment and melancholy in his recollections and adds support from his own observations: "For all my love of the prairies I can understand how it was that they affected Charles Dickens so disagreeably and how it was that some of the pioneer women grew melancholy under the influence of their unchanging mood. It may be that the faded eyes, the drooped eyelids of some of the old women of Sandridge were caused by years of gazing over the level stretches of grass to the rims of the forest that seemed to bound a happier land." (*S*, 16). These are not the thoughts of a partisan romanticizer or a "poisoned" satirist, and the tone of his recollections is as changeable as the varying moods derived from the sense of place. What was at one point a source of somber brooding could also be New Salem's robust "Chaucerian material of the richest sort" (160). The mood was often celebratory as in accounts of how Lindsay "turned the fiddle into the lyre" and used tales of the prairie as his "classical dictionary" (219), or somber in the constant refrain that "something has departed from the haunts" of what once was rich in its own myth. In the end, Masters' prose accounts of his midwestern origins remain a quest for hidden meanings rather than analyses of what was: "I'd like to know what it is that catches the imagination like a strange touch on the very heart, the very spiritual being of prenatal memories that persist with reference to earth-places" (87–88).

Masters' attitudes toward the land broke away early from both stereotyped romanticizing and the laments of bitter "expatriots." Beginning with *The Great Valley* (1916), his lesser-known poetry also presented a complex mythology of a people and culture emerging from the land. The symbols and characters of his land-locked verse are richly diverse as they transplant a Shelleyan longing for the eternal into intensely localized explanations of midwestern experience.

"Autochthon" (*GV*, 33–42) is an intricate narrative which follows, in a three-part parallel, the lives of Tennyson, Darwin, and Abraham Lincoln. The emphasis is on Lincoln, the subject of the poem's title which means literally "one who has arisen from the land." Masters portrays the man of the soil as a poet who is "moving in higher spaces." He is "moulding stuff / Too tough for spirits practical to mould." The poem records Lincoln's rise from "rude" beginnings to public life and reflects the ambivalence of the poet who became a "patrician." Although there is some of the tone of Masters' controversial Lincoln biography, the final impression is again the Shelleyan "windless flame."

The Midwest in *The Great Valley* is a complex place. It is thick with "fertile stuff" in "Gobineau to Tree" (*GV*, 53), a pointed satirical retort to American heroism in "The Typical American?" (68), the "simmering sands" of a midwestern fishing tour in "At Havana" (78), the narrowness of small-town life in "Winston Prairie" (120), and the Shelleyan "fiery seed / Of mad Prometheus" in "The Radical's Message" (211). Among the often stunning character sketches in the volume is "Having His Way" (190–197), the story of two boys sprung from the village and out to face "babbling multitudes." The poem is a narrative of "two boys in the early twenties / Fresh from the quiet of fields, / And the sleepy silence of village life." The inventor travels the world; the writer stays nearer to home where his "grind is a column a day." The world traveller laughs, while the writer goes to "where the youths were thinking, / Painting and writing, / And talking of the revolution." One man flees from his origins and dines with friends; the other stays home where the "elevated . . . roars" beneath his window. The Midwest is a tough place compared to a life of wandering through the ruins of Rome. It is cloudy and wintry, while tourists pick flowers under the sunny Italian sky. Yet, the poem questions, "Can a man or woman alive escape / The granite's edges or ditch's mire. . . ?" While reading his friend's letters from abroad, the toughened and unobtrusively proud resident of the Midwest wonders why life has not yet "caught" his friend: "Is the asp at your breast in spite of laughter? / Or when is the asp to sting you?"

Two years later, *Toward the Gulf* (1918) presents further portraits of the variety in midwestern life. In his dedication "To William Marion Reedy" (vii–xiii), Masters describes his own poetic techniques as a "sculpturing of the clay taken out of the soil" from which he and Reedy came. He says the volume is "a continuation of the attempts of Spoon River and The Great Valley to mirror the age and the country in which we live," and he characterizes his subject as "the life around us as we view it through eyes whose vision lies in heredity, mode of life, understanding of ourselves and of our place and time." A few samples illustrate these techniques and themes. The title poem "Toward the Gulf" is a Whitmanesque catalog of midwestern geography and the histories of settlement across the plains. "The Lake Boats" localizes the "great mystery" and mythic shadows in the Michigan landscape. "Cities of the Plain" shifts the scene from the expanse of the prairies to "the psychic cackle" of the "soul-less" in "fumes of pitch."

Two poems in *Toward the Gulf*, "The Landscape" and the richly complex "Excluded Middle," are among Masters' most resonant early statements on midwestern consciousness.

"The Landscape" (*Gulf*, 91–98) is a dramatic monologue which matches the moods of the auditor to those reflected in a "sea of tidal grass":

> You and your landscape! There it lies
> Stripped, resuming its disguise,
> Clothed in dreams, made bare again,
> Symbol infinite of pain,
> Rapture, magic, mystery
> Of vanished days and days to be.

Throughout the poem the "secrets of the landscape" embody "past and present," and their scenes lodge themselves in memory as the "soul's interpreters." In a version of the "you can't go home again" theme, the auditor will "lose the landscape through / Absence, sorrow, eyes grown true." The scenes, of course, change, and what first "on your vision burst" is no more and "you return and find it bare."

But the startling revelation of this poem is the speaker's discovery that his own vision and experience either invest meaning in the landscape or make it barren. He discovers that the sense of place receives its energy from within and then reflects back the human soul:

> O, landscape I am one who stands
> Returned with pale and broken hands
> Glad for the day that I have known
> . . . .
> And you who nourished me and bred
> I find the spirit from you fled.

These regrets are Masters' version of "the glory and the dream" which fled in Wordsworth's "Intimations Ode." His sense of loss arises from the collapse of his own powers to transform his soul through the landscape as he once could:

> Now the familiar landscape lies
> With breathless breast and hollow eyes.
> It knows me not, as I know not
> Its secret, spirit, all forgot
> Its kindred look is, as I stand
> A stranger in an unknown land.

The mood of this poem is significant because it suggests not a nostalgia for a romanticized homeland or a longing for the good old days but rather a growing realization that one's imaginative powers are failing. Again as in Wordsworth's Ode, the big question is "whither has it fled," and here the devastating collapse of vision is presented in the metaphor of dislocation from the landscape.

The movement of this metaphor is alternately dislocation and an urge toward reunification with one's sources:

> Are we not earth-born, formed of dust
> Which seeks again its love and trust
> In an old landscape, after change
> In hearts grown weary, wrecked and strange?

Masters' midwestern longing to go "home" is not sentimentality but an inner urge to regain a wholistic experience:

What though we struggled to emerge
Dividual, footed for the urge
Of further self-discoveries, though
In the mid-years we cease to know,
Through disenchanted eyes, the spell
That clothed it like a miracle—
Yet at the last our steps return
Its deeper mysteries to learn
It has been always us, it must
Clasp to itself our kindred dust.
We cannot free ourselves from it.
Near or afar we must submit
To what is in us, what was grown
Out of the landscape's soil, the known
And unknown powers of soil and soul.

"The Landscape" is Masters' version of the fall and the struggle to achieve once again a state of wholeness.

This early poem (1918) anticipates Masters' extended reworkings of the themes of separation and reunification in the thirties and marks his entry into the visionary mysticism (much of which he learned from Shelley) that is so typical of the "regionalist" poetry of his final years.

"Excluded Middle" (*Gulf*, 18–33) is an historical polemic and a mild satire on using logical rigor (with its "reductions") as a way of life. The poem is about Masters' Midwest in two ways. First, the image of the "middle" itself as a geographical locus describes hybrid experiences of great intensity. Here is one haunting description of midwestern experience:

Long ago it was over for them,
Massachusetts has done its part,
She raised the seed
And a wind blew it over to Illinois
Where it has mixed, multiplied, mutated
Until one soul comes forth:
But a soul all striped and streaked,
And a soul self-crossed and self-opposed,
As it were a tree which on one branch
Bears northern spies,
And on another thorn apples. . . .

This image of the mixed and self-crossed breed describes Masters' norm of whole and meaningful experience which is then fragmented and distorted by Calvinism, profit-mongering, and a life of total "logic."

But the chief meaning of "middle" in the poem is in the satire on logic which develops an opposition between a life of pure thought and feeling, intellect and soul. This opposition celebrates finally the simple life of experience on the land and in the truth of what is beyond logic:

> See
> A universe of truth pass on the way
> Cleared by Excluded Middle through the stuff
> Of thought and visible things, a way that lets
> A greater God escape, uncaught by all
> The nippers of reductio ad absurdum.

Metaphorically, these logical perversions are the inverse of the healthy prairie hybrids from which soul comes forth:

> And so this man
> Went through the years of life, and stripped the fields
> Of beauty and of thought with mandibles
> Insatiable as the locust's, which devours
> A season's care and labor in an hour.

Somehow the life force is "whacked . . . back and forth" and finally murdered, the "color fades," the "heart is sick," "spectral speculations" fill the brain, and the only hope is for the return of "a sudden feel of life" with its "wonder" and "terror." Amidst the somber tones and sense of loss in *Toward the Gulf*, the conclusion of "Excluded Middle" is a rallying cry of midwestern optimism:

> with an out-worn self
> Crying for burial on your hands, a life
> Not yours till now that waits your new found powers—
> Live now or die indeed!

Between *Spoon River Anthology* (1915) and *The New Spoon River* (1924) Masters set out "to interpret and memorialize Illinois and the country which had given so many distinguished men to America." He called the books he published between 1916 and 1921 "epics of a land" (*ASR*, 375). Soon after this period, his reflections on his midwestern origins began to deepen and turn inward. In the early thirties he referred frequently to what he called the "haunt of the infinite." In a decidedly Far Eastern cast, many of his poems were meditations on the mystical dimensions of "earth places." He was attracted at this time to Taoism, Confucianism, and Buddhism and the access they provided to visionary breakthrough. The thinking of Confucius matched his own "worship of the earth" and a growing commitment to the "life of feelings." Asian aphorism complemented as well what he admired in the wisdom of Emerson.

Lichee Nuts (1930) was his most explicit venture into non-Western thought. The best known poem in the volume, "Ascetics and Drunkards," captures the tone of the work: "'Denial,' said Yang Chung, 'has as much sensation / As indulgence'" (*LN*, 11). The mystical intimations of the land are repeated in several haiku-like tone poems. "City Hall Park" looks beyond the city, "beyond houses to meadows / Where the eye can look as far as the heart longs" (13). "Letter From Peking" explains how "the peace and the indifference of China" helped dissolve anxiety (41). In "Pictures and Women," Wah Tom sums up what Elmer Chubb has trouble learning: "Who speaks the wise word, / The word to be obeyed, you or Nature?" (97). "Chinese Religion" hints at the interiorizing of the landscape which is to come in Masters' next half-dozen volumes. The mystic wants "to make the inner life full / And to gain the center of Being." To that end, the prairies and plains will take on new dimensions. The new goal is to

> make the heart a clear pool
> Which mirrors Nature:
> To become a pine tree, a mountain, a river;
> To ride moonbeams;
> To adore the sun and become a flame.
>
> [117–118]

No longer is it enough merely to learn the lessons in the landscape. Now the speaker seeks to *become* the landscape, to merge into a perfect harmony with all of nature.

In a moment of revealing self-assessment in *Across Spoon River*, Masters compared the skepticism of his early satires to a mystical serenity which was always an inseparable part of his deeper vision: "I know as well as anyone that there is a devil in me which turns that cyclopean eye of mine upon what I have revered and tried to cherish and keep, when it has fled me and left me to go on alone; and after gazing upon it has poured skepticism upon it." He then alluded to an appropriate symbol for this restlessness in an early poem: "I am the mad Frederick whom I pictured in a poem called 'The Star' published in *Songs and Satires* in 1916, who saw the star imaged in a pool and cried to have not the image but the star itself, confessing that the star would not be escaped, but had to be served" (*ASR*, 415). Mad Frederick's struggle was the same kind of energetic quest which dominated Masters' work from *Spoon River Anthology* through the dramatic monologues of the early thirties.

Yet in his later years through a kind of Taoist letting go, Masters experienced what he called a "renascence of feeling and thinking" evident especially in the mystical chants celebrating the life forces of the land in Illinois. His own symbol of this transformation is the Bodhisattwa, the eternal woman who "emerges to the heightened imagination everywhere." As a result, "that old, watchful, almost cruel Panlike daemon of mine was changed into a nature of understanding and devotion to nature, of love and forgiveness." The resolution in the later poem turns out to be this calmed quest, "like the movement of swift, white hands, swift with intuition, white with suffering" (417).

The same symbols were there in *Spoon River Anthology*. There the allusions were to the driving power of the river itself, the restless quest of the people, and the brooding sorrows of the graveyard. The struggles continued in the "census spiritual" of *Domesday Book* and the monologues of *The New Spoon River*; the use of place as metaphor for an eternal truth beyond literal space was a dominant feature of the landscape poems of *Toward the Gulf* and *The Great Valley*. In these early collections the "Panlike daemon" had been urged on by the classics, by Goethe, by Masters' sources in the English and American traditions.

In Masters' later poems the quest was to be calmer, and it would be conducted in silence. At last, the struggle for unity would come to rest in the optimism of mystical union. From Goethe, Shelley, and the Greeks he caught the vision. Whitman and Emerson showed the way to eternal song. Browning taught him how to release that energy in dramatic form. But as the vision matured, the landscape became invisible and the optimism which had been there throughout his career overtly triumphed.

Proponents of the "one-book author" view charge that, after *Spoon River Anthology*, Masters merely produced a series of unrelated books, one after the other. But beginning in the early thirties and extending for ten years, a definite pattern can be seen. First there are anguished struggles to possess the pure energy of the life forces. Then these Promethean quests break out into the realm of science fiction, into new universes and unexplored realities. But what goes up must come down, and soon the despair of the wide-eyed dreamer sets in. The disillusion is conquered only by the eternal truths found in serene pastoral settings. Content with a vision of eternity in the invisible and internal landscape, the poet pours forth hymns of celebration on the silent prairie.

In October, 1932, this pattern began to take shape in "Beethoven's Ninth Symphony and the King Cobra," published in *The American Mercury*. The epic begins in the days when life was "fermenting and crackling, and trying to escape / The trance of Nature, and get beyond itself." The poem has always been popular—partly because of the exposure it received before Mencken's readers and partly because of its own fierce energy. In one reading, it is a consciousness epic, a record of what it takes to endure the torments of existence in order to reach the peace of a mystical state.

The problem of the poem is simple: how can human consciousness deal with awareness of its own limitations? How can a conscious being who wants to rise above physical limitations endure the entrapment? The problem is stated directly in part two of the poem and deserves lengthy quotation:

Nature is a sleeping spirit.
Nature is a trance, a mass drugged by eternity,
A petrifaction, a solid jelly, a self-containment,
A contemplation which cannot arise from itself,
Or get out of itself, or look upon itself.
Man has escaped from this deep catalepsy:
He has soared up, and can look down;
He has flown forward, and can glance back;
He can turn upon the past, and see the future.
But as he ages he ceases gradually to be outside himself,
Or see himself.
He becomes again all self-contained, reduced to one mood of
    nature,
Reduced to the eye which contemplates, but does not know.
So he descends to the mind of the cobra,
On the way to the unconsciousness of Nature,
Which is Death, the cobra's cousin.

The quest is thus to overcome death by reaching knowledge. The lessons of the landscape hold clues to a higher life, as the quester will find out; but even the messages revealed there only create more pain along the way. Masters uses Emerson's sense of nature to sketch the process:

> Nature is spirit, but the spirit of calm swamp-slush;
> Nature is unconscious, but it casts upon matter
> The reflection of what has created Nature.
> Nature as the whole of things lies locked in the unconsciousness
> Which is the primal condition of all terraqueous things.
> The same power which slumbers in the stone,
> And dreams in the flower, and sends half-legged beings
> Out of the water to the land, then back to the water,
> And into trees, and on to rocks—
> This same power awakes in the cobra;
> It awakes in Beethoven.
> It awakes when anything separates itself from Nature,
> And becomes two instead of one;
> And becomes outside as well as inside;
> And becomes something more than a landscape's mood,
> Something more than a motionless eye;
> Becomes in truth an eye that knows enemies,
> And a head that knows that pain is in the flesh,
> And comes from turning from one to two;
> And that pain brings something into existence
> Which is an advance upon a mere stare.

What comes into being is pain and fear—"both births of consciousness." Here the separation that takes place "between Nature the creator, / And any mind created" increases the sense of dualism between what Emerson called the "me" and the "not me" and ultimately between spirit and matter. Into this quest to restore a wholeness come the mutual tortures of Beethoven and the cobra. The problem is "separateness," and the only solution is to recapture the "vanished aeons of earth / When there was peace in the pulse of the earth mood / Which made a oneness of plants, rocks, ooze, and primordial plasm." The whole movement of the poem reproduces the direction of Masters' thinking at the time: sorrow and suffering result from separation, fragmentation, duality; truth and happiness can be found only in unity and wholeness of the mystic's vision. This complex work moves brilliantly toward that vision.

All this may seem a long way from the Illinois prairies, and certainly this brief summary oversimplifies a poem of astonishing complexity. But when suddenly Beethoven triumphs, it is worth noting the mystical Nature scene that gives rise to the scherzo:

> Beethoven's soul stepped from darkness to brilliant light,
> From despair to the rapture of strength,
> Overcoming the world.
> Beethoven caught the spirit of a fresh May morning,
> And it inspired him to exult with trumpets and strings,
> And drums and trombones.
> There are no such mornings in the jungle.
> The rhythm of three bars changed to the rhythm of four bars
> Is nothing less than the secret ecstasy of May;
> It is nothing less than the thrill of life,
> Making the worm feel the blisses of creation,
> And making man himself a dweller with Eternity.

This ecstatic breakthrough stands somewhere along the way between the energy of Masters' Shelleyan hymns and the later serenity of his prairie poems. The resolution just seems to happen too soon and too easily for the earlier prophetic tone; yet the calm acceptance of a healing vision is very predictable in the later mystic.

In the middle thirties, Masters' Shelleyan fervor frequently reached this kind of a breaking point and gave birth to a mystical calm very like the prairie stillness of his origins. In the nature hymns of *Invisible Landscapes* (1935) the deeper realities intimated in nature scenes began to dominate over the recollection of actual people and places. The opening "Invocation" (*IL*, 1–2) to the Earth goddess addresses the healing power the land offers to "the life-worn children of men." "Invisible Landscapes" (3–7), the title poem, begins to interiorize the visions of eternal hills and plains. As "Each generation films / Its landscape" and then "rises / From Earth and floats away," still a "soul that prizes / The Earth . . . stays in the land" and "keeps the landscape true / To men who toiled and planned / Their days of living through." The passing away of all that is so fleeting is also a message earth brings to man. But in the end an internal wholeness endures:

> There are landscapes hidden and piled
> One after the other forever:
> That was one when evening smiled,
> And one that dock by the river.

When the prairie moon dips and races
By hills as you speed in the train,
That's the drawing anear of faces
Who have sunk as leaves in the rain,
And become the soul of the soil,
And the memory passed from mind,
But remaining a sorcery coil,
And an unheard voice in the wind.

You cannot have millions of men
Who march, who harvest and plow,
Who grow and die as grain,
Who feast, who laugh, who bow
Their heads in churches for tears,
For kindred gone into the Earth,
For broken and meaningless years,
For love, for labor, dearth,
Save invisible landscapes rest
In layers like fallen leaves,
Whose voice is the wind from the West,
Where the middle meadow grieves;
Whose voice is the frozen lips
Of Earth, which echo Space,
As Earth lies under eclipse—
But the shadow is that of a Face.

The land's internalized and mystical visions thus redeem centuries of futility.

Throughout *Invisible Landscapes* the external manifestations of those visions turn increasingly inward to a mystical celebration with calm, deep tones. "Hymn to the Earth" (8–18) sings of the "Earth-stuff" that lives forever and "the rhythm of the universe" through which the life force daily impresses itself on the human mind.

Invisible Landscapes revisits the actual places of Masters' boyhood—but now from the perspective of "cultivated indifference" and with a "matchless power of dumbness." All the external scenes become invisible even as their lesson becomes fixed in the inner eye. "Sandridge" (*IL*, 120–121) is a good example of that transformation. The sense of actual place "fades and flies" as "Time makes a landscape ashes." People and places are "not merely forgotten, they are even / As the unborn." Half-expecting to recapture the people and places of an earlier time, the speaker returns to find the external scene long gone but the inner landscape very much intact:

> Though in this sky there is no shadow of turning,
> And every field and hill appears
> As of old, the long dead pioneers
> Took with them the landscape's soul, and left it yearning.
>
> Yet the same sunlight hides the meadow lark;
> For an instant the scene resurges with its cry,
> And with the crow, ranging the hollow sky
> Amid the descending dark
>
> Over the Shipley corn-crib and the wood
> Toward the Hills, which seem still to possess
> A brooding spirit, being witnesses
> To the landscape's secret mood.

The yearning of the land's brooding spirit made Masters a "regionalist" to the end. But throughout the thirties and extending into his posthumously published works, the landscape's inner secret replaced the fading external scene.

In 1938 "Hymn to the Universes" appeared in *The University Review*.[7] On the surface, the work has nothing to do with the Illinois prairies. But its ever-widening vision helped Masters trade the external for an internal landscape.

The hymn begins with a disclaimer as the poet announces that he sings not to Demeter, Pan, Apollo, or Uranus but rather to "star clusters and vast islands of light" rising "above this whiff of air." He will journey 135 million light years away to 500 trillion universes, "all receding, all eternally expanding, / All changing into matter and back into radiation." "Into the endless sea of space," the journey will be "lighted by the self-sustaining light of mind"; it will "traverse the darkness of the universes / Seeing that there is no end to space and energy."

Finally, there is the homeward journey, and once back on earth the enlarged view of earth and its single universe. "Hymn to the Universes" is about an enlarging experience, the revelation of widening perspective in which meditations on the landscape become visions of the mystic. After the journey, nothing is ever again as it was before. Philosophies, creeds, governments, good and evil, the arts, emotions, and nature itself come in for "reconsiderations":

> I will consider why nature exalts and debases
> And creates the loneliness of sea shores,
> And evokes the breathless ecstasy of mountain peaks;
> And what it is that makes the human heart desolate,

> And whether it is the suction of the receding universes
> That pulls at his breast and draws his wonder on
> That fills him with ever unquiet dreams.

These, of course, are not new questions. But after the cosmos-spanning journey, the familiar quest takes on a different tone. Nature has its lessons of "correspondences," and those lessons are also not new. But in the endless expanse, the answers are fuller, calmer:

> I will sing the spirit of man,
> Which whether it emerged from earth and rocks,
> Or was separately created, is the transcendent miracle
> And may fitly face the universes as an equal,
> And eye them with satire,
> Wisdom and solemn music.

At the time Masters wrote these poems he sat in New York longing for the Illinois prairies where his vision could complete itself. In the next two years he published three books celebrating the land and the rivers of Illinois. Although he returned only to visit, the poetry of his later years is devoted to the prairies and to the symbols of eternity he learned on those prairies and carried with him wherever he went.

Several recreations of the midwestern landscape in *More People* (1939) are seen through the eyes of people returning to the place of their origins after a long absence. "Return to the Lost Orchard" (*MP*, 182–188) begins as the speaker fears such a return and "lingered near The Lost Orchard, trying to command / Courage to see it again." He needs the courage in part because he senses Emersonian correspondences arising as much from within as without, and the loss he fears is a loss of his own inner power:

> As a cloud brightens and fades
> When wind and sunlight sweep the amplitude
> Of heaven, so my dreams were crossed
> By dreams of the orchard that was lost,
> By dreams of the whole world made my own,
> Lived as mine. This is the heavy cost
> Of imagination which broods alone.

Years later it is not sentimental memories that linger but that imagination-feeding dream creation that must suffer solitary brooding. The poem is, then, a mood piece as the speaker wanders through his former life of "earth's changed mood" until he can endure no more. The weight of the lesson stays with him as he moves on:

So I had seen The Orchard Lost,
And to what use? Back to the village then
I walked and watched the stars. I weighed the cost
Of Fate that overtakes both trees and men.

In a volume not dominated by poetry of the land, "Lands End" (*MP*, 189–192) best captures the tones of land-locked experience. Through the metaphor of a journey to the sea's edge, all is "going forward" to reach the "eternal tides" below the sea-edge cliffs. Here "There is no turning back to Springtime pastures" but instead the relentless marching of one who may at least "walk this shore with unaffrighted will." Along the way the heart "grows / Larger with understanding and with longing / As life shrinks down and narrows along the way, / And leaves the soul through losses so much the greater." The educative power has been nurtured in the soil, and at Lands End is found death as well as a fullness of imaginative wisdom:

Year after year imagination gathered
Into itself the roar of Time, the madness,
The tumult of humanity, the world of grief.
Now these must counterpoint the sea and listen,
As to a shell, the burdens of stilled music,
And matches them with the dirges of the deeps.

Thus the sea must imitate the music of the land, teaching endurance and transformation through the visionary powers of memory:

That world-ache of the long interior country
Is turned the petrifaction of this granite,
The pitiless Medusa which makes bloodless,
And heaps this shore with flesh transformed to stone.
That country's voice now mingles with the sea's.
And thus life's music lingers here by Lands End,
And thus the world of memory remains.

What comes at last at Lands End is the peace of "union with a love whose gravity / Cannot be stayed," a "yielding to the current, / Which flows through all things, by swimming with its streams."

Illinois Poems (1941) and *Along the Illinois* (1942), the last two collections of poetry which Masters published, are a fitting resolution to the questing spirit and the restless urges central in all his earlier verse. In their mystical celebration of the internal landscape, these two volumes go beyond the regionalist's spirit of place. The poems are more than landscape portraits, character sketches, or local history.

Instead, they reach for the mystic's vision beyond words. The metaphors begin in the silence of mute memory, in the lonely and brooding expanse of the prairie and soon build to the vastness, fullness, and solidity of messages not spoken but felt in the quiet. On Masters' prairie, silence is more than the absence of sound; it is the fullness of a pause on stage or a skipped beat in a musical score. The quiet of the Illinois prairies is accentuated by the shrill noises of birds and winds as it breaks through to the transcendent.

Masters' prairie poems are photographs of the countryside, penetrating to the hidden meanings of the mystic. In *Illinois Poems*, the landscape itself creates the mood for meaning beyond words. The hills speak to the centuries. The Illinois Ozarks exude history lessons. The flowers recall pioneers who struggled to achieve beauty in "far solitudes." The gravestones of Petersburg stir up in visitors "wonder" about "what we mean and what they meant." The "vastness of the valley" becomes even more vast when the "quiet majesty" of snow brings icicles and their "hypnotic dream." No silence is more still than that scene in "Starved Rock in Winter" (*IP*, 23–24) when the dead descend "to lock / The land about, the river and the Rock / Against all sounds." In this "enchanted hush" the silence is deafening.

In poem after poem, the quiet deepens until "the earth is measured" and the mystic is able at last to penetrate to the vision. In "Near Fourth Bridge" (*IP*, 25–26) the November marsh "lies stiff in silence under a sunset sky," the dregs of sunset give way, and "the sun is gone with one expiring flash." With that flash comes the silence beyond the quest:

> Night deepens, and absorbs the solitude,
> A zephyr out of nowhere seems to run
> Along the waste of cattails, and reveals
> An inner meaning, as if the summer's face,
> Or some memorial thing sought now this place
> Of noisy mallard ducks and blue-winged teals.

As silence creeps in "like a wave," the vision becomes clearest in the paradox of illuminating darkness:

> The sun has hidden, and the marsh is caught
> As by enchantment. Finding what they sought
> The ducks are silent, and the marsh is still.

This same stillness is captured in the photographic detail of "Corn in the Shock: Menard County" (*IP*, 27–28). Like the frozen flux of a photo album, a picture of hills, prairies, fences, barns, and schoolhouses comes into view in "The mute trance of its contemplation." As "the fans / Of a windmill pause thoughtful and motionless," the moon "in fullness" shines its "bright immensity" on the "lonely oak tree." Again the poem breaks off as the mystic finds the message beyond words:

> If you would find unknown
> Secrets, stand by the oak tree all alone,
> Where the falling leaf just touches earth and ticks,
> Just as a twinkle from the moon is blown.

On the prairie such secrets are carefully locked away. In "Havana and Lewistown" (*IP*, 29–30) they are in "bungalows, old dwellings / Of brick, bespeaking the past with wellings / Of memory which the quiet scenes arouse." In "The Old Salem Mill: Petersburg" (*IP*, 43–44), the secrets are locked in the "lonely and phantom-like" mill "which looked on the solitude / Of the hilly east."

The prairie silences are somehow made louder in these portraits when solitary sounds break through. The waters of the Sangamon rush through mills and dams. The lark revels and the hawk "broods above the silent lands." The sounds of streams and rivers merge in the rush of the sea as "All waters and all souls forever yearn / For the deep secret of eternity." Even the mute swan seeks "a pasture-pond in Illinois," on the "fat weeds" of the inland shore "heavy with mud"— sitting there "a thing of awe, / Like something that regretted it was born, / And seeking so this prairie solitude." On the prairie also can be found the rooster, the archetypal "oracle of night," the "reader of dreams before the light" who "hides mysteries from sight." Presiding over "meadows dumb / Tranced with thought, with no words," the rooster pitches a "mystical" note:

> The night is the prairie's odeum,
> It is the churchyard's rune.
> The night is the peace of sleeping herds,
> Near falling Concord Church that stands
> A ruin above the prairie lands.
> These need a voice their secrets to express,
> Their memory, sorrow and their loneliness.
> The rooster crows afar, the misted scene
> Cries out, unveils its grief,
> And in a mood, how bright, how brief
> Dreams come of vanished hands

That no more bind the sheaf
And centuries pass revealing what they mean.
["The Prairie Rooster," *IP*, 49–50]

The same secrets are released by other birds. "Wild Geese" reflects "the urge of life that never rests." In "The Nightingale Sighs for the Moon's Bright Rays," the "soul of the song" is for "those that were gone." "The Robin" in ecstasy "warbles forth its joy" with rapture and "swelling throat." In "Meadow Larks," the "haunting" song roars in the breeze "chorals of the earth's unease."

Hundreds of varieties of birds are a major part of the landscape Masters studied on the Illinois prairie. Over the silences in "vast spaces of unending sky," the buzzards "circle and survey." In "Turkey Buzzards" (*AI*, 29–30) that wheeling "round and round" amplifies the silence while the "horizon is crying / For something, in distance loneliest / Of lonely things, save only man's lonely breast." Again the birds portray the landscape drowned in sunlight and drowsing in dreams:

And the prairie grass from swale to mound
Races in waves, with scarce a sound
Of the animate wind, with secrets sighing—
And the buzzards wheel round and round.

The same fullness beyond words is conveyed in the song of an inland bird in "Kildeer" (*IP*, 53):

Fellow to the winds, and to the green flags kindred,
Messenger of the prairie, and spirit of the hills,
Lost in the levels, hastening unhindered,
Soul of the landscape, heart that mourns and thrills.
What a lonely melody, speaking the pioneer,
Winged grief that startles, and dies far away;
When his wings have vanished still you hear "kildeer"
Over dimming acres where the sky is gray.

Finally in "Cicada" (*AI*, 61–63), Masters compared man's limited knowledge to that species of insects that watch the moon and "vibrate their membranes on their breasts until the valley / Sounds with their rhythmic shrills, praising and dispraising / That full ark of light." Such penetrating vibration on the still prairie suggests centuries of learned thought as philosophical theories "change various words affirming and denying, / Thus making the symphony of this little sphere." "Cicada-man" thus stares at the skies, wondering about the universe of "empty space" with its "right magic" broken by the love-trance moon. Man as one "lone soul" broods on "the soul's eternal loneliness, / Hearsed in silence, and looking forever / Through meaningless space"—trying to grasp that "God is all, is fire, is light, is energy, is mind." The mystic thus breaks through as all else collapses:

> Thus sing cicada-men as they trick with numbers
> Into a trick-box of summation the desert darkness
> Spread out between galactic light.

At last "pressed to strangulation," new truths and laws wipe out one another and there is in the end only the chants vibrating across the deafening prairie solitude.

Although it appears nearly half-way through *Along the Illinois*, "The Prairie: Sandridge" (*AI*, 34–36) is a keynote statement for all the songs of the countryside. The voice of the poem is Edgar Lee Masters in meditation. It is the poet sitting in the Hotel Chelsea, eyes closed, envisioning his kite high above the flatlands. The poem begins and ends in contemplation that is a "guess at infinite space," a discovery of "Earth-spirit in a dreaming mood." The Illinois prairies are, for this dreamer, as close as man comes to "soul." The poet is a seer, "a muse of distance eyeing the solitude." The vision is a correspondence between nature and higher realities; what he sees is the soul reflected in grass all the way "to the horizon's rim." It is Whitman's grass—what he called "hopeful green stuff." It is a "sea of earth" with "waves / When the wind sweeps over them." Miles of grass are "dotted with barns and houses" and "long heaped graves / In country yards." A cock crows to at once break and accent the pervasive "stillness." Birds fly over carrying secret messages in their very movement, and even "the sunlight's glare / Mingles with the stillness." Merging together is "a river's flow," a "drift of hills," expanding banners of corn, the blinding light of sun, and "a hoard / Of sweetness for the harvest."

Midway through the poem, the scene becomes too full and breaks out into a hymn to "the spirit of the scene," an acknowledgement of "the mystical / Presence, not wholly nature, and not man, / But made of these." The rest of the song celebrates the unquantifiable ingredients of the mystical presence. The dead cultivated the "vastness" and now live on as a part of the soil ("they have become the earth"). The muse of "toil and mirth" continues to sing the memory of "a ruined liberty." Corruption comes and goes but the source of the vision—the "brooding" prairies, the "soil's fertility"—cannot be ruined. In miniature we have the themes of all the other hymns to invisible landscapes and new universes. In the quiet of the prairie, a vision of indestructible wholeness takes hold of the mystical spirit of man. It is a fullness that words can only reduce, and it is celebrated by the wind, the songs of birds, the lives and deaths of farmers and pioneers, and the unexplainable presence of the ever-renewing land itself. What begins as a distant memory of origins or a regionalist tribute to the landscape becomes a meditation beyond even language itself. The metaphors throughout both volumes capture this mystical dimension when they break into what is "voiceless," "overflowing," "benumbing"—always finally "silent" and "full."

Masters celebrates the land and its people, and he sketches in miniature his disillusion with "progress" that has no regard for nature:

> Kincaid, McDoel, Ensley, Watkins, Miles,
> Houghton and Masters speak here as the Muse
> Of this domain, they whisper of toil, of mirth
> In the gracious days, before the Republic grown
> With the lust of trade to power imperial,
> And battleships to man the farthest seas
> Sapped all this realm, and gnawed to the very bone
> The substance of their descendants, to the fall
> Of liberty and bread, even as tyrannies
> Did this, for now is tyranny
> Masked as a benefactor. A slow disease
> Fatal, progressive has ruined liberty.

No matter how much "progress" tries to corrupt what is eternal, the prairie keeps the vision of wholeness intact:

> Man cannot ruin the good earth. All the scars
> Of spears upon Acadia, Macedon,
> Thessaly, Sparta, did not blind
> The recreative shining of the sun,
> Nor take away the soil's fertility.
> These prairies will be here when man has done
> His worst to ruin life, long as the sea
> Rolls round this earth, these prairies here,
> Surviving the death of hope, of liberty
> Will brood upon the centuries year by year,
> And tell of plenty, peace, domestic joy,
> And labor recompense, and rugged health,

And hearths unanxious, and honest wealth
In this beneficent land of Illinois.

In hymns to orchards, trees, leaves, and corncribs, Masters dissected "landscapes which suggest / The mystery of man in this strange sphere" (*AI*, 28). "Oak Leaves" matches the rustling of autumn with "the yearning of Schumann's soul" and reaches the "clairvoyant," "whispering," soul slumber in "the mystery of the heart." "River Towns" (*AI*, 19–21) describes the changeless, enduring, peaceful towns that "grew out of the land." Again the "quiet sounds" express an eternal yearning as the geography releases deeper breaths:

The town is memory longing for the places
Far up the river, never found
By the river's winding spaces
Which the heart forever follows.

That longing must always reach beyond consciousness. In "Orchards in Summer," the meditative quiet is a "waking woman" who, "full of sleep," dreams beneath a "fathomless sky." In "Oak Trees," Apollo's tree rises on "the symbol of this land" as the doves "pour forth their plaintive song" and the cows simply enjoy the pastures. And the lonely corncrib on Shipley's hill feels "the vastness of the sky" and appeals "with longing, with memorial dreams" to "the unnamed something." Under "the vast omnipotence of the sky," the simple corn-crib shines forth like Walden pond:

Look no farther for a scene
That will stay thought and waken pain,
Or stir a wonder in the mind or fill
The heart with longing for what has been,
And will not be again.

[*"Shipley Corn-Crib," AI*, 27–28]

From his earliest poems in *Songs and Satires* to the epitaphs of *Spoon River Anthology* and the prose celebration *The Sangamon*, Masters sought eternity in the local. In the later volumes, the deepening of a calmer quest is reflected in the mystic's advice: "Beneath these elm boughs / Walk and commune; / With spirits that linger here and importune." Those spirits move in "still solitude," either in a "grieving mood" or "so quiet in delight." In "Spring Lake Village" (*AI*, 82–83), the gleaming river "rushes motionless as in a trance." The village spire stands eternal, "evoking what is expressed / Never, so deep it slumbers in the breast, / Where strives the infinite with the diurnal."

Though the doctrine of correspondences expressed in these prairie poems is most often a gentle soothing, the vision is, nonetheless, a pain-bought calm. "T'ang At the Window" (*AI*, 70–71) reflects such a struggle in the contrasts between one who walks the road "seeking a shrine" and another who looks out the window "laughing and drinking wine." The window separates "hunger and pain" outside from the full cups inside. Outside, the wanderer pays "the price of the quest," while inside the drinkers feast "to dull the pain of the breast." Somehow at feast or fast the result is the same as "The heart that longs and sings / Will hear alone or with wine / The beat of mystic wings" (71).

The ultimate symbol of Masters' undefinable mystical vision is repeatedly the land itself. "Invulnerable Earth" (*AI*, 49–50) is a catalog of warriors from Attila to Napoleon, of battles Shiloh to Waterloo raged on the "uninjured," "unmoved," "deep and passionless," ever "triumphant" earth. Leveled towns arise again on ruins; slaughtered troops "glide into earth and are earth again." The earth folds them in with a "sealing spell" and the solidity of granite makes them safe as the hills set them free. The mystical vision is at once an unbroken unity and rush of silence:

> The dignity of mountain heights once again is theirs,
> Their freedom is a pine tree looking to the stars;
> They are a river flowing so swiftly that it hears
> No lumbering of legions, no thunder from the wars.

Though there are echoes of Bryant in most of Masters' landscape poems, his vision is not pantheistic. His questers are always too individualized, too introspective to merge completely into thanatopsis. One major artery to the mystic's vision is the celebration of human consciousness itself—enacted on the plains in Wordsworthian portraits of the men and women of the Illinois countryside. In one such portrait Masters notes that "Judge Mallory" was "an American bloom / That must not be forgot." Like the earlier "people" poems, these later portraits celebrate the heroes who arose from and then returned to the earth.

"Eduard and Katrina" (*AI*, 31–33) is that kind of portrait of a cabinetmaker and his wife who tilled the soil, kept a few animals, paid their mortgage, and then watched orchards, bushes, and house fall down around them. Only the town's "ancient folk" keep alive the memory of a way of life long gone. "Ballad of Ruby Lucas" (44–48) is a sordid tale of a prairie maiden raped and killed by August Meyer who "hummed a maniac song" in the "prairie solitudes." Another strange psychological study is "The Loon" (25–26), a story of "intensest thought," and an "hysterical," "insane cry." Many "sit and look for long," trying to decide what went wrong, making plans, contemplating with great seriousness; the Loon, after he has "looked long and thought it through," decides to laugh out loud with the laughter that is "half mystical." Perhaps Masters' best tribute to "an American bloom" is found in "The Green Hill" (68–69). In a scene worthy of Wordsworth's most memorable rustics, a man pushes a cart up a lone road, himself "sound and part / Of this entranced, this numb / Landscape asleep and without will." Along his journey the landscape goes into a swoon, and "what beats in his heart" is itself "the Earth's secret." In step with the best of Wordsworth's *Lyrical Ballads*, the closing scene is a photo-album shot good for years of attic meditation:

This Earth-man cramped and bent,
These horses with lean bones,
This grass-green hill, these stones,
This sky whose depth is without measurement
Over this scene in syncope
Capture infinity.
It is a heart's mood, as when the wind
In a lone woodland ceases to lament,
And in the stillness something is divined
Whose voice fails, being spent
With grief of a brooding mind.

Masters saved his highest praise for the personal memoir of his uncle "Wilbur D. Masters"—appropriately slotted on the last page of *Illinois Poems*. While he was living in New York in the thirties and forties Masters often spoke and wrote to friends about the possibility of returning permanently to his native Illinois. Though he visited regularly, he never lived there again. The portrait of his uncle is a eulogy as well as a lament for a way of life forever gone. "Something real is you," the poet writes, "something native," from "the true American folk." But a certain "something that blesses a neighborhood" soon fades:

Strange breeds may take our country, what
We lived and loved may all be lost;

> Strange accents, dialects spoken may blot
> The Illinois language, with bitter cost
> To the America we loved and hoped to keep.

That lament is more than nostalgia for what can never be relived. It is a fear also that "the secrets" locked in the land may be lost to future inhabitants and a hope that Wilbur Masters' voice may come again, like a wayward broadcast signal, to bring the mystical prairie vision:

> But some day a youth to secrets tuned,
> A radio sound may pick up, as out of sleep
> A sound that shall shame down imperial noise,
> The wars of robber nations, and souls dragooned
> That out of the past will be your voice!
> My hope is that the voice will then command
> A vision of the Sandridge land,
> And all the story of greed and wrath
> That took America from the path
> By the fake log cabin that replaced the true:
> How Jackson's work was ruined by that crew
> Of Henry Clay, with this the consequent woe
> Of America walking where no man can know.

In all the prairie meditations, the sound of the wind as it accents silence remains a unifying symbol. Like Shelley's prophetic west wind or the calmer "correspondent breeze" of other English romantics, Masters' "Prairie Wind" (*AI*, 54–58) brings messages where words leave off. As windows whine, sycamores sway, the apple trees "break the enchantment of light and speak, / Then lapse again to meditating peace." The wind itself is a "deserted soul," and its "moan" is a "cry with longing and patient pain." The poet finds all these lessons and cries out to the "voice of the infinite":

> O prairie wind! O ever seeking soul
> That wanders like time, and even when at rest,
> Surrounded by silence, speaks the unfathomed whole
> Of human feeling by your kindred breast,
> You voice us, for we as souls are wind,
> Who wander, seek, lament, are blind
> Sole audible genius of eternity,
> Intangible being hastening ever between

The orphaned earth and homeless infinity,
Mourning for what man is, what earth has been,
And for his aching heart, his hopeless woe.

This celebration of the eternal cycle repeats Shelley's "Ode to the West Wind," perhaps the most famous poem of its kind in the language. The parallels with Shelley are unmistakable:

O unseen presence, singing the ebb and flow
Of human sorrow, O winged and free
Spirit over the meadows from slopes below
The Mason County Hills, who touch the strings
Of hearts, and make them question what you are
In all your wanderings
From magic lands, some place afar.
In moments rare our inner eye perceives
Unutterable things half understood:
As when you spring from whispering leaves,
Parting the branches of a wayside wood,
And breathe upon the heart a secret bliss,
A fleeting something of an inwardness.

All the moods of Shelley's west wind can be found in these prairie winds, from "enchantment" to the "moan" of a "soul across the plain." The seasons pass through their corresponding breezes. Travelers, cabins, crops, whole lives come and go until at last the speaker breaks off into the climax of his quest:

I would know what you are, and what you say,
Crooning at windows, singing as you stray
The long miles from the hills, moaning in coigns
Of house walls, shrieking as you cross
The rippled rivers—is it death or loss,
Is it life defeated, is it hope that joins
A consummation never that you sing,
Are you eternal light given a voice, a wing?

Are you infinity pacing the never ceasing flow
Of human feeling, and with soul too vast
For man's weak heart? O unquiet soul
Touching man's thought and waking desperate dreams
Through earth-sounds, or the evening's glow,
Or wrecks of clouds that sail the blast,

Or the moon you toss and roll,
Or float upon the current of prairie streams?

Are you a lamentation, an endless dirge
For dying man, for lone lands where his bones
Waste else unsung, while earth's defeated urge
Is chanted by your mourning tones,
That seem to speak all tragedies, all wars,
And the bright indifference of far visible stars?

From his anguished struggles of the early thirties through his silent meditations on the fullness of the prairie ten years later, Masters' vision became more certain and peaceful, calmer and more deeply mystical. The mystical harmony of the later poems progressed to what Masters himself called "a higher happiness" with "deeper rhythms," "memories sweet as wine."

Illinois Poems (1941), *Along the Illinois* (1942), and *The Sangamon* (1942) were the last books Masters published. In those years he had become especially disenchanted with publishers, and he chose James A. Decker's press in Prairie City, Illinois, as a further tribute to that region. Yet people who visited him at the Chelsea Hotel and wrote about their visit reported that he had many unpublished poems stuffed in drawers or piled on his desk. In 1947 he told August Derleth that he was going to publish another collection entitled *Far Horizons* and then would "write a book about Petersburg, Illinois, my home town."[8] Neither book ever appeared.

Most of the unpublished manuscripts have been collected in the Masters Collection of the University of Texas Library in Austin. In a review of the holdings, Frank Kee Robinson notes that the collection includes "12,000 items of correspondence, both from and to Masters" and an estimated 3,500 manuscript pages of poems from "The Minotaur" (1884) to "Proteus" (1943).[9] The next year a catalog of holdings appeared in *Texas Quarterly* and a selection of 29 poems was published under the title "Posthumous Poems of Edgar Lee Masters."[10] More recently the Humanities Research Center of the University of Texas has published *The Harmony of Deeper Music: Posthumous Poems of Edgar Lee Masters*, a collection of 34 poems written between 1927 and 1942.[11]

The posthumous poems now published display a remarkable sensitivity to symbols available in the midwestern landscape. Masters continued to use the landscape to depict his ever-deepening mystical vision. The "deeper" music is exactly that serenity reflected in the harmonious fullness of the mystic's perspective. The previously unpublished songs of Masters' later years are brooding yet hopeful meditations on nature, death, memory, and the ever-resurgent energies of the spirit. His mystical chants fall into three headings: (1) exuberant celebrations of life forces symbolized by "the eternal earth," (2) explorations of eternity as a felt process which create consciousness of a "deathless existence," and (3) commentaries on human memory as the preserver of indestructible visions beyond the boundaries of time and place.

The hymns to the earth in the manuscript collections are consistently bittersweet songs of praise combined with a sense of loss and impending death. "I Have So Loved This Earth" (*Harmony*, 19–20) is a curious poem of praise to the state of unconsciousness which saves a dead person from the especially difficult pain of remembering what can no longer be experienced. It is good to be "nothing but insensate dust," the speaker claims, in order to escape "the nameless punishment" of unrealizable dreams. Yet in the midst of this sober philosophy, energetic praise for the beauties of nature manages to take over:

I have so loved this earth! No grief
Has robbed the lilac of one leaf,
Or blotted from the solitude
Of Tennessee the white dogwood;
Or ever Virginia's valleys erased,
Or Oklahoma's levels effaced,
Or taken away the dips and swells
Of Taos and its citadels
Of red and yellow rocks; or dimmed
The look of water where Huron meets
Superior by the islands rimmed,
And ever the mystic tale repeats.

While embracing unconsciousness, the speaker finds in the "mystic tale" a triumph over death itself. Almost in spite of itself the poem becomes a celebration of fullness:

I have had all of this; to have
None of it in the midnight grave,
And yet to think of it, is more
Than heart can bear—

as well as a sublimated lesson which the vision of death teaches about living:

But what if in grave-dreams should come
Beautiful things your eyes ignored,
Something for which your lips were dumb?
What if you lay and ached with love,
For earth you had not loved enough?

That same insight is found in "At Midnight in Mytilene" (22–24) where the mystic's vision, the poet's song, and the achieved union of passionate love merge into one:

Earth's beauty consumes me;
The lyre makes my heart leap like a fawn,
Then sink as a fawn struck by an arrow.
For the passion of women is in the lyre
O the agony for understanding the passion of women!
Love makes a poet of the veriest boor,
What has it not done to me?

The energizing force of passion enables the poet, the lover, the mystic to

Mingle
The music of words with the harmony
Of your face, your breast
And interpret each other,
As the sun and the sea exchange enchantment.

Some of the posthumous hymns to the life forces are calm, poignant, ever serene; others are restless, tortured, defiant. Finally, simple straightforward hope is the dominant tone. In the series "Vignettes from Vermont" (*Harmony*, 46), Mrs. Malatesta Meyerbaum describes herself as "one of the pioneers in the back-to-land trek." She lives with nature and memory "quite alone, / Very happy, and not in the least lonely." "Wind From the West" (62) broods on "The joy of breath." "The Hills of Big Creek" (65–67) tells the story of the "race of men" who, "like the new creatures of each passing spring / Are born, grow old, and mix with earth again." "A New Day Dawns" (68–69) enacts the coming of a new generation in "the mystical stirs of the dawn."

These mystical stirs bring hope even in the face of death. They bring a vision of the "soul's ecstatic horoscope" to a mind that transforms the fullness of experience into eternity itself. This process of transformation is the subject of "Club Fellows" (*Harmony*, 42–43), a portrait of Thurston and Conway and Seward who are "Approaching eighty," sitting about all day with "vacant unconcern," turning "the

pages of the twice-read magazine." Their day ends as it begins—
drowsing from nicotine and gin, and their wisdom is derived more
from an inner strength than from any orthodoxy. In a brilliant passage, Masters describes what, for the Village Atheist, would qualify as
the achievement of immortality:

> They are wise, but their wisdom is unavailing;
> They knew their state, and they remember
> What life was, and what it is in their December.
> God's love and storied philosophy
> Are an empty cup whose failing
> Wrinkles their understanding irony,
> They are not terrified but calm,
> Quiet of desire and will;
> Epithalamium and psalm
> Take their reflection as a water still
> With ice, and what they failed to live,
> Or lived, has now no qualm.

Calm and quiet, like the ice yet wrinkled with uncertainty, these club
fellows begin to experience the ongoing process of felt experience
beyond the grave.

That same vision of serenity answers "the heart's deep ache" in
"The Sleepers" (*Harmony*, 21). In the long life continuum "between
the unawakened souls and those who sleep" come that short time and
that small space of weariness and waste and the burning "madness" of
the quest. The only "final wisdom" must be an understanding of "the
scheme that wakes / The sleeper who to sleep so soon returns."

Many of the posthumous poems examine in detail that paradoxical scheme and find in death itself an extension of life energies.
"Medusa" (*Harmony*, 29–30) uses that classical image of arrested motion to describe the horrors of "lifeless matter." With reference to
cells that had been alive with motion, two crucial questions are posed
in the poem. First the paradox of death: "Whence was fled / The
spirit that made them whirl and dive, divide?" Philosophically, there
is never any comforting answer to that question. All that remains in
theory is "eternal darkness, and a swoon / Of ice where souls, like
lifeless cells, are brought / By winged Medusa." But for Masters,
there is another more important question: "Then is there in these
cells, / So Gorgonized, a something not all bereft / Of motion, but
still active, though improved?" And the answer goes beyond the resources of theory:

> Perhaps with this regard one hope is left:
> As substance still the nucleus goes on
> Dancing, though slower to the harmony
> Of deeper music, that of tranced stone;
> With cells of flesh, therefore, this thing may be.

This slower dance to a deeper harmony sets the direction for the intimations of the landscape and the hopeful visions of the post-humous poems.

Death becomes a mere extension of life energies when the deeper music slows and enriches the tempo. "There is Labor Whither Thou Goest" (*Harmony*, 31) describes death as a process in which "flesh has become / A part of other whirling." In the grave "life will go on, not cease" because "death cell-energy" also has thought:

> Shelley described this as the sea of love
> In which we sink, a sea unconscious, deep.
> But as in life our flesh works while we are asleep,
> Death may an endless labor prove.

That "endless labor" surprises a recent corpse in "First Night in the Grave" (33–34). Rather than the Medusa stare, the dancing of cells continued that first night like "the warmth of gathering mold / In the grave" which the lifeless body "found." The cells will dance and that grave will become external with the prairie land.

A most curious tribute to a stuffed pig, "Dressed Hog in a Window" (*Harmony*, 35–36), returns to the same questions about the life force which had will, desire, and "hunger that made you grunt and squeak, / When you were in your prime." The question is worthy of Keats' odes:

> That you feared dogs, and feared the fire,
> And fearing had a mind,
> Is past denying, and where went
> Those things intangible,
> And left this hulking tenement,
> This fat, insensate shell?

Again, "the hog-mind," like "the man-mind," is eternal. "Though what in just the body grew / Has lost the living touch." The horror is not death but the terrors of the "sleepers" who must remain "awake" a while longer:

> I think that all of you just cross
> A bridge barred by a gate
> And leave the living with their loss
> To wonder, stare, and wait.

The pain is left to those who wonder, while the dead, who have for long "known the change of grass and tree," enjoy "the meadow's peace" and move on "by some progression to larger happiness" ("An Old County History," 37).

That progression to a higher awareness is a discovery of "The Widow" (*Harmony*, 44–45)—a funeral-parlor poem about a very recently breathing person who is suddenly a "voiceless mind," "condensed in thought," "sealed in a coffin." The first stage of death is far from lifeless but instead "a crystal with a light," reflecting "the spirit that thinks and knows; / Which does not instantly take flight, / But lingers in a sweet repose." When at last "from the body the soul is drawn" the tenseness of life also vanishes and gives birth to "a consciousness / Turned in." As the years pass by, the buried corpse seems ever more distant, and a "blankness" takes over. As the distance widens the progression to mystical harmony mounts:

> We buried him, he still seemed near,
> Closer than life, and day by day
> He grew more intimate, more dear
> By being gone and put away
> In the body, which left his spirit free
> To be itself, commune with mine.

The mystical communion summarizes the lessons of the landscape as well as the triumph of the life forces:

> Then I remember, as a star
> Can fade into the void and then
> Appear and shine, from realms afar
> He seems to pass me once again.

As a catalyst of mystical experience, memory is both creative and terrifying in the posthumous poems. Memory can create eternity by celebrating rhythms that have long slowed into the deeper harmonies, or memory can terrify the human spirit by reminding the living of their loss. The "mystic tale" of "I Have So Loved This Earth" is a bittersweet plea that unconsciousness will triumph over that acute sense of loss. The "hulking tenement" of a pig carcass in the window is terrifying because it reminds those on the outside staring in of the terrors of the incomprehensible. Medusa is horrifying because it seems as though "death moves life at will, but is by life not moved." The expectations turn out to be worse than the realities of that "first night in the grave." In "The Hills of Big Creek" memory becomes synonymous with the ongoing painful process of the life experience itself. A narration on the theme "you can't go home again," the poem poses the problem of return to the places of one's origins. The essential problem is that nothing and no one remain in those places except in the visitor's memory.

But the sorrows of the failed attempt to recapture the past lead the speaker to insights on the mind's own participation in the achievement of immortality. In "The Hills of Big Creek" (*Harmony*, 65–67), memory at first is the cause of terror and then an essential part of the healing mystical vision. First the lament:

> And here again are youths
> And maidens who repeat my happiness,
> My wonder at the sailing cloud, my shouts
> To comrades hidden in the fastness.
> They know me not. They know not as a boy
> These hills were mine.

This is, of course, one of those "heart's deep aches" left to the living who must wonder at their loss. It is not yet the "mystic tale." But even this lament recognizes that what was once life's breath still moves, though "hidden in the fastness." And that recognition breaks through to another kind of earth-hymn to the eternizing powers of memory:

> O Earth,
> Growth is forgetfulness, and within ourselves
> Life has its eras, and with senseless stone
> Walls in the heart, till to its inner core
> Remembrance, like a fallen acorn caught
> Between the crevice of great boulders, dies
> For light and rain, grows pale and withers too,
> Forgetting what it was.

Even though so many have "glided to the grave," the power of memory creates an inversion wherein life and death change places. The skeptical question sets up the mystical resolution: "If death end all remembrance, what is life / Which blots remembrance of the soul you were / But death?" Life without memories is death and yet life with memories of what is no longer attainable is the pain of experience itself. With the discovery that he cannot relive the past and at the same time cannot afford the "convenience" of forgetting it either, the speaker finds the deeper music of mystical awareness beyond philosophies and creeds. "To know, the heart must feel," he discovers, and again "to remember, it must live again its love." Through memory the experience can be recreated and the vision brought to life:

> All this I know,
> But with the mind, as if an eye should bud
> Upon the branch's tip, and backward look
> To the parent trunk, but being but an eye,
> Without a heart to make the vision life,
> Would stare without a tear. And not to feel
> Is not to live; it is the loss which life
> Exacts for living; it is the death which creeps
> With years into the flesh.

At death's door, the lessons of the old man trying to go home again are the same as the messages in the landscape:

> I see
> This landscape in a light that shows each bare,
> Each empty spot, each shrunken height, each vale
> Made narrow, and these grassy banks reduced
> By the cold glare which is Eternity's.
> That we forget the soul we were is death;
> But that we neither live the past nor grieve,
> Proves Death the healer, since he heals in life.

That paradox is no longer a contradiction for the prairie mystic.

So it is actually better to be unable to go "home" again. When one cannot relive the past, that past still lives in the memory and helps transform the present into that "larger happiness" and "deeper music" which mystics talk about but never attempt to define. In the posthumous poems, memory takes on this mystical dimension. No longer an attempt to relive years gone by, the remembrance of things past becomes a transforming power energizing life in the present. In "An Old County History" (*Harmony*, 37) the heroes of the past are celebrated not for what they were or did but for what they still are and are still doing:

Born like the swallows or the swine,
Judge Clark and Isaac Scott
Aunt Sally and Parthena Green
Made houses and left memory sweet as wine.
Up from invisible life their strength begot
The beauty of a neighborhood and a scene
Of pioneer truth upon their chosen spot.

When they rest in "the meadow's peace" their life energies will progress "to a larger happiness" through the creative agency of the memory of those who come after them.

In "Memories of *Pinafore*" (*Harmony*, 38) souls depart from the Sangamon Valley "like the blood beating and returning to the heart." They later live again through memory: "They live being a higher existence which sprang / From our love." They live on in a "sphere of crystal, in which we gaze"; it is a "deathless world." Those who come after see in the crystal themselves and memories of people and days gone by. The language to describe what happens breaks off into mystical song at this point as the "influence" of those astral powers shines down:

This is immortality standing over
The headstone and the sunken sod,
Partaking of the life of song, the lover
God who is Beauty, Beauty who is God.

Here what Masters calls "Eternal Mind" takes over, and there is never any thought of going home again. "Not to See Sandridge Again" begins as a longing for the prairie country but quickly reaches the conclusion that "All changed, but changeless in my memories." People, events, and places move on, are forgotten, change from one form of life into another; the eternal truth of the inner eye's invisible landscapes remains unshakable:

Earth even may change, but if the love it stirs
Remains, is Earth then changed? If man must pass,
And generations of cattle, if harvesters
Themselves are gathered, and old men sink like grass
Into the quiet of the universe,
Yet memory keeps them, they are never less.

Nothing can ever be less when the mind's own transforming powers create an eternity from the lessons of the landscape.

Within that vision of eternal truth, an irreducible wholeness is captured. Limitations of time and space fall away. Individuals are merged into a unifying beauty, and the lessons of correspondences are no longer needed. There is no need to go home because there is no place but right now and right here as it is recreated from the then and there:

> That is eternal life for them, for me.
> For what is living save it be that what
> Was beauty is preserved in memory?
> If gazing on a dead face is to blot
> What the dead was in life, so not to see
> Sandridge again may be the better lot.

These and other posthumously published works document the growth of Masters' mystical vision in the thirties and forties. The aging poet living in New York never went home again. He didn't need to. Perhaps he actually thought it better not to. His visions of life and death had become as calm as the quiet of the club fellows he celebrated. His music had reached deeper harmonies. He was progressing to a larger happiness. He could still see his kite over the Illinois prairies. And those landscapes had at last become invisible enough to see straight through to eternity.

near The Lost Orchard, trying to ....
again." He needs the courage in part because he senses Emersonian
correspondences arising as much from within as without, and the loss
he fears is a loss of his own inner power:

> As a cloud brightens and fades
> When wind and sunlight sweep the amplitude
> Of heaven, so my dreams were crossed
> By dreams of the orchard that was lost,
> By dreams of the whole world made my own

Notes

Chapter 1. An Omnivorous Reader

1. For a slightly different view of Masters as lawyer-writer, see Charles E. Burgess, "Edgar Lee Masters: The Lawyer as Writer," in *The Vision of This Land*, ed. John E. Hallwas and Dennis J. Reader, *Essays in Literature* (Macomb, Ill.: Western Illinois University, 1976), pp. 55–73.
2. Edgar Lee Masters, "Learning to Write," *Writer* 3 (January 1889): 11–13.
3. Masters, "The Genesis of Spoon River," *American Mercury* 28 (January 1933): 44.
4. As quoted by Lois T. Hartley, *Spoon River Revisited*, Ball State Monographs, no. 1 (Muncie, Ind.: Ball State Teachers College, 1963), pp. 11–23. The letters are in the Dreiser Collection at the University of Pennsylvania.
5. Masters, "Genesis," p. 46.
6. Ibid., p. 50.
7. Brewster Ghiselin, *The Creative Process* (New York: New American Library, Mentor, 1952), p. 29.
8. Masters, "Genesis," pp. 50–51.
9. See *Influx: Essays on Literary Influence*, ed. Ronald Primeau (Port Washington, N.Y.: Kennikat, 1977).
10. T. S. Eliot, *Selected Essays*, new ed. (New York: Harcourt Brace Jovanovich, 1960).
11. Lionel Trilling, "The Sense of the Past," in *The Liberal Imagination* (New York: Viking, 1950).
12. Claudio Guillén, *Literature as System* (Princeton: Princeton University Press, 1970).
13. Harold Bloom, *The Anxiety of Influence* (New York: Oxford University Press, 1973), p. 5. And see also idem, *Yeats* (New York: Oxford University Press, 1970); idem, *A Map of Misreading* (New York: Oxford University Press, 1975); idem, *Kabbalah and Criticism* (New York: Seabury Press, 1975); idem, *Poetry and Repression* (New Haven: Yale University Press, 1976).

14. Walter Jackson Bate, *The Burden of the Past and the English Poet* (Cambridge: Belknap Press of Harvard University Press, 1970), p. 134.

15. Ibid., pp. 3, 66–71.

16. Robert Van Gelder, "An Interview with Mr. Edgar Lee Masters," *New York Times Book Review*, February 15, 1942, pp. 2, 28.

17. Bloom, *A Map of Misreading*, p. 163.

18. Charles E. Burgess, "Masters and Some Mentors," *Papers on Language and Literature* 10 (1974):175.

19. Ibid., pp. 177, 191, 201.

20. Preface, "To William Marion Reedy," in *Toward the Gulf*, pp. vii–xiii; see also Masters, "Literary Boss of the Middle West," *American Mercury* 34 (April 1935):450–455. In the latter, a biographical tribute to Reedy, Masters recalls that he "had read nearly every book of moment among the Greeks, the Romans, the Italians, Germans and English and French. Thus he was able to identify the derivation of a new work" (p. 450).

21. Masters, "Genesis," p. 48.

22. Masters, "Histories of the American Mind," *American Mercury* 35 (July 1935):341.

23. Ibid.

24. Ibid.

Chapter 2. "While Homer and Whitman Roared in the Pines"

1. Masters, "Learning to Write"; "The Poetry Revival of 1914," *American Mercury* 26 (July 1932):272–280; and "The Genesis of Spoon River" (pp. 38–55).

2. Edmund Clarence Stedman, *An American Anthology, 1787–1899* (Boston & New York: Houghton, Mifflin & Co., 1900).

3. Masters, "Genesis," p. 47.

4. Ibid., p. 52.

5. August Derleth, *Three Literary Men: A Memoir of Sinclair Lewis, Sherwood Anderson, and Edgar Lee Masters* (New York & Copenhagen: Candlelight Press, 1963), pp. 39–56.

6. Van Gelder, "An Interview."

7. Masters, "Learning to Write," p. 13; "The Poetry Revival of 1914," p. 274.

8. Karl J. Shapiro, *In Defense of Ignorance* (New York: Random House, 1960).

9. Ernest Earnest, "Spoon River Revisited," *Western Humanities Review* 21 (1967):59–65.

10. Cesare Pavese, *American Literature: Essays and Opinions*, trans. Edwin Fussell (Berkeley: University of California Press, 1970); Henry Hahn, "Evolution in the Graveyard," *Midwest Quarterly* 10 (1969):275–290.

11. Sherwood Anderson, "Lindsay and Masters," *New Republic*, December 25, 1935, p. 195.

Chapter 3. "I Am a Hellenist"

1. See John T. Flanagan, *Edgar Lee Masters: The Spoon River Poet and His Critics* (Metuchen, N.J.: Scarecrow Press, 1974), pp. 33–35, 44–45.
2. Willis Barnstone, Introduction to *The New Spoon River*, paper ed. (New York: Collier, 1968), pp. xvii–xxvi.
3. For more on Reedy's observation, see Max Putzell, *The Man in the Mirror: William Marion Reedy and His Magazine* (Westport, Conn.: Greenwood Press, 1972), pp. 193–216.
4. Van Gelder, "An Interview."
5. Masters, *A Book of Verses* (Chicago: Way & Williams, 1898).
6. The principal texts are Irving Babbitt, *Rousseau and Romanticism* (Boston: Houghton Mifflin, 1919); T. S. Eliot, *The Sacred Wood* (London: Methuen, 1920); and T. E. Hulme, *Speculations*, ed. Herbert Read (London: Kegan Paul, Trench, Trubner & Co., 1924). The pertinent documents are collected in *Romanticism: Points of View*, ed. Robert F. Gleckner and Gerald E. Enscoe, 2d ed. (Englewood Cliffs, N.J.: Prentice-Hall, 1970).
7. Hulme, *Speculations*, p. 126.
8. For a fuller treatment of Hulme see my "On the Discrimination of Hulme: Towards a Theory of the 'Anti-Romantic' Romanticism of Modern Poetry," *Journal of Modern Literature* 3 (July 1974): 1104–1122.
9. Hulme, *Speculations*, pp. 119–120.
10. Hulme, "A Lecture on Modern Poetry," *Further Speculations*, ed. Sam Hynes (Lincoln: University of Nebraska Press, 1962), p. 67.
11. Ibid., pp. 70–71.
12. Ibid., p. 126.
13. Masters [Dexter Wallace], *The Blood of the Prophets* (Chicago: Rooks Press, 1905).
14. For more on Reedy see Masters' "Literary Boss of the Middle West." Masters notes that when Reedy became discouraged about the state of modern literature "in his desperation he would take to Homer" (p. 452).
15. Masters, "Hymn to the Universes," *University Review* 5 (Winter 1938): 81.

Chapter 4. "Awakened and Harmonized"

1. David Levin, ed., *Emerson: Prophecy, Metamorphosis, and Influence* (New York: Columbia University Press, 1975).
2. Bloom, "Emerson and Influence," in *A Map of Misreading*; see also idem, "Emerson and Whitman: The American Sublime," in *Poetry and Repression*.
3. Van Gelder, "An Interview."
4. Bloom, *A Map of Misreading*, p. 177.
5. Emerson, "The Uses of Great Men," quoted in Bloom, *A Map of Misreading*, p. 169.
6. Henry David Thoreau, "Reading," in *Walden*.

7. Emerson, "Experience," quoted in Bloom, *A Map of Misreading*, pp. 169–170.

8. Ima Honaker Herron, *The Small Town in American Literature* (Durham, N.C.: Duke University Press, 1939).

9. Charles E. Burgess, "Masters and Some Mentors," *Papers on Language and Literature* 10 (1974): 175–201.

10. Van Gelder, "An Interview."

11. Charles E. Burgess, "An Unpublished Poem by Edgar Lee Masters," *Papers on Language and Literature* 5 (1969): 183–189.

12. "Epic of America," *Times Literary Supplement* (London), January 1, 1938, p. 8.

13. Vachel Lindsay, *The Litany of Washington Street* (New York: Macmillan, 1929), p. 42.

Chapter 5. "The Natural Child of Walt Whitman"

1. Ezra Pound, "Webster Ford," *Egoist* 2 (January 1, 1915): 11–12.

2. *New York Times*, April 4, 1915, pp. 7–9.

3. Flanagan, "An Anthology Is Born," *Edgar Lee Masters*, chap. 3, pp. 21–50.

4. For a list of criticism on Masters from 1950 to 1975, see *The Vision of This Land*, ed. John E. Hallwas and Dennis J. Reader, pp. 114–128.

5. Allen Tate, "Whitman in America," *Poetry* 50 (September 1937): 350–353; Newton Arvin, "Whitman As He Was Not," *New Republic*, April 14, 1937, pp. 301–302; Carl Van Doren, "Behind Spoon River," *Nation*, November 14, 1936, p. 580.

6. Pavese, *American Literature*, p. 201.

7. Ralph Waldo Emerson, "The Poet," in *Selections from Ralph Waldo Emerson*, ed. Stephen E. Whicher (Boston: Houghton Mifflin, 1957), p. 231.

8. Ibid., p. 233.

9. Charles E. Burgess, "Masters and *Whitman*: A Second Look," *Walt Whitman Review* 17 (March 1971): 25–27.

10. Masters, "The Poetry Revival of 1914," pp. 274, 277.

11. Earnest, "Spoon River Revisited," pp. 59–60.

12. Shapiro, *In Defense of Ignorance*, pp. 203, 193.

Chapter 6. Hymns on the Midwestern Prairie

1. Masters, "Genesis," p. 43.

2. "Amphimixis" was unpublished in Masters' lifetime. The poem appeared for the first time, by permission of Ellen C. Masters, in my article "Shelley and Edgar Lee Masters' 'Amphimixis,'" *Old Northwest* 1 (1975): 141–157.

3. There is no complete standard edition of Shelley's poems. Here and elsewhere I quote from *The Oxford Anthology of English Literature*, vol. 2, ed. Harold Bloom et al. (New York: Oxford University Press, 1973). References are to line numbers of poems cited.

4. Harold Bloom, *The Visionary Company*, rev. and enl. ed. (Ithaca, N.Y.: Cornell University Press, 1971), pp. 340–341.
5. Percy Bysshe Shelley, *Shelley's Prose*, ed. David Lee Clark (Albuquerque: University of New Mexico, 1954), p. 292.
6. Ibid., pp. 293, 291–292.
7. Ibid., pp. 282–283.
8. Masters, "Beethoven's Ninth Symphony and the King Cobra," *American Mercury* 27 (October 1932): 129–139.
9. Masters, "The Triumph of Earth," limited-circulation edition, 1940, in the Arthur Davison Ficke Collection of the Yale University Library.
10. *Oxford Anthology*.
11. Pavese, *American Literature*, p. 47.

Chapter 7. Intense and Subtle

1. Bloom, *The Anxiety of Influence*, pp. 19–45.
2. Letter from Ellen Masters to the author, May 23, 1977.
3. Bloom, *A Map of Misreading*, pp. 19–20, 24.
4. Pavese, *American Literature*, p. 200.
5. Flanagan, *Edgar Lee Masters*, pp. 66–78.
6. Burgess, "Edgar Lee Masters: The Lawyer as Writer."
7. Robert Browning, *Pauline*, in *Poems of Robert Browning*, ed. Donald Smalley (Boston: Houghton Mifflin, 1956), p. xi. Smalley follows the 1898 Florentine edition.
8. *Poems of Robert Browning*, pp. 241–249.
9. Bloom, *A Map of Misreading*, pp. 106–122. See also Bloom's *Poetry and Repression*, pp. 175–204.

Chapter 8. Invisible Landscapes and New Universes

1. Flanagan, *Edgar Lee Masters*, pp. 156–159.
2. Herron, *Small Town*, p. 355.
3. Bernard Duffey, *The Chicago Renaissance in American Letters* (East Lansing: Michigan State University Press, 1954), pp. 147, 167.
4. Dale Kramer, *Chicago Renaissance: The Literary Life in the Midwest—1900–1930* (New York: Appleton-Century, 1966).
5. Michael Yatron, *America's Literary Revolt* (New York: Philosophical Library, 1959), p. 70.
6. David D. Anderson, "Notes Toward a Definition of the Mind of the Midwest," *Mid America III* (East Lansing, Mich.: Midwest Press, 1976), p. 16.
7. Masters, "Hymn to the Universes," *University Review* 5, no. 2 (Winter 1938): 81–83.
8. Derleth, *Three Literary Men*, p. 53.
9. Frank Kee Robinson, "The Edgar Lee Masters Collection: Sixty Years of

Literary History," *Library Chronicle of the University of Texas* 8 (1968): 42–50.

10. Frank K. Robinson, ed., "Posthumous Poems of Edgar Lee Masters," *Texas Quarterly* 12 (1969): 70–115.

11. *The Harmony of Deeper Music: Posthumous Poems of Edgar Lee Masters*, ed. Frank K. Robinson (Austin: Humanities Research Center, 1976). Subsequent references cited as *Harmony*.

Index

silence under a sunset sky, the dregs of sunset ... is gone with one expiring flash." With that flash ... beyond the quest:

Night dese...

DATE DUE			

Primeau   180209